PENTECOSTAL PIONEERING

To Conna Hodges, from
George and Stella Flattery,
on July 17, 1997

PENTECOSTAL PIONEERING

An Autobiography

by
George W. Flattery, Sr.

Published by the Author

George W. Flattery, Sr.
3218 N. National
Springfield, Missouri 65803
Second Printing - March 1995

Library of Congress Catalog Card Number: 92-93564
ISBN 0-9634670-0-X

Printed in U.S.A. by Litho Printers at Cassville, Missouri

Dedicated to:
Stella, our four children,
and their families

TABLE OF CONTENTS

PART ONE: *BEFORE AFRICA*

PART TWO: *FRENCH WEST AFRICA*

PART THREE: ***WORLDWIDE CHRISTIAN MINISTRY***

PREFACE

I began preaching the gospel of Christ, as a beginning exhorter, in the Fall of 1931, almost 61 years ago—about 3 months after my conversion to Christ. I have never, for a moment, turned from Christian ministry to anything else as the main vocation of my life. I have not chosen "Pentecostal Pioneering" as the title of my autobiography because my part in such pioneering is outstanding, when compared with the Pentecostal ministry of many others in the worldwide, century-long outpouring of Pentecost. I've chosen this title because it accurately summarizes my 61 years of ministry. I wish many other ministers would write autobiographies on the same subject.

I have carefully excluded imagination and fantasy from the story of my life. Those qualities have some positive aspects, but realistic, well-documented autobiographies exert better influence on their readers than those which are founded on fiction. My wife, Stella, and I feel that the very heart of our lives was the 20 years that we spent between 1944 and 1964 as pioneer missionaries to French West Africa. And the very heart of the documentary source for my autobiography is the hundreds of letters which we wrote to our relatives, or received from them, during those 20 years.

Some reasons why I undertook the arduous task of writing my life's story are: 1) to provide myself with better understanding of and appreciation for my own redemption through Christ; 2) to improve the good spiritual and social relationships which exist between my wife and myself; 3) to improve these good relationships which exist between us and our children and their families; and 4) to provide myself with better understanding of and participation in the one Family of God.

I hope that reading my story will help provide readers with better understanding of a well-balanced biblical life, and will help cause them to live more nearly like God wants them to!

George W. Flattery, Sr.
Springfield, Missouri
August 1, 1992

PART ONE:
BEFORE AFRICA

Foreground (left to right): George Flattery at 4; his cousin, Maurice Houser; his sister, Helen, by hand water pump. Background (left to right): Horse-drawn buggy, small barn, horseless buggy (Model-T Ford). Site: The Flattery 40-acre farm on South Hydraulic Avenue, a mile or two South of Wichita, Kansas, in 1918

CHAPTER 1: MY EARLY LIFE

When and Where

I'm 78 now and using the term "early life" to refer to my first nineteen years. I was 19 when I left my home at Wichita, Kansas, to attend Bible School in Enid, Oklahoma.

In 1914, I was born at the small Kansas town of Clearwater—a few miles southwest of Wichita. My birthplace was, and still is, surrounded by great fields of wheat. Often it is very hot in the summer and very cold in the winter in that part of our country. I was only 4 when my parents moved in the spring of 1918 to a 40-acre tract of farm land just outside Wichita's southern edge at that time. This land is bound by South Hydraulic avenue on the east and on the north by a road which, after World War II, was named MacArthur Road. I lived for eight years on that tract of land which is now made into city blocks filled with Wichitans.

A few impressions from my childhood in Clearwater still linger in my mind. I remember standing at the base of its ordinary-sized water tower and thinking it was the biggest thing in the world. Something I remember even better is the occasional coming to our house of Rebah Rodgers—a neighboring high school girl. From my lowly point of view (near the ground, of course, at only 3 or 4) she looked so tall that I would exclaim: "Weedy is as high as the sky!"

George about 2 (right) and his sister Helen about 4

Parents, Brothers, Sisters

My mother was Rose Houser before marrying my father, James Perley, in 1910. While still single she was the teacher at a country grade school for several years in Butler County, east of Wichita. She had little free time from her duties as farmer's wife and mother to little children. During her moments of relaxation between chores, she was often reading something! Her background as school teacher had helped to prepare her for the enjoyment in reading which she experienced (both before and after the invention of radio), while helping to rear her family.

My earliest recollections of my father are of him as a thresher of wheat—before the invention of wheat-threshing combines. He threshed wheat until about 1921, then took up truck-gardening to make his living. Much of his threshing was in central and western Kansas. It stretched westward to the town of Plains and beyond! This operation included the threshing machine or separator, a large steam engine to furnish power for it, and sometimes more than twenty manned, horse-drawn bundle wagons.

Threshing wheat in Kansas about 1920, J. P. Flattery by front wheel of steam engine

My parents lived good moral lives, and their children have gracious memories of them. My father's reading of Hurlbut's story of the Bible to me (at about 8) was positive spiritual influence upon me. But my parents seldom found time to go to church while they were rearing their children. They were poor tenant farmers who felt that taking time out for church would lower even more the standard of living that they were able to maintain for themselves and their children.

If my parents had been more faithful to the church, God would have given them the more abundant spiritual life that he gave to Harriet Flattery (my father's mother) who lived more than 90 years. She was a faithful, old-fashioned Methodist in Butler County. On occasions when Cyrus S. Nusbaum visited her home, they must have enjoyed singing together the now widely known and used hymn he had written: "His Way With Thee."

I am the second of six children of J. P. and Rose Flattery. These six with dates of birth are: Helen, 1912; me, 1914; Ellis, 1916; Frank, 1919; Iva, 1921; and Wendell, 1926. I think the lifelong faithfulness of our parents to each other has contributed much positive influence toward the success of our marriages. Neither I nor any of my brothers or sisters has ever been involved in the increasing modern tragedy of divorce. All my brothers and sisters are still living—except Frank who died a year ago.

Left to right: Helen, George, Ellis, Frank, Iva, Wendell, in August, 1965

Elementary and Secondary Schooling

I entered the first grade of Riverside (now Funston) School in the Fall of 1920. At that time it was a country school, a couple of miles south of Wichita. But it is within the enlarged city. I was usually a model student at Riverside but was occasionally involved in something which showed that "through one . . . sin . . . came to all" (Romans 5:12, NIV): one day I (along with other boys) stole turnips from Grove Stuckey's patch across the street from the school. We outran Grove when he tried to catch and punish us. And oh how sweet that stolen turnip tasted to me, an unsaved boy of about 8 or 10! I should have asked Grove Stuckey to forgive my theft of his turnip, but being "without God in the world" (Ephesians 2:12) I was unable to bring myself to do so.

In the spring of 1926 our family moved about 3 miles northwest to a 33-acre farm that was even closer to the southern boundary of Wichita. It was near the Enterprise School where I completed the 8th grade in the Spring of 1927—a year early, since I had completed the 5th and 6th grades at Riverside in one year.

In the school year of 1927-28, I completed the ninth grade at the Hamilton Intermediate School on South Lawrence (now Broadway) Avenue in Wichita. In my woodworking class, I made a cedar chest and some other furniture. (This class helped to prepare me to work with wood in the building of churches and mission houses later in life.) That year, the faculty-sponsored students' yearbook contained prophecies concerning what each 9th grade student might become best known for. Concerning me it was: "George Flattery for his seriousness." My serious attitude toward life (even before my conversion to Christ at age 17) helped me to maintain complete chastity. I never did yield to any temptation to commit fornication—either before or after my conversion.

In the Fall of 1928, I entered the tenth grade at Wichita High School on East Douglas Avenue. When North High School was completed the following year, my school became known as Wichita High School East. I completed my high school training at Wichita East in August, 1931.

Conversion

My main interest before my conversion was in athletic activities. I preferred baseball and participated in amateur baseball. In 1930, I played for the Model Clothing Company's team at Wichita in the American Legion Junior League. Just before conversion, I attended the Grace Methodist church in Wichita, and played on its baseball team in 1931. For several years (while helping my father with truck gardening), my greatest recreational joy had been to attend periodically (with Ellis) the Western League's professional baseball games at Island Park. Wichitans of that era will remember that old ball park near the Broadview hotel.

I was converted to Christ on Sunday evening August 16, 1931, at the Pentecostal Tabernacle, an Assemblies of God church in Wichita. And at the same church, I received the Pentecostal baptism of the Holy Spirit, according to Acts 2:4, in April, 1932. Reverend and Mrs. H. B. Garlock had built this church and were pastoring it at the time of my conversion. I don't remember ever having thought about Pentecostal religion until one day, while on my way to high school in a streetcar going north on Main Street, I was impressed by the extremely large inscription PENTECOSTAL TABERNACLE written across the front of this church's rectangular wooden building at the corner of Lincoln and Main Streets.

Kenneth Haines (now deceased) was about my age and lived near me. On the day I was destined to be converted, God impressed him to invite me to go with him to the evening service at Lincoln and Main. I accompanied Kenneth to that Pentecostal meeting and listened intently to Mrs. H. B. (Ruth E.) Garlock's sermon. Then Kenneth invited me to go forward with him in response to her altar call.

I went to the altar with Kenneth and confessed all my sins to God (including my unforgiven stealing of Grove Stuckey's turnip so long ago). Then, according to 1 John 1:7-9, God immediately forgave me and cleansed me "from all unrighteousness" (v. 9) through "the blood of Jesus" (v. 7). I gratefully remember Kenneth Haines for his godly influence upon my life! My lifelong friend, Glen Ahlf, witnessed my conversion, and returned to God as I was being converted.

Kenneth Haines (right) and George Flattery, Sr., about 1968

At the time of my conversion in 1931, God began to impress me that I should become a missionary to Africa. Garlocks had been missionaries to Liberia, West Africa. They were preparing to return to West Africa, and encouraged me to prepare to go to Africa. (Reaching ahead in my autobiography: about 1943, Garlock became the first field secretary for A. G. missions in Africa. And it was about 1944 when, with his recommendation, the A. G. Foreign Missions Committee appointed Stella and me to Upper Volta—now Burkina Fasso—West Africa.)

Romance

Before my conversion at 17 I had experienced wholesome activities with neighborhood girls and girls in my classes at school. But I had never had a date with any of them. My conversion greatly increased my awareness of the teaching in Genesis 2:20-22 that God's purpose for creating woman was to bring "her to . . . man" (v. 22, NIV) to be a "suitable helper" (v. 20, NIV) to him. This awareness produced thoughts of romance in me. Stella Engel was a girl of my age in the young peoples' group at the Assembly of God church where I was converted. And the first time I saw her I fell in love with her!

I had never met a girl who seemed to care as much about all people as she did. Her interest in old people and children was extraordinary. When I first met her, she was seated at a large sand table in one of the church's Sunday School rooms, and was conversing with some little children. We had a cordial interchange of remarks—but I don't think she fell in love with me at first sight, as I did with her!

During my almost three years of courtship with her (between August, 1931 and marriage to her in May, 1934), it was my task to help create in her a love for me like the love I already had for her. (Fifty-eight unbroken years of married life with her testify to my success.) With God's help I was able to win Stella's love, largely through the sincerity and tenacity that He had created in me. Although no person can be saved spiritually by merit of these qualities, they can be very valuable to any person—saved or just needing to be saved! If one is "sincerely wrong" his fault is wrongness rather than sincerity. And correction is in departure not from sincerity but from wrong! The more conditional quality of tenacity is desirable only if directed toward something good.

I think my first date with Stella was our winter-1932 trip from Wichita to Hutchinson, Kansas, to participate in a young people's rally in the Assembly of God church. (It was the first time in my 18 years that I had been 60 miles away from home!)

I was the rally speaker and she drew a picture during a special musical presentation before I spoke. Our 3-year courtship was partly by correspondence, because Stella moved with her parents to Deercreek, Oklahoma, when I had known her for only about a year. The correspondence was cordial even though it revealed that she was dating a young man in Deercreek. But I couldn't bring myself to date any other girl while she lived in Deercreek—even though other young people at our Wichita church encouraged me to do so.

Another year had gone by and my journey to Enid, Oklahoma, to enter Southwestern Bible School in the Fall of 1933 was just ahead. By that time I had begun to think (to myself only) that if Stella did not enter this school along with me as she had thought of doing, I would begin to allow myself to think that God's plan for me might include some other young lady as wife to me. But I have never been happier than when I learned that in response to her Gideon's-fleece type of testing (see Judges 6:36-40) regarding going to Bible School or to New York to work, she had enrolled in Southwestern for that year! This brings me to the end of my nineteen years of early life, and I will describe my engagement to Stella in the next chapter.

Entire family of the parents of George Flattery, Sr., in 1937—the year he completed his Pentecostal training at Southwestern Bible School in Enid, Oklahoma. Back (left to right): Helen, George, Ellis, Frank, Iva, Wendell. Front: mother (Rose) and father (James Perley)

CHAPTER 2: PENTECOSTAL TRAINING

Have you ever experienced difficulty in trying to outline something you were writing—an essay at school, or just a letter to a friend? You were trying to create the outline but thoughts just wouldn't come to mind. Then suddenly the outline appeared to you on a mental screen, as it were! And you hurried to jot the outline down before the screen vanished. All this resembles my learning, later on, of four tribal languages during the twenty-year period that I was a missionary to Africa: I tried to keep a slip of paper in my pocket on which to jot down each new word the first time I recognized it, because I might not soon recognize it again.

In a very real sense my "Pentecostal training" here on earth began on the day of my conversion and will continue until the day God takes me to heaven. But I am using this phrase with reference to the part of my life between 1933 and 1937: my years of most intensive training for Pentecostal pioneering. I spent three of these four years at Southwestern Bible School. (It took me four years to complete Southwestern's three-year program because my financial circumstances caused me to miss a year after I had completed the first year of it.)

First Year at Southwestern

My big problem in 1933 concerned how and where I would receive the needed Pentecostal training for missionary work. I thought of trying to enroll in Central Bible Institute of Springfield, Missouri. But even though its charges for room and board were not excessive, they were more than I could afford. Then, one late-summer Sunday, Dr. P. C. Nelson visited the Assembly of God Church in Wichita, and told us about Southwestern Bible School in Enid, Oklahoma—the Pentecostal training school where he was president. Its charges were at a level that poorer students, like myself, could pay. So, I enrolled that day in Southwestern.

"He who finds a wife finds what is good and receives favor from the Lord" (Proverbs 18:22, NIV), and in some cases favor from the Foreign Missions Committee of the A. G. concerning his application for missionary appointment. This committee sometimes postpones a young man's application for missionary appointment until he can find a wife! In such cases, acquisition of a wife is an important part of his preparation to become a missionary. The entire courtship between some missionary couples has been carried out during their years at Bible School together. But I had already courted Stella for over two years before we arrived at Bible School in the Fall of 1933. When we arrived at Southwestern, we had not yet become officially engaged, but I knew that her love for me had become as much as my love for her since the day I first met her.

Now, how could we establish our engagement without breaking Southwestern's severe rules which prohibited private social activities between its men and women students—even between a man and woman who were contemplating engagement? These rules were ostensibly the same for couples who had experienced early stages of courtship before arriving at Southwestern as they were for couples who met for the first time at the school. The dean of women, Mother Bamford, told Stella and me after our marriage, following our first year at

Southwestern, that she wished she had allowed us some social times together during that year. Well, during the following year she cooperated with other leaders of the school in easing those rules a little—making them more realistic without endangering their propriety.

How Stella and I did establish our engagement within a few weeks after arriving at Southwestern is an interesting story: one day, Dr. Nelson told me that he and his wife had to drive to Wichita, and he invited me to accompany them so I could visit my family. Stella learned about this and, knowing that Deercreek was on the route between Enid and Wichita, asked to go along so she could visit her family. Daddy Nelson's rather eccentric but saintly wife wanted me to sit in the front seat while Stella rode in the back seat, but he placed us in the back seat together! Stella's parents had not had time to inform her that they had moved to Three Sands, Oklahoma, to pastor the Methodist church.

So, Stella went on to Wichita with Nelsons and me, where she stayed with some friends during the couple of days that Nelsons were in Wichita before returning with us to Southwestern. She and I were off limits to Southwestern's rules as well as its campus. So, we became officially engaged at Wichita while enjoying two precious, chaste, midfall days together. It was much nearer the time of our marriage when we set the day after we would complete the first year at Southwestern as the exact date for it. On May 8, 1934, Stella's father, Reverend George Engel, performed our simple wedding ceremony in my home. Stella's close friend Evelyn Heard was her Maid of Honor, and my brother Ellis was my Best Man. We had no wedding picture made.

Married Life and Preaching

Here, I will review the first 17 months of my married life, and of my preaching (if I omit the few occasions when I had spoken in my home church, or at a youth rally somewhere else).

These months include Southwestern's 5 vacation months in 1934, its 7-month 1934-35 school year which I missed, and its 5 vacation months in 1935.

Stella at 19, in 1933

George at 19, in 1933

What is the Pauline philosophy regarding a gospel minister's engagement in work other than that of his ministry? In 1 Corinthians 9 Paul says that "those who preach the gospel should receive their living from the gospel" (v. 14, NIV), and indicates that his own secular work was confined to "work for a living" (v. 6, NIV). When a gospel minister engages in secular work for material gain beyond his needs for a living, his potential for achievement of fruitful spiritual work in God's kingdom is reduced. I have tried to limit my secular work to that from which I needed help with my family's living expenses.

Just one week after Stella and I married, we set out with the late Charles Craighead and his wife Florence to engage in

Pentecostal pioneering in Tennessee. They too had studied at Southwestern during the 1933-34 school year. (At a subsequent time Charles became district superintendent of the Assemblies of God in Mississippi. After that, he was a prominent A. G. pastor in New Orleans, where he and Florence kept Stella and me in their home in 1960, and helped us to get back to West Africa for our fourth term of missionary service.)

On the memorable day in May, 1934, when the four of us crowded into Charles's one-seated Durante coupe to begin our long journey from Three Sands, Oklahoma, to Red Boiling Springs, Tennessee (75 miles northeast of Nashville), Charles had not yet preached a sermon. And I had preached very few times! Charles and I alternated in driving the little coupe. And each of us held his wife on his lap while the other drove. We enjoyed holding our wives, but being held was a little more difficult for Stella than Florence because she was the taller lady! Muskogee, Oklahoma; Russellville, Arkansas; Brinkley, Arkansas; Memphis, Tennessee; and Old Hickory, Tennessee; were among the places enroute to Red Boiling Springs where we stopped and held one-night meetings.

Our long journey ended at the home of Sid Langford and his wife Ora (Charles's sister), where we spent much of our time in the Red Boiling Springs area. We were among hillbillies: the gangling Sid popped little homemade biscuits in his mouth whole before sitting down to breakfast, and used catalogue paper to roll cigarettes from home grown tobacco! To show appreciation for room and board, Charles and I helped him hoe his tobacco, while Stella and Florence helped Ora with the housework. We stayed for a few days in a hotel at Red Boiling Springs. Sometimes couples who attended our meetings kept us for a night or two in their log cabins. When it was a one-room cabin, the couple would make their bed on the floor beside the bed they had given us!

Local men donated help for building a large brush arbor just outside Red Boiling Springs. We conducted meetings day and night under it for about a month. Charles alternated with me in preaching. The meetings were well attended, and we had converts. Many people had no cars and walked long distances to the meetings. A young single lady, Clio Ray (about 18 or 20), was among our converts under the arbor. Soon after her conversion, Clio went to Enid and completed Southwestern's three-year diploma course. During her years at school, she worked for a living in a factory that processed turkeys. Clio sent us her graduation picture with this comment:

> *Dear Stella and George, you will never know how much I appreciate your kindness and goodness to me. May God bless you and make you a soul winner forever. Please pray for my family. Your friend Clio Ray. Red Boiling Springs, Tennessee.*

Southwestern Bible School graduation picture of Clio Ray

After the brush arbor campaign, we and the Craigheads conducted Pentecostal meetings for about two weeks at Gregory's Chapel—a dirt-floored, tabernacle-type church at Windy City, Tennessee. All four of us stayed in a one-bed trailer house beside the church, taking turns sleeping on the floor! At Windy City, old Mr. Gregory said, jokingly, that marks of an itinerant preacher were "playing the guitar and the itch." Well, I almost qualified! I was trying to play a trombone and, no joke, did have a serious case of the itch. Also I had a little malaria that summer in Tennessee. But God helped me through everything, and it was all good training for my later years in West Africa.

Room and board were almost all that we received as remuneration for our Pentecostal pioneering in Tennessee during the summer of 1934. We were working among poor people who were even poorer than they had been before the great depression of that era. In August, the Dewey Slates (with whom we had stayed at Red Boiling Springs) invited us to ride with them to Eureka Springs, Arkansas, to attend the Assemblies of God tri-state camp meeting which Kansas District Superintendent Fred Vogler was conducting.

By that time we were wanting to visit my parents. So, enroute to Wichita, we went to Eureka Springs with the Slates. We were glad to be in the camp meeting, even though we arrived there with hardly enough money to buy a small bag of beans! Imagine our feelings while listening to Howard Carter's excellent sermon on evil desire for money which he termed "filthy lucre." After visiting my parents, we returned to the home of Stella's parents. They gladly kept us while we awaited the birth of our first child.

At about 1:00 a. m., Sunday, February 24, 1935, our son James Warren was born in the home of Stella's parents at Three Sands, Oklahoma, where her father was still the pastor of the Methodist church. After the morning service, almost the entire congregation came over to the parsonage beside the church to see our newborn son. It was a time of special joy for all of us!

Throughout Warren's life we have rejoiced in his care for others. First, we rejoiced in his special concern for his brother and sisters in our home. Then, later on, in his loving care for his own dear wife and daughter. For about 26 years Warren and his wife Jean have been missionaries: in Jordan (during wars of 1967 and 1970), in Europe, and now as a vice-president of the A. G. International Correspondence Institute at Irving, Texas.

Warren Flattery at 9 months

About a month after Warren was born, I moved my family to the small town of Billings, Oklahoma (near Three Sands), where I pastored the very small A. G. Church. We stayed there only about four months (until about mid-summer, 1935). We received almost no financial support from the church, and I could find no work there. How could I support my family in Billings?

In the summer of 1933, I had taken over someone's country

bread route around Wichita and, from operation of it, saved 90 dollars toward the 125 dollars I needed for my first year at Southwestern. So, I asked the Billings baker to allow me to take his bread and try to create a country bread route within a radius of 25 or 30 miles around Billings. I use the term "create" advisedly here, for I know that it is by God that "all things were created . . . and in him . . . hold together" (Colossians 1:16-17, NIV).

God alone has power to create out of nothing! But God has given man the ability to create or bring about new combinations and forms of things which already exist: the bakery already had the bread and people already lived around Billings. My job was to persuade them to be my bread customers—and I did! That bread route not only supported my family at Billings but also afforded opportunities to me for Pentecostal pioneering of spiritual bread among my customers.

During July and August of 1935, Stella and I held revival meetings at Cherokee, Oklahoma; Liberal, Kansas; and in a schoolhouse near Forgan, Oklahoma. Recent dust storms had been very severe and, at that schoolhouse, I had to scoop out literally bushels of dirt before I could hold meetings in it! We enjoyed staying with Roma Potter (Stella's sister) and her husband Ed while holding the meeting near Forgan. It was Pentecostal pioneering in all these meetings, and souls were saved in them.

Then in September we stayed a few weeks with my parents, who had moved (before we were married) to a 32-acre tract of farm land about a mile east of the 33-acre tract I mentioned in the first chapter. During those weeks I helped my father with the drilling of wheat. The 32-acre tract has now become part of Watson's park in south Wichita.

Back to Southwestern

In October, 1935, I took my family back to Southwestern Bible School and enrolled for my second year of study. Soon after enrolling, Stella and I saw that our financial circumstances would not permit us to continue in school. (I washed kitchen walls at the Youngblood Hotel, delivered the Enid Daily Eagle, peddled calendars and donuts—nothing paid me enough to keep my family.)

When I told the school of our plans to leave, students in my class (some even poorer than I, and others almost as poor) took up a collection among themselves to help me stay. It was only a few dollars, but its impact on us was far greater than its monetary value. I am grateful to this day for what those students did! I stayed in school throughout that year and the following year, and received my diploma from Southwestern in May, 1937.

Now back to the fall of 1935 for a few observations from my final two years in Southwestern. Soon after school began in 1935, we were attending the daily morning chapel service in the A. G. frame church building right beside the brick school building. And the church caught fire and burned completely. Reverend Robert McCutcheon was conducting the chapel service, I was playing my trombone in the orchestra, and Stella was attending the service with our 8-month-old Warren. Smoke was appearing below the ceiling above the platform, and McCutcheon was first to speak out of it.

Misunderstanding him, students thought he was speaking of holy, spiritual smoke. Many of the students knelt to pray. Stella also knelt to pray, after placing Warren on the bench where she had been seated. When McCutcheon immediately spoke out again, all understood that he was referring to the literal fire which was spreading in the building. Stella, carrying Warren, was accidentally run over from behind by a fleeing student. But neither she nor the baby was hurt. No one was hurt in the evacuation of the burning building.

While the church was burning, it was thought that the school might burn also. So, all library books were hurriedly removed from the school building. This did considerable damage to the books (many of them very old and all of them very valuable). A book repairman was needed to repair the books. Although I had not yet repaired books, Brother Nelson thought I would be the man for the job. He took me to a large bindery in Oklahoma City where I learned quite a bit in a short time about repairing books. From that time until I graduated from school—about 18 months—I repaired books for Southwestern. My pay (two or three dollars a week plus daily rations of milk, bread, and leftovers from the school cafeteria) would have been insufficient for current living, but was sufficient to support my family then.

I had received an exhorter's permit from the Kansas District of the A. G., when I visited its District Council meeting in November, 1935, at Topeka. Then, when I became the temporary pastor of the Okeene, Oklahoma, A. G. Church, for the summer of 1936, the Oklahoma District of the A. G. issued me my first license to preach. Stella and I were appointed as custodians of the Southwestern campus and buildings for the 1936 vacation months. And I continued to repair library books during this vacation period.

We returned temporarily to the home of Stella's parents in Three Sands for the birth of our second son, George Manford. He was born on September 10, 1936. We have rejoiced in his excellent childhood attitudes and his subsequent accomplishments (with the help of his dear wife Esther) for the kingdom of God.

Early in life and under their mother's direction, Warren and George studied in Africa by correspondence, and learned how valuable such study can be. In the early 1960's God gave George the idea of an International Correspondence Institute. He was outlining plans for such an institution while he was earning a doctoral degree in religious education. Then, he sought and received the A. G. Foreign Missions Committee's endorsement of those plans in 1967. Through combined efforts of this Missions Committee and dedicated ICI workers, ICI has become a very successful worldwide Christian outreach.

After graduation from Southwestern in May 1937, I went with Stella and our two sons to my parents' home at Wichita to await an opening for pastoral work in Kansas.

George Manford Flattery at 9 months

CHAPTER 3: PIONEER PASTORATES

During the seven and one half years following my graduation from Bible school at Enid, Oklahoma, I pastored two A. G. churches in Kansas: two and a half years at Wellington and five years at Leavenworth. Both were "pioneer pastorates" if we define the term as relating to a church which has not yet become able to supply all the financial support that its pastoral family needs. The Wellington church had struggled through its first six years under more than six pastors when I was called to it—none of them had stayed as much as one year. (I may have been its first pastor who required his term to be an indefinite time rather than only one year.) The Leavenworth church had existed for only six months when I began to pastor it.

Since neither church could completely support our family, I continued my binding of books (especially old Bibles) while pastoring each of them. I had been told that some students were letting their Bible School debts go unpaid for years. I was hoping to pay my modest school debt of about one hundred dollars within a year after my graduation. I was able to do that with my earnings from binding the Wellington City Directory.

Both the Wellington church and the Leavenworth church are doing well. The "1991 Thrust Report" of the Kansas District Council states that Wellington averaged 85 in weekly attendance and gave $15,465 to world ministries. And it states that Leavenworth averaged 99 in attendance and gave $10,894 to such ministries. In recent years, it has been the privilege of Stella and me to participate in the 50th anniversary celebration for each of these churches: at Wellington in 1981, and at Leavenworth in 1989.

Wellington

We had owned a car at Enid but did not have one when we arrived at Wellington in June of 1937, to begin our pastoral work. We needed to visit many people throughout the city: people who had not yet attended our church, or infrequently attended it, as well as the small group who were faithfully attending it. We wanted to take our little sons (Warren 2 and George 9 months) with us in this visitation work. We felt that their presence with us in the homes of new people would help to bring those people to our church. The boys were too heavy to carry about in this work! What would we do?

We needed a vehicle. But the worsening of the Great Depression in the late 1930's made it financially impossible for us to buy a car during our first few months in Wellington. We did buy, from a secondhand store, a four-wheeled vehicle right after arriving there—but it was only an outdated, wicker baby buggy! (Coincidentally, it was the same kind of baby buggy that I had used while in Bible School to wheel donuts around Enid.) We put our babies in the buggy from week to week and, pushing it here and there in Wellington, accomplished our church visitation work. Most of the people we visited were friendly, and some invited us for meals. Several times we visited Mr. Mounts who was then 99. He was a veteran of the Civil War in the U. S. A. After a while we were able to buy an old car for our work.

The only financial support of some of our church people at Wellington was from WPA (Works Progress Administration), a national relief organization which provided work for people during the Great Depression. People received some (but not much) money from the United States government for this work. In addition the government gave them (from surpluses) such foods as butter, cheese, powdered milk, and grapefruit. We too enjoyed these food surpluses, as our church people brought to us a tithe of them. We shared this food with hungry hobos who got off railroad boxcars nearby and came frequently to our door. The parsonage door must have been marked. During the depression there was a shortage of many things—but not hobos!

When we accepted the pastorate in Wellington, the church people had not been able in six years to complete the siding of their 40 ft. by 60 ft. frame building. So one of my first jobs was to complete the siding of the west end of the building, paint the newly sided part, then paint the entire building. Up to that time I knew little about the construction and maintenance of buildings. This job taught me a little more.

The church's wooden front steps needed replacing. Construction of new concrete steps presented quite a problem to me. The steps were long enough that two-inch forming lumber was needed for the risers. But I used one-inch forming lumber for them because it was all I had. Like a bad golf shot that sometimes turns out better than a good shot, my forming of those risers turned out better than if I had used the right lumber in forming them: the one-inch forms bowed just enough to produce an unplanned set of beautifully curved steps which serve the church to this day—55 years later!

Stella directed the church women's helpful quilting projects, and their preparation of meals for people who attended our sectional rallies. For one rally in particular, I remember her buying of large supplies of chicken, eggs for noodles, jello, and other foods with funds that the women had saved up for the occasion. About 125 (or more) attended the rally and enjoyed the fellowship of a lovely meal together in the Wellington city park's spacious dining facility.

While we pastored the Wellington church, Brother Mumford, one of its men, began the digging out under the church which resulted (many years later under the supervision of Pastor N. B. Rayburn) in the completion of a finely finished basement with Sunday School rooms. When Rayburn completed this project in 1971, my wife and I were among the former pastors of the church who attended the dedication of the new basement.

George Flattery, Sr. (left) and N. B. Rayburn, in front of the Wellington A. G. church in 1971

In the summer of 1939 (a few months before our time in Wellington ended), Stella, Warren, George, and I (accompanied by my sister Iva and Mrs. Moore of our church) made a trip to Southern California to visit my grandmother Harriet Flattery and her daughter, my Aunt Eunice Flattery. Grandmother was 92 and died about a year later. She was blind but still very alert. One of my most cherished memories is that of her singing (in a rocking chair) "Would you live for Jesus, and be always pure and good? Would you walk with Him within the narrow road?" from Nusbaum's hymn. During this 1939 visit, we attended the Santa Ana A. G. church where Ernest Friend was pastor, and he invited us to participate in his Sunday services. Years later in Africa (about 1945-1948), we enjoyed fellowship with Friend and his family, while we were missionaries to Upper Volta and they were missionaries to the Gold Coast.

Back: Aunt Eunice Flattery (left), and George. Front: Warren (left), Grandma Harriet, and George, Jr. At Santa Ana, California, 1939

Leavenworth

Leavenworth, Kansas (a city of about 20,000 people) is older than the much bigger Kansas City, Kansas. It is known as the pioneer city of Kansas. The first effort to establish an A. G. church in Leavenworth was begun in the Spring of 1939, by a minister who stayed there only about six months. Stella and I (with our two small sons) moved in November, 1939, from Wellington to Leavenworth to continue the work he had left so soon. (Since the first minister stayed only a few months and we stayed five years, I was honored during the church's 50th anniversary celebration in May, 1989, as the founding pastor.) In 1939, under the pastoral leadership of Reverend and Mrs. H. B. Garlock, the First A. G. Church at Seventh and Riverview in Kansas City, Kansas, helped substantially to establish our new A. G. church in Leavenworth.

Just before we moved to Leavenworth, Garlock's church had bought for Leavenworth's newly formed A. G. congregation a small Methodist church building. Leavenworth was a pioneer pastorate for us in an even stricter sense than Wellington had been. We had moved into the church parsonage at Wellington in June, 1937. There was no parsonage for us in Leavenworth in November, 1939! And it was financially impossible for us to rent a house in which to live.

The winter (usually colder than in southern Kansas) was at hand. It was with reluctance that I moved my family into the rough, one-room, unceiled, basement apartment of the small church building located at Wilson and Vilas streets (on Billy Goat Hill), in the southern part of Leavenworth, near the west bank of the Missouri river. This was even better than boot-camp training for our time at Corabie, Upper Volta, in West Africa—about seven years later!

The church people had brought food into the basement for us the day we arrived. That encouraged us but we were discouraged that first night by large river rats that came through the holes in the basement floor and damaged those food supplies. Those rats caused us to be "troubled . . . but not in despair" (2 Corinthians 4:8, KJV). We used traps to catch any that remained in the basement, and plugged the holes to keep others from coming in!

It was so cold in that rough apartment that each of us had to stand close to the pot bellied wood stove—warming his front and back sides alternately! In further effort to keep warm, we strung up bed quilts around the stove and stood between them and it. When summer arrived we accomplished the rather extensive task of putting a ceiling and new floor in our basement apartment, then enjoyed much greater comfort during our second winter in it.

Wadsworth, Kansas (just a few hundred yards south of the southern boundary of Leavenworth), is a large facility for the care of veterans of wars. Many of the veterans were unsaved, and were impaired mentally as well as physically. Knowing that "it is not the healthy who need a doctor, but the sick" (Luke 5:31, NIV), we invited them all to attend our church. On pay day some of the more evil minded among them would slip over into Bain City (a small center of great wickedness between Wadsworth and Leavenworth), buy its free-flowing liquor, get drunk, and sometimes commit murder. All this was enacted almost within earshot of our little church on Billy Goat Hill. What a milieu from which to draw a congregation! But God blessed our Pentecostal pioneering among those veterans. Some, like William Schwerdfager, matured beautifully in Christ while attending our church.

William Schwerdfager, a veteran of World War I

At Leavenworth God blessed our Pentecostal pioneering with a not-large-but-faithful congregation from the city itself. Most who had attended the Methodist church just continued to attend when it became an A. G. church. We were able to help them come into Pentecost. And we also won new converts from the city.

I will not devote a large amount of space to the naming of people who formed our congregation in Leavenworth, but will refer to one family as an example of others: Orville Rutter and his wife Faye were brought to the Lord through our Pentecostal pioneering effort. They lived on a small tract of land near the church, grew many vegetables, and kept a cow. Orville (now deceased) worked skillfully for many years at the Wadsworth facility for veterans. He donated as much labor to our building projects as any man in the church. And Faye, a very proficient housewife, often supplied our table with milk, butter, eggs, her delicious custard pies, and other foods. (What a joy it was to visit with her again during the church's 50th anniversary celebration in May, 1989!)

As to the Rutter children: Charlie went into the U. S. Air Force, and in more recent years has helped with maintenance of the A. G. Bethany Bible College near Santa Cruz, California. Juanita married Herman Karriker and for several years has helped him to pastor the A. G. church in Tonganoxie, Kansas. And David helped to win his neighborhood chum, Arthur Sorg, to the Lord. (Sorg became a well-known A. G. minister in Kansas, preached the Sunday morning sermon during Leavenworth's 50th anniversary celebration, and is now pastoring the Medicine Lodge, Kansas, A. G. church.)

While in Leavenworth we were able to minister from time to time in the Kansas State Prison at Lansing (just 4 miles south of Leavenworth), but were not allowed to minister in the Federal Prison on the northern edge of the city. Just outside Leavenworth to the north is Fort Leavenworth with its huge army prison. One officer at the Fort attended our church with his wife quite regularly, and invited us to their home (within the Fort) for meals.

Shortly after the Japanese raid on Pearl Harbor on December 7, 1941, Fort Leavenworth became an important reception center for American soldiers who had been drafted into military service for World War II. Many draftees, including my three brothers (Ellis on his way to the South Pacific, Frank on his way to Okinawa, and Wendell on his way to Europe), attended our church during the short period they were there. We ministered spiritual help to these draftees during their tearful "goodbyes" to their families.

Warren (left) and George in front of school building across street from A. G. church at Wilson and Vilas streets

In Leavenworth we lived for about two years in the small church basement at Wilson and Vilas, then during our remaining three years, we lived at three other places in the city: 420 Second Avenue, 222 Spruce, and 411 Sheridan. On Second Avenue we lived on the upstairs floor of the house where the

Charles McKinney family lived on the first floor. McKinney with his wife Louise and two daughters came to our church from Aaron Wilson's large A. G. church in Kansas City, Missouri. The whole McKinney family helped our young church in various ways. On Spruce street we lived on the second floor where Warren and Mayme White and their children (of our church) lived on the first floor. Mayme was a friend of Stella's family in western Kansas, when Stella was a small girl. Then we purchased the small house on Sheridan and lived there until we left Leavenworth.

As I write for you about our building of a new church building at a new location in Leavenworth, I will draw information from my articles of November 28, 1943, in "The Leavenworth Times" and of January, 1944, in "The Kansas Fellowship News."

We knew from the beginning that our church on Billy Goat Hill was (because of its isolation) poorly located. We planned from the beginning to find a suitable property and build a new church. After two years in Leavenworth, our first step toward a new church was to move ourselves out of the church basement at Wilson and Vilas and sell that church. Because of our having made the basement into suitable living quarters, We received $525 for this little (I started to say "2x4" but it was 24x35) church which had been purchased for $300. We put this $525 with $300 which we borrowed from Springfield, Missouri's "A. G. Revolving Church Extension Fund" and began the $10,000 project of building a new church with only $825 cash in hand!

We decided to build the new church on the city bus route at Fourth (U. S. Highway 73) and Sheridan, where we could maintain our contact with the southern part of Leavenworth, and also be more conveniently located to serve those who would want to attend our services from the entire city, and vicinity. In the fall of 1941, we hired J. O. Fisher as our construction foreman for the building of the 40x60 full basement for this new church. The rest of the labor was donated by church men and myself. We completed this basement and had our first service in it on Pearl Harbor Day (Sunday morning, December 7, 1941).

We were building on the pay-as-you-go plan, and it was about 18 months after finishing the basement before we had money to begin building the superstructure of the church. The roof over the basement was the floor for the second story of the church. That made the basement more expensive but saved money in the long run. Since we had built a sloping floor for the superstructure, some people driving by the basement thought the builder had "lost his level."

About May or June, 1943, I hired a carpentering gospel minister of Coffeyville, Kansas, Paul W. Kincaid, to help me frame the entire superstructure of the church. Then with the help of our church people, I completed the entire building. While helping me to nail the rolls of roofing over the wooden sheeting, my son George, then 7, said, "Dad, I'm an expert."

Although our family has teased George about saying this, I feel that he has, indeed, developed expertise throughout his life in his projects for the Lord! Many others feel the same way about George's accomplishments. Central Bible College of Springfield, Missouri, conferred upon him its honor of alumnus of the year, in 1977.

Church women, as well as men, helped with the building of the superstructure. The women applied the first coat of paint to siding boards before those boards were nailed in place over the boxing. One day Stella was standing on a nail keg inside the church while varnishing a window frame. She lost her footing, struck the base of her spine against the top of the keg and, in physical anguish, rolled on the floor. (Fortunately, she was not permanently injured.) Her rolling on the floor resembled the rolling of Pentecostal people on church altar floors which (quite often back then) caused bystanders to call them "holy rollers." But rolling at the altar was seldom caused primarily by a physical condition. Usually, it was caused mainly by "anguish . . . of . . . evil" (Romans 2:9, KJV) or "joy in the Holy Spirit" (Romans 14:17, NIV).

God supplied (with our cooperation) much of the material for the superstructure in an unusual way: Helmers Furniture Company had vacated their large lumber shed (150x45 feet) and sold it to us at a bargain. We tore the shed down and received 20,000 board feet of sound lumber for only $500. We felt that this cured, used lumber was at least as good for the building of our superstructure as new lumber would have been. The shed not only furnished us with enough lumber to frame and box our entire superstructure, but also with much additional lumber to exchange for new finish lumber, windows, doors, paint, etc.

I did most of the dismantling of the lumber shed myself, because my church men were working overtime in the civilian war work of the era. Passersby, seeing me with crowbar atop that long shed, would refer to me as the "lone eagle." Some of them even thought there was facial resemblance between me and the famed "lone eagle" of early aviation, Charles A. Lindberg. Well, I've no claim to fame but have sincerely tried to be "faithful in all things" (1 Timothy 3:11, KJV). Paul wrote this concerning wives, but it applies to me and every other Christian believer!

When we had completed all of the outside work of the superstructure, a Leavenworth building and loan association lent us $1500 with which to finish its entire interior. When we completed our building and held our first service in its superstructure on Easter Sunday, in April, 1944, it was worth about $10,000 and we only owed $1500 on it. During the five remaining months of our five years in Leavenworth, our church did better in every way than it could have done on "Billy Goat Hill." Then under the ministry of pastor Frank Tatum (after we had gone to Africa), it paid off its $1500 building indebtedness before it was due.

Leavenworth Assembly of God church completed in 1944

Conclusion

In concluding this chapter on "Pioneer Pastorates," I will refer to the revival campaigns in our churches at Wellington and Leavenworth. At each place we called evangelists quite frequently to conduct revivals. Some of the campaigns produced more genuine revival than others, but all of them were worthwhile. They brought in new people to our Sunday School and church. One of our first revival campaigns in Leavenworth brought the record attendance in Sunday School up from about 100 to 145!

Some of the evangelists who helped our church at Wellington were: Wanda Faye Wells with Beulah Sears, Doug Friesen, and the Zook party. Some at Leavenworth were: Ray Murphy, Sister Cleever, Jimmie and Madge Mayo, Brother and Sister Cotton, Bob Sellers, Alma Bryant, E. C. Lagmay, Cordelia Donnell with Mildred Holler, and Floyd Dennis.

Our evangelists nearly always stayed with us to avoid the unnecessary expense of room and board. Back then we couldn't always do everything in the modern fashion that has marked our way of life in recent years. For example, we sometimes bathed our children only once a week in an old-fashioned wash tub—instead of every day in a lovely shower room. Once a lady evangelist asked my wife about arrangements for bathing, and our five-year-old son George, overhearing her, spoke up and said: "This ain't Saturday"!

Evangelist E. C. Lagmay at Leavenworth, Kansas in 1942

CHAPTER 4: STUDY OF FRENCH

In Leavenworth

I did not study any foreign language in elementary school or in high school. Nor did I have much interest in foreign languages during those school years. When I received my call to foreign missionary work (shortly after my graduation from high school and conversion to Christ), I began to be more aware of the value of foreign language study. During 1934-35 (the year that I was forced by financial circumstances to miss school at Southwestern), I thoroughly studied (on my own) a college-level Spanish grammar book. (As yet, my wife and I had no indication as to what foreign language we would use in missionary work.) I studied Spanish that year because I thought such study was a valuable way to occupy my time, while awaiting the birth of our first child.

The Foreign Missions Committee of the A. G. in Springfield, Missouri, called us to Springfield in 1940, to interview us concerning the application for missionary appointment that we had placed with them, back in 1937. They were very considerate of us and helpful to us, while informing us that because of World War II in Europe, we could not receive appointment in 1940. Then this committee encouraged us to keep open hearts and minds toward receiving missionary appointment (perhaps to the Upper Volta in French West Africa) after the war ended.

The committee wanted our children to be with us when we met them. Warren 5 behaved well during the meeting but George 3 needed a spanking. So I excused myself and took him out and spanked him. While spanking him, I was thinking: "Oh boy, this will hinder our chances for missionary appointment!" But when we went back to the committee, its spiritually mature members seemed to think that during such a meeting it was quite normal for a three-year-old to need a spanking, and just as normal for his father to take him out and apply it!

Before World War II, A. G. missionaries to French West Africa were not required to learn French, and few of them learned very much of it. But world conditions after that war made it very desirable that missionaries to French-speaking areas of the world be able to communicate in French as well as in tribal languages. It was during the summer of 1943 when V. G. Greisen (Kansas District Superintendent of the A. G.) came to us in Leavenworth and told us we had been appointed to the Upper Volta.

We were then certain that we had to learn French. I thought back (about nine years) to how well I had succeeded (on my own) in the study of Spanish. So I went to the Leavenworth public library, checked out a French grammar book, and began to try to learn some French without a teacher. Very soon I saw that French was more difficult for an English-speaking person to learn than Spanish. Then I abandoned study on my own, and engaged Laverne Dale (a member of our church and one of its pianists) to teach French from a high school textbook to my wife and me. Dale had been an interpreter of French for American soldiers in France during World War I. He taught us for about a year and helped us to get a good start in French.

In Springfield

When we left Leavenworth in September 1944, we moved

to the house that was then at 1410 North Clay street in Springfield, Missouri. The A. G. foreign missions committee had invited us to continue our study of French in Springfield at Central Bible Institute, while we waited for world conditions that would permit our going to Upper Volta. It was a few months before the battle of the Belgian Bulge in Europe when we arrived in Springfield. For about four months, Madame DeLattre of C. B. I. taught us French. Our assignments from her included the memorization of the entire fourth chapter of the Gospel of John.

I felt that I could accomplish a little more than she was assigning us. So, I purchased a phonographic record course in French and thoroughly studied it during our time in Springfield. The course included the reading matter of grammar, vocabulary, and idiom booklets, as well as fifteen double-sided records to listen to. Between about September 10, 1944, and January 1, 1945; my wife and I learned much from Madame Delattre, and I learned much more from the excellent phonographic course.

While we lived those four months on Clay street, we enjoyed a six-week visit from my mother who came over from Butler County, Kansas. This visit was very special to both her and us: it was her farewell to us before our leaving to spend several years in Africa. One day, we all took my mother to the Branson, Missouri, area. Back then (the fall of 1944), that area had been developed very little as a tourist attraction. My mother (then past 60) joined us in descending a little ways down into Marvel Cave, by means of a rickety wooden ladder. Stella's sister, Roma, came from Forgan, Oklahoma, with her beautiful little daughter, Roma Ann, just before we left Springfield, and told us good-bye.

In Canada

Near the end of December, 1944, the A. G. Foreign Missions Committee seemed pleased with the progress in the study of French that my wife and I had made in Leavenworth and Springfield. I think the Allies' decisive victory over Hitler in Belgium helped to convince this committee to authorize us to begin On January 1, 1945, the trip in our car to New York. We were to wait in New York city (and continue our study of French by phonograph) until improving world conditions would permit us to go on to Africa.

George Flattery Sr. and his mother Rose Flattery with Warren (right) and George in 1944

During the latter part of December, 1944, we used the little garage back of our house on Clay street as the place to pack our drums and other freight for shipment to Africa. On December 30, a big van picked up this freight and took it to the railroad depot in Springfield. Two days later, at 7 p. m. January 1, 1945, we finished packing our car for our trip to New York. It was about 7 a. m. next day when we left Springfield on this trip. We traveled rather slowly with the heavily packed car, arriving about 4 p. m. in St Louis that day. We then visited my brother Wendell who was stationed at Scott Field in preparation for going on to the European battle fields.

On January 3, we went on to Chicago and stayed in its A. G. missionary rest home that night. The next day before proceeding further eastward, I visited the French consulate in Chicago to inquire about our visas for Upper Volta. The French official had no word as yet as to when they would come. The road began to cover with ice and we had to stop at Lagrange, Indiana, for the night of January 4. The next day on the ice (and in the snow—worst in 12 years in that area), we got to Cleveland about 3 p. m. and it took 2 hours to drive through it. We stayed at nearby Willoughby that night. We had planned to follow the Great lakes route to Syracuse, N. Y., so Stella could visit friends there. But at the beginning of our journey on January 6, the snow and ice caused us to turn southeastward for the turnpike and Pittsburg, Pa.

When that day our car slid headfirst into a ditch, my first thought was "Satan must be disputing with the Lord about our going to Africa in the manner that he disputed with Him about the life of Job" (see Job 2:3-6). But the ditch was shallow and we suffered no damage! Satan would have preferred to cast us into a deep ditch, but the God who had limited what he could do against Job "stilled the storm" (Psalm 107:29, NIV) for us by providing a shallow ditch. We continued slowly but steadily on our way and arrived in Pittsburg about 6 p. m. The 150 mile trip on ice from Willoughby had taken 12 hours! On Sunday, January 7, we attended the A. G. church in Pittsburg where Reverend McKinney was pastor. I preached at his church that morning. Then our sons enjoyed ice sledding in his yard that afternoon.

Early January 8, we began our trip to Harrisburg, Pa. Between Pittsburg and Harrisburg we stopped at a truck stop on the turnpike. And its radio announced that New York city might be bombed any moment by missles launched from nearby submarines. It seemed to me as though there were a voice whispering "better give up this idea of going to Africa via New York City." Satan was trying to combine "an alarm of war"

(Jeremiah 49:2, KJV) with the terrible ice and snow in an effort to turn us away from our "heavenly calling" (Hebrews 3:1). I said to Satan just what Jesus said to him in Matthew 16:23 (NIV): "Get behind me!" Then we drove on to Harrisburg. On January 9 (seven days from Springfield, Missouri), we crossed over the George Washington bridge into New York City.

When We met Reverend C. B. Smith (the general superintendent of the Pentecostal Assemblies of Canada) at Pastor Mckinney's church in Pittsburg, we did not yet have plans to go to Montreal while waiting for our visas for Africa. But Smith, having learned of our need for further French study, suggested that we go to Montreal to study French at the Pentecostal Bible School there. Then two days later at a previously scheduled meeting with Garlock in Toronto, Smith informed him of the opportunity for us in Montreal. It was only a few days after our arrival in New York City when we received word from Garlock to go to Montreal as soon as possible to study French.

This was our first time in New York City. We spent 11 days there before putting our old Ford in storage and going by train to Montreal. One night during those days, I preached in English in a church in one of the slums of New York City. Warren and George attended a New York City school. The Empire State Building and Rockefeller Center were prominent among many marvelous sights for we midwesterners to see! Another of those marvelous sights was the 5-layered subway system which wound its ways down under the great buildings. We enjoyed riding in the subways.

During the baseball season, our sons (like me) were always interested in checking the sports page of the paper to see how the major league teams were doing. The Polo Grounds where the New York Giants had played for many years was in view from the back rooms of Mizpeh Missionary Home at 1003 Summit Ave. in the Bronx—our home during those 11 days in New York City. It was winter, but we enjoyed just looking out our back window at the famous baseball stadium!

On January 20, 1945, our train to Montreal followed the Hudson River and Lake Champlain. We had a joyful trip through beautiful winter scenery. W. L. Bouchard, principal of Montreal's Berea French Bible Institute (a Pentecostal school), met us at the Montreal train station, took us to his home at 1750 Gouin Blvd. E., and provided lodging for us in his home adjacent to the school. We ate at the school to gain the advantage of French conversation during meals.

Berea French Bible Institute at 1750 Gouin Blvd. E., Montreal. Home of Bouchard at left end of school building

We immediately placed Warren and George in the elementary division of this French school. Stella and I entered some special classes in French. Part of our classes were taught by teachers in the elementary division, and the rest of them were taught by teachers in the Bible School. Mme M. A. Tasse, a former Catholic nun, was the Bible School teacher of advanced French. We learned that Montreal was then about two-thirds French. It was a city of about 1,500,000 people and mostly Catholic. Soon after our arrival, we toured its renowned St. Joseph's cathedral.

There was an ice skating rink in the school yard (such rinks are numerous in Montreal). Warren and George learned to skate quite well during the winter we were there. One day, Warren cut his chin while skating. It is commendable that he always keeps his chin up, but he's been prone to minor chin injuries from various things. We've always joked with him about "leading with his chin." Warren was 10 just a month or so after we arrived in Montreal. French-Canadian boys average smaller than boys from the U. S. A. Many people in Montreal thought Warren was about 12. I tried to skate a few times but didn't accomplish much. Although I was only 30, I was already "an old dog trying new tricks" when I would put on skates and get out on the rink!

Because of my diligent study of French in Leavenworth and Springfield, I was able to preach my first sermon in French about 2 or 3 weeks after we arrived in Montreal. I'm sure many in my audience thought my French was slow and faulty. But I knew it was best for me that I begin to try to preach in French as soon as possible. During our almost six months in Montreal, we attended regularly a French Pentecostal church which was then located in a large room over a store building in a section of downtown Montreal. Reverend E. L. Lassegues, a rather young bachelor, was the very capable pastor of this church. It was a blessing to us just to witness the great joy of worship expressed by these French Pentecostals.

On May 8, 1945, the war in Europe ended. Montreal wildly celebrated the event with great fanfare that stopped almost everything—even street cars! We knew that our permits to enter Upper Volta, French West Africa, would soon be granted. We had been in Montreal almost four months, and all four of us had made good progress in French. By this time the A. G. Foreign Missions Committee in Springfield, Missouri, had sent about 21 other missionary candidates to Montreal to study French—and more were on the way. We knew when we were sent ahead of all the others that we were like "guinea pigs" in that the committee would not send others if we failed to make good progress in French.

U. S. A. Assemblies of God missionary appointees to French-speaking countries in the yard of the Berea French Bible Institute in Montreal, about June, 1945

We were impressed that Montreal was probably as good a place for English-speaking missionary candidates to study French as any other place that was open to them during World War II. Our positive attitude toward studying French in Montreal helped us to do well in our studies up there. Those who came later were doing well too. When the French Pentecostal church asked we missionary candidates to conduct one of its services in French, we complied and did all right: Raymond Sanders led the song service, Amelia Schewe and Stella led in prayer, and I preached the sermon. Toward the end of our time in Montreal, I taught, in French, the young men's Sunday School class at the French Pentecostal church, and preached in French at several other Pentecostal churches in and near Montreal.

As the time for our departure from Montreal for Africa was drawing near, I was helping other missionary candidates with their French: by teaching phonetic sounds to beginning classes, and Hugo's grammar to middle classes. Also I translated into English some of the instructions given by Mme Tasse to missionary candidates in the advanced French classes. When we were leaving Montreal on July 9, 1945, some of the missionary candidates wanted me to stay on and continue to help them with French. I would have enjoyed doing that, but could not because it was time for me and my family to leave for Africa. I will begin the next chapter by telling about our two weeks in New York City before flying to the Bermuda Islands on our way to Africa.

Back: Stella (left), George, Sr. Front: Warren (left), George, Jr. Beside Berea French Bible Institute in Montreal—just before leaving for Africa

PART TWO:

FRENCH WEST AFRICA

Rev. and Mrs. George W. Flattery

George Warren

The Fields . . . Are White Already to Harvest.
John 4:35

PRAY FOR AFRICA

Foreign Address:
Ouagadougou
Upper Ivory Coast
French West Africa

Home Address:
336 W. Pacific St.,
Springfield, Mo.
U. S. A.

Flattery Missionary Card of 1944. Back: Stella (left) and George, Sr. Front: George, Jr. (left) and Warren

CHAPTER 5: FIRST TERM, UPPER VOLTA

From Montreal to Ouagadougou

We arrived back in New York City from Montreal by train on July 9, 1945. Much of our time during the next two weeks was spent in buying the remainder of our outfit for Africa. We had purchased beds, a stove, and some other things in Montreal. One day while I was shopping in New York City, Stella and our sons went sight-seeing by boat up the Hudson river to a point about 30 miles north of the city. During this excursion, they enjoyed fellowship with the Foths, an A. G. missionary family to India who were also staying at Mizpeh at the time.

On July 25, we flew from New York City to Bermuda in one of the four Pan-American Clipper Ships. Just before getting on the plane, we and some other missionaries went together (in an impromptu fashion) to a secluded place near the passengers' waiting room to pray God for His protection during this flight over a large expanse of the Atlantic Ocean. The war with Japan was not over yet when we made this flight. We knew that we would be put off the plane and left temporarily in Bermuda, if there happened to be priority military personnel there who needed our seats on the plane. How happy we were when after an hour or two in Bermuda, we were called to get back on the plane to proceed on our way toward Africa!

But after a flight of about 600 miles toward the Azores, our plane had to turn around and go back to Bermuda. The swells on the Azores' harbor were bigger than the plane could land on. Then when the plane started again for the Azores, priority personnel were given our seats and we were left behind! At first we were saddened, but soon learned that God had planned a lovely two-week vacation for us in Bermuda. We needed that relaxation because we had been in a difficult, full-time, study program for a year without a vacation. In Bermuda, Warren and George learned to swim in a swimming pool, and I played some golf.

Warren 10 and 1/2, and George almost 9, enjoying a vacation in Bermuda

Pan-American Airways paid all our expenses during those two weeks in Bermuda—but only because we had been included on the plane the day they had to return to Bermuda! Our family was given England's Queen Mother's suite of rooms in

Bermuda's elegant Belmont Manor hotel. Every time we crossed over the bay from the hotel to the town, we enjoyed a lovely ride on a ferry. On August 8, we flew on another one of the Pan-American Clipper Ships from Bermuda to the Azores. We arrived at the Azores during the morning of August 9, and, after just an hour there, flew by the same plane to Lisbon, Portugal. We arrived in Lisbon during the afternoon of the same day.

When we went to a restaurant to eat in Lisbon, a glass of red liquid was placed on the table before each one of us. We wondered what kind of beverage it was. We didn't know whether it contained alcohol or not, whether it was fermented or sweet liquid. So I tasted it to see, and it was bitter. Then we knew that it was a red alcoholic drink. I told the waitress to take it away and bring us water to drink. When Daniel asked the king of Babylon for "nothing but . . . water to drink" (Daniel 1:12, NIV), he was asking for the best of beverages for a healthy person. Paul's admonition to "stop drinking only water, and use a little wine because of your stomach and your frequent illnesses" (1 Timothy 5:23, NIV) is valid advice for a sick person. But it does not contradict my estimation of the value of water to health!

We noticed that the people of Lisbon ate fish twice daily, and that many industrious fishermen live there. Streets are filled with women who go barefooted about Lisbon carrying on their heads big baskets of fish to sell. We saw one woman carrying a big sewing machine on her head. Many Portuguese women resemble African women in carrying heavy loads on their heads, and in going barefooted. We enjoyed our visit in the Lisbon area to two ancient castles. The oldest of the two was wrested in the 12th century by the Portuguese from the Moorish people (Mohammedans).

We had to stay two weeks in Lisbon before we could get a plane for Dakar, West Africa. Although we were enjoying our time in Lisbon, we would have preferred to go sooner to our work in Africa. It seemed that in Lisbon some people without plane tickets to Dakar were paying extra money for such tickets and immediately given seats on the plane. Missionaries could not do that and, consequently, were being held longer in Lisbon before they were granted passage to Dakar on the tickets they had already had for some time.

Stella with George (left) and Warren at a famous Square in Lisbon

"Pop" Martin, a veteran missionary of the Christian and Missionary Alliance (whom we had met in Bermuda), had gone on to Lisbon a week ahead of us, and had, with some success, intervened in Lisbon for stranded missionaries. Without his intervention, we would probably have been forced to wait even longer there. On August 23 (two weeks after having arrived in Lisbon), we flew out of Lisbon for Dakar on still another one of the four Pan-American Clipper Ships. It was an 11-hour flight.

My first glimpse of the African continent was of the western edge of the great Sahara Desert from our plane at 6000 feet above it. What I could make out of the landscape below was absolutely nothing but sand. I felt glad to be in an air-conditioned plane above that desert's heat, instead of down there in it! As we progressed southward over Africa toward Dakar, the landscape below changed from desert to steppes, and we could begin to distinguish signs of human habitation: some vegetation, little clearings with small huts, and even man-made roads.

We were supposed to have landed at Dakar, but there were swells on the harbor which prevented our sea-plane from landing. We had to proceed about 75 miles down the African coast to Bathurst for landing. Just before landing, the plane was shut up for spraying within it. This operation gave us some stomach sickness. We were glad to breath some fresh African air as we stepped out of the plane! We were cared for at the British Overseas Airways Headquarters, and flown in an R. A. F. Dakota plane the next morning to Dakar. It was a 50-minute trip from Bathurst to Dakar.

After having been in Dakar for only a day or two, Stella wrote her parents:

> *Africa is just as we had pictured it in our minds. They wear anything to cover them. The more they can get wrapped around them the prouder they are. And of course even in a city you see them in their birthday clothes.*

I preached my first sermon in Africa on Sunday, August 26, to about 100 men at the Dakar American Army Camp. I was asked to fill the pulpit for their chaplain who was vacationing in the Holy Land. The assistant chaplain took us to the meeting in an army vehicle. After the church service, Stella and I with our sons were invited to an excellent dinner at this army camp. The captain of the base (a Californian) ate with us in the officers mess.

After we had been in Dakar one week, a much-used, threemotored, French military plane began its journey with us from Dakar to Bobo Dioulassou (about 200 miles west of our destination at Ouagadougou). The plane maintained a low altitude. We had an excellent view of everything (people, housing, animals, vegetation) as we flew eastward over West Africa. The plane stayed overnight at Bamako and went on the next day to Bobo.

A. G. missionary Vivan Smith met us at Bobo and took us the remaining 200 miles of the long journey from Dakar to Ouagadougou in the Upper Volta Field's mission truck. More than once the absence of toilets along those 200 miles caused us to improvise (make do for the occasion): Smith would stop the truck, each of us would get behind a private roadside bush, then look carefully in every direction before taking care of nature! It was on the 50th day following our departure from Montreal on Monday, July 9, that we arrived in Ouagadougou on Tuesday, September 4, 1945.

Among the Mossi at Ouagadougou

This section of Chapter 5 covers our first 14 months in Africa. The day after we arrived at Ouagadougou, Stella wrote her sister Roma the following about its A. G. mission compound (our home during our first 16 months in Africa): "The compound . . . is quite attractive. The buildings are all washed with lime which makes them white . . . the missionaries all have nice furniture." Then she contrasted the nice condition of our mission compound with disappointing conditions she had seen in run-down, wartime Dakar.

Veteran missionaries Arthur and June Wilson were temporarily at Ouagadougou (just before opening the Dahomey field) when we arrived, and the Smiths boarded the Wilsons and us for a while. After dinner was Wilson's time to tell gruesome stories of Africans killed by lions—stories that tended to keep us awake at night! After all, missionary Emile Chastagner was reporting (from time to time) that an African had been killed by a lion. He had caught 16 lions in two years in his lion pits beside the Mossi Bible School building at Koubri, about 20 miles south of Ouagadougou. And he was quite frequently bringing an African in to the Ouagadougou hospital who had been scalped by a hyena.

George, Sr. (center), Warren (left), and George, Jr. in front of our first home in Africa on A. G. mission compound at Ouagadougou

A. G. missionary ladies at Ouagadougou (left to right): Stella Flattery, Cuba Hall, June Wilson, and Florence Smith

Newly arrived missionaries were obligated in various ways to the ruling French officials at Ouagadougou, the capital of Upper Volta: I had to visit their offices to accomplish necessary paper work, and Stella and our sons had to accompany me to their homes for meals. All of this was enjoyable to me because I could communicate with these officials in French. Up to that time, many of our American missionaries to French-speaking colonies had found this part of their work difficult because of their inability to communicate very well in French. Right away Stella and I began our study of the tribal language of the Mossi people. And right away she began her supervision of Warren and George in their study of Calvert correspondence courses.

After I had been at Ouagadougou only a few days, I was asked to accompany missionaries A. E. Wilson and Vivan Smith to Navrongo, Gold Coast (British colony which bounded Upper Volta on the south, and is now the independent country of Ghana), to supervise the trucking of Wilson's baggage to Ouagadougou. It was my task to follow, in a passenger car, the truck which was heavily loaded with this baggage. The truck crew included an African foreman with other Africans working under him. I will never forget how unmercifully the foreman whipped his men when they did not do their work in a manner that pleased him—especially when the task was to move the truck forward through a mud hole.

About mid-November, 1945, the Greenaways (our fellow missionaries at Tenkodogo, Upper Volta) telegraphed the Smiths at Ouagadougou that their baby Sandra was ill, and they needed missionary help. Since Florence (Mrs. Smith) was not well enough to make the trip at that time, Stella and I and our cook Timpiga made the 120 mile trip to Tenkodogo (in the Ouagadougou mission's Chevrolet station wagon) to help Charles and Mary (Greenaway). Sandra got well, and I left for the Gold Coast to get my Ford car which had arrived there from New York. An African who could change a tire was with Stella and Timpiga as she was driving the station wagon back to our home in Ouagadougou.

She was only about ten miles from home when a tire blew out, and there was no inner tube to fix it. Stella started riding one of two bicycles toward Ouagadougou. Timpiga accompanied her on the other bicycle—leaving the other African to watch the broken down car and its contents. During their bike rides, it was distasteful to Stella when Timpiga took care of nature beside the road—without going behind a nearby bush for privacy. And her thoughts of man-eating lions lurking behind nearby bushes thoroughly scared her!

Stella soon got too tired to ride the bike further. So Timpiga tied her bike to his and started pulling her. That went alright for a little while—until twice Timpiga's bike, having hit ruts, stopped without warning; and her bike banged into his, throwing her to the ground each time and skinning her leg "pretty bad," according to her letter to her parents of November 29. (Actually her injury was worse than she described in her letter—but she suffered no permanent ill aftereffects from it.) By then it was pitch dark and Stella was afraid to get on the trailer-bicycle again! On her crippled leg, she (suffering from thirst) and Timpiga pushed their bikes the rest of the way to Ouagadougou.

Timpiga wearing white jacket, in front of his home behind the Ouagadougou mission station

I began trying to preach in More (language of the Mossi) in November, 1945—just two months after having first heard it spoken. It is the easiest to learn of the four African tribal languages that I eventually learned and spoke during our 20 years of Africa mission work. On January 2, 1946, Stella wrote of my preaching to her brother Manford and his wife: "George has been preaching in More a couple of months now. He has had two converts." The time that I remember best among my earliest efforts to preach in More was on a lonely roadside, beside my broken down Ford car, about 15 miles north of Po.

When we went to Africa in 1945 for our first term, the A. G. Speed-the-Light, fund-raising program for missionaries' vehicles had not yet begun. Our 1939 Ford had served us well for over five years before we went to Africa, but we had much difficulty with it while in Africa. We learned firsthand more about why, in 2 Corinthians 11:23-27, the Apostle Paul listed "journeyings" (v. 26, KJV) among the perilous things he had to suffer for Christ's sake. At the end of our first term in Africa, I told a veteran fellow missionary that I had spent (during that term) a total of nine days and nights in the bush with my broken down Ford. He observed: "That's a record!" Then I replied: "If so, it's an unenviable one!"

Just before the Ford's battery went dead at that point north of Po, I had replaced (in Po) its broken transverse rear spring without proper tools for the job. I was so relieved to accomplish that task without the car falling on me! Then I had to improvise regarding what I ate during the two days I had to wait beside the lonely (no car passed by) road for missionary Vivan Smith to come (by motorcycle) the 75 miles to me from Ouagadougou with a good battery. I bought a guinea fowl from a native passing by, cooked it in a smelly kerosene tin, and ate it without salt.

God gave me an audience of Mossi men to preach to when a large caravan of traders (on their way down to the Gold Coast) stopped to greet me beside my broken down car. When I finished my sermon, they thanked me for it. It may have been the first time some of those men had ever heard about Christ. In spite of my trials during those two days in the African bush, I felt (after enjoying the unexpected opportunity of witnessing to that caravan) like Stella did when she wrote her parents on March 29, 1946: "I like Africa more and more. I can't explain the feeling of satisfaction one has in a heathen land witnessing for Christ."

Caravan of traders that George preached to in More beside the Po road in 1945

During our first year in Africa, Warren and George thoroughly enjoyed their studies and play time outside the protective walls and roof of our mission house. They remained in the house most of the time between mid-morning and late-afternoon. Stella's work during her first year in Africa included many interesting things besides her heavy load of entertaining new and returning missionaries and teaching our sons: some of those tasks were her study of More, playing the accordion for church services (accompanied occasionally by Warren's guitar), making copies of the unpublished More dictionary for us to use, occasional attempts to preach in More, and much letter writing.

Here are excerpts of a letter Stella wrote to Marjorie Carter, a young person in our church at Leavenworth, on December 18, 1945:

Dear Marjorie: Greetings from Ivory Coast. Its been a long time now since we left Leavenworth . . . there is much missionary work to be done here . . . the natives

. . . receive no joy or peace in their hearts from their heathen worship . . . Mr. Flattery is screening in our house which will keep out the mosquitos . . . hope you are still attending S. S. and church . . . Warren and George like Africa very much. Yesterday they took about 15 little black children for a ride on their bikes . . . Oh! how thrilled they were.

The A. G. Missionaries appointed me, in their business meeting on October 3, 1945, at Ouagadougou, to begin evangelistic meetings in French in downtown Ouagadougou. I wanted to do this because thus far our missionaries at Ouagadougou had not attempted it. Right away I began holding Sunday meetings in French in the yard of a French-speaking Mossi man who was an official at the Ouagadougou post office.

From time to time during the next year, we mentioned (in our letters to various people) the progress of this Ouagadougou French work: On March 13, 1946, we remarked that "it was going to be a slow task." There was great opposition to this work from the Roman Catholic leadership in Ouagadougou. It was said that Ouagadougou had the strongest Catholic work in French West Africa. But on April 13, we remarked that "we had a lovely service . . . in Ouaga . . . all in French last Sun." Then the following week "We had another good service in French . . . three more ask pardon."

Right after we arrived in Ouagadougou in September, 1945, I began using Myer Pearlman's Adult Teacher Quarterlies to condense and translate Bible lessons into French for future use in Upper Volta. Then it was about mid-May, 1946, that I started using them in Bible studies on Thursday nights in the post office man's yard in downtown Ouagadougou. Regarding this French work in Ouagadougou, I wrote my mother on June 29:

We are having very encouraging results in our French services. One young man who seems to have promise of being a native evangelist led in prayer for the first time last

Thursday night. I had been trying to get him to take courage and lead in prayer for several weeks. He wanted me to write him a prayer so he could memorize it, but I felt that if I waited he would eventually pray without a written prayer. I told him to talk to God as he would talk to a friend because God is our greatest friend.

In early February, 1946, all our Upper Volta missionaries and 500 Africans gathered for 10 days in Ouagadougou for the Mossiland Christian convention. When Stella and I visited the heathen head Mossi chief just before this convention, he expressed favorable recognition for it by donating a cow for the natives to eat during the convention. H. B. Garlock (A. G. field secretary for Africa) and his wife, Ruth, arrived in Ouagadougou on April 26, 1946, for some conferences with the Upper Volta missionaries and Mossi church leaders. (They devoted five weeks of their itinerary throughout Africa to Upper Volta.) Garlock outlined missionary furloughs, and encouraged the missionaries and Mossi leaders in several ways regarding progress of God's work in Upper Volta.

Henry and Ruth Garlock at Ouagadougou in May, 1946

Missionaries and Africans at Ouagadougou in May, 1946

Screening in our house was the biggest manual task that I accomplished during our first 14 months in Africa. I had to rip by handsaw the hard mahogany lumber for the screen frames. Other manual tasks included making of school desks from our packing-case lumber for Warren and George, making of steamer chairs from mahogany, and laying of 16x8x4 mud blocks for modifications to our house.

When my son George had been asked at Leavenworth what his father was, he (then about 4) replied "a preacher and a bookbinder." Later, when he wrote his Uncle Manford on January 19, 1946, about my work in Africa, he said "dad . . . is going to be a preacher, a carpenter, and a block layer." Many times in my life, I think I have qualified as the proverbial "jack of all trades." But when I had to work on my car, I wished for my brother Ellis who was an auto mechanic during most of his life.

Another important part of Stella's work (during our first 14 months in Africa) was helping missionary Marie Johnsrud with the native girl's school on the Ouagadougou compound. It turned out that Stella taught these African girls each morning from 7:30 to 8:30. On February 8, she wrote her parents:

> *To-morrow Marie and I intend to start the girls' school. I will help her until her co-workers get here . . . we will give the girls reading lessons, memory work, sewing, etc. . . . one of the main things I want to teach the girls and women is to wear clothes. The girls have been told they were donkeys and can't learn but it is not so.*

The most basic reason for starting this girls school was to provide a home for girls who had been cast out of their homes when they refused to become the wives of men they did not want as their husbands. French laws were favorable to the founding of this school for the homeless, in that they set a girl free from her buyer (often an old man) if she did not want to be his wife.

Marie and Stella not only told the girls to wear clothes but also made clothes for them. Stella's note of April 5 says, "Marie and I made 5 skirts in two afternoons for the girls in the school." One day, soon after this school was started, all the girls in it came in a group to our front door and clapped. When Stella asked them what they wanted, they replied, "we just want to visit!" This was an expression of their desire for her friendship—an indication that they were benefitting (spiritually and socially, as well as physically) from all that she and Marie were doing for them.

Mossi converts usually did not go to the altar to decide whether or not they wanted to be converted to Christ. They went as an outward expression of decision for Christ that they had already made. Either way is a good way if one is brought to Christ in it! Mossi converts included both children and adults. On June 18, 1946, Stella and I rode together on a small motorcycle to Mossi Pastor Zitenemia's church at Conge (12 miles southwest of Ouagadougou) for a water baptismal service. I baptized six converts in a nearby water hole that day.

Dahomey Trip

Arthur and June Wilson went to the French colony of

Dahomey (renamed Benin in 1976) in October, 1945, to open the first A. G. mission station in Dahomey at Natitingou. They went in their passenger car, taking with them only the small portion of their equipment that they could pack in the car. By early February, 1946, they needed their truck load of baggage which they had left at Ouagadougou.

George and Zitenemia standing in a water hole behind the six candidates for baptism

Mossi church and congregation at Conge, Stella at right end of group

On February 8, Charles Greenaway and I began the 300 mile journey in the Upper Volta mission field's truck with this baggage. We arrived at Fada N'Gourma (140 miles east of Ouagadougou) about 9:00 p. m. During the hour we were there we enjoyed fellowship and a meal with S. I. M. missionaries. Then we proceeded southward toward Natitingou. We needed to travel in the cool of the night to protect a weak tire on one of the truck's front wheels. Lions in the tall roadside grass along our way kept us awake! I remember shooting at one and missing it.

Traveling slowly, we arrived about 2:00 a. m. at a dry sand-filled creek bed which crossed our road at Pama in northern Dahomey. We proceeded carefully down into the creek bed, and the truck's rear wheels got stuck in the dry sand. Its differential gear broke when we tried to drive on out of the creek bed. Charles and I decided that one of us must stay with the truck to protect its baggage against theft, and the other must ride his small motorcycle toward Natitingou (about 65 miles south of Pama) in search of help. Charles had learned very little French as yet. So, we chose me for the motorcycle journey!

When I arrived on the motorcycle at the first telephone station, I used my French to call Natitingou for help. Poor telephone connection made it difficult for me to hear the man at Natitingou, but I hoped that I got this message across to him: "Go to missionary Wilson and tell him to come with help for the broken down baggage truck at Pama." I rode on, knowing that I would have to ride the motorcycle clear to Natitingou, if my message did not get through—but knowing also that I would probably meet Wilson (on his way to the broken down truck) before I reached Natitingou, if my telephone message did get through to him.

I suffered a little, from the extreme heat of the day, as I proceeded on the motorbike. But I remained alert and seldom stopped. At one point a brush fire on each side of the narrow road ahead of me helped to keep me alert: the fire was nearing road ahead of me helped to keep me alert: the fire was nearing the road from each side of it, and I wondered if I could make it past that point without getting burned! I went a little faster and was not harmed by the fires as I passed between them.

I learned when I reached Tanguieta in late afternoon that Wilson had received my telephone message. I would not have to ride the motorbike over the mountainous 15 miles between Tanguieta and Natitingou. Wilson (having covered those miles in his car on his way to Pama) met me at Tanguieta. I stayed that night in Tanguieta while he went on his way to Pama to get Greenaway. Being quite tired from my 50 mile motorbike ride through the heat, I thoroughly enjoyed a cold bucket shower and a tasty meal at the primitive French rest house. Then I went to bed early and slept well.

The next morning Wilson (having left the truck and baggage in Pama) arrived, with Greenaway, back in Tanguieta. All three of us then went on to Natitingou in Wilson's car. I fulfilled a Pentecostal pioneering assignment by preaching in French to the rather large group of Sombas that the Wilsons gathered together in their new church. Greenaway and I began looking immediately for a truck that would go up to Pama and tow the mission truck with the Wilsons' baggage to them in Natitingou. After one week of searching, we got a truck to start out for Pama. But because it was too heavily loaded with government salt, it broke down and we were right back where we were!

Trucks at Natitingou were busy with the peanut harvest, and it was three more weeks before we finally got a truck to go to Pama. When its African chauffeur got to Pama, he almost refused to try to tow the heavily loaded mission truck—thinking that to attempt to do so would ruin his truck. We persuaded him to begin towing it with a chain. (But he still averred that his truck would not be able to pull the load over the hill between Tanguieta and Natitingou.) The mission truck's brakes were ineffective so it was banging into the front truck when ruts caused the latter to slow down without warning.

Arthur and June Wilson standing beside the foundation for the new A. G. mission station at Natitingou, Dahomey

Then the African chauffeur displayed ingenuity by improvising a solid trailer hitch from tree branches which he roped together, then tightened the ropes by pouring water on them. Drinking alcoholic liquor is usually detrimental to the one who drinks it, and to what he is attempting to do. But when this African chauffeur drank native beer along the way, it buoyed him up in a manner that made him confident that his truck could pull the truck and baggage over the high hill at the end of the journey.

When we passed Tanguieta and started up this hill the lug nuts started coming loose from one of the rear wheels of the African chauffeur's truck. Greenaway and I took turns at keeping them tight while the trucks slowly moved along. After an all-night journey of 65 miles from Pama, we rolled down the other side of the hill into Natitingou with both trucks and all the baggage, at 5:00 a. m.!

Greenaway and I then got a ride from Natitingou to Tenkodogo (where he lived). But he had to go on to Ouagadougou with me to get his wife and baby who had spent the month we were in Natitingou with my wife and boys at Ouagadougou. Tenkodogo was about 30 miles to the south of the main truck route between Natitingou and Ouagadougou. So Greenaway route between Natitingou and Ouagadougou. So Greenaway and I had to get back up to that main route to catch a truck to Ouagadougou. He had no car at Tenkodogo, but did have his small motorcycle and a bicycle. So he tied the bicycle behind the motorcycle, leaving perhaps 20 feet of tow rope in between them. And we started out with him on the motorcycle, towing me on the bicycle.

Everything went fine until he hit some deep sand which slowed him down without warning. My bicycle banged into the motorcycle, but I avoided what could have been very serious injury to myself by alertly leaping off the bicycle just before it tangled with the motorcycle. I did sustain some rather deep cuts on my arms and legs when I hit the ground. Because of his empathy for me in my plight, Charles suggested: "George, you get on the motorcycle and tow me on the bicycle." But I didn't want him to suffer as I had, so I replied: "I'm used to it now, I'll continue on the bicycle!" I did and suffered no more injury.

Having proceeded over to the main truck route, we got a ride to Ouagadougou and arrived on March 8. When Charles and I left for Dahomey, we told our families we would be back in a week, but it took us a month to get back to them. And now you've read my whole story of our Dahomey trip!

Gold Coast Trip

At 4:00 a. m. on September 17, 1946, Marie Johnsrud, Stella, Warren, George, and I left Ouagadougou in our old Ford for the Gold Coast on a vacation and business trip. We were pulling a heavy trailer and the car's radiator kept heating up. We left before the rainy season was over because waiting any longer would have ruled out a vacation for us before our mission field's business meetings which would begin on October 22. We arrived at Po about noon and had to wait until 2:30 p. m. to see the customs man. Then the African official at Navrongo was so slow that it took him until 5:00 p. m. to finish checking our passports. We stayed that first night of the trip in the British government rest house at Navrongo.

The next forenoon, in the 11 miles between Navrongo and Bolega Tenga, we encountered three washed out bridges (very simple bridges of logs and branches). We had two of our African house boys in our car with us. They with other nearby Africans laid big rocks across the streams, then shoved our car and trailer across them on the rocks. We had to leave our Ford at the Catholic mission in Bolega because the road ahead between Bolega and Wale Wale was impassable for our car in certain places.

We hired a truck to take us and our baggage 3 miles beyond Bolega where there was a washout that not even a truck could pass over. Then we hired about 15 African men to carry our baggage over the washout to another truck which had been trapped between the washout and the river further on. The owner of the trapped truck was making lots of money off passengers who, like us, had him haul their baggage the 11 miles between the washout and the river.

We arrived at the river about 3:00 p. m. and the ferry wasn't operating! It took 3 hours to get us and our baggage across the river by means of 5 trips in a dugout canoe. Gold Coast A. G. missionary Floyd Thomas met us at the river and took us in his jeep—on to his mission station at Wale Wale. (We had telephoned him to meet us at the river when we were in Bolega Tenga.) We had to hire another truck to take our baggage to Wale Wale. By the time Thomas left the river with us, darkness had set in on the second day of our trip from Ouagadougou.

Mrs. Thomas had supper ready for us when her husband arrived with us. After staying with the Thomases 2 days, Thomas took us on down to Tamale where Hal and Naomi Lehmann were the A. G. missionaries. The H. B. Garlocks had founded the mission in Tamale in the early 1930's. The Gold Coast mission field's superintendent, Homer Goodwin, was at Tamale while we were there. He said the field could spare the gasoline for us to go on to Kumasi in Lehmann's station wagon.

Along our way to Kumasi we passed through beautiful tropical forests. What a contrast to the comparatively barren grass lands of Upper Volta!

We stayed with A. G. missionaries, Burdette and Doris Wiles, while in Kumasi. Our friendly association with the Gold Coast A. G. missionaries and the refreshing weather of the tropical rain forests provided us with a needed vacation from our work in Upper Volta. I took the train down to Accra and bought a small motorcycle for my missionary work. When I returned to Kumasi, we started our journey north to Ouagadougou to get started in our second year of work in Upper Volta. While at Wale Wale again we (Warren, George, and I) enjoyed going hunting with Floyd Thomas. We arrived back in Ouagadougou from our month-long Gold Coast trip on October 16.

Among the Kasena at Corabie

Just six days after we returned home to Ouagadougou from our Gold Coast trip, the annual business meeting of the Upper Volta A. G. mission field began on October 22, 1946. One year before this (as I've already pointed out), the A. G. missionaries appointed me in their annual business meeting to begin evangelistic meetings in French in downtown Ouagadougou. I had worked faithfully at this for a year and God had blessed my effort. But now (October, 1946) God was speaking to me about beginning evangelistic meetings among the Kasena tribe at a place called Corabie (about 110 miles south of Ouagadougou). The Kasena of that area had not yet been reached with the gospel of Christ.

It was the general policy of Upper Volta A. G. missionaries to veto the opening of a new mission station by a first-term missionary. But when I informed them during their business meeting that God was calling me to Corabie, I was "accepted by the Field Committee" (see *The Missionary Challenge*, April 1949) to open a new station among the Kasena. I think this committee made an exception (in my case) to general policy because I had pastored churches for over 7 years, and had already built the A. G. church in Leavenworth.

This entailed a lengthy postponement of my previously assigned work in French in Ouagadougou. But I did resume that work about 10 years later when I built the large concrete and steel church building in downtown Ouagadougou (which I will write of at length in proper sequence).

The Mossi called the people of Corabie "Gourounsi" but they used this same designation for other tribes to the south and west of them. The Kasena of Corabie, Po, and Leo (numbering about 100,000) were just one tribe of the Gourounsi Peoples. Before our arrival in Upper Volta, its A. G. missionaries had chosen Corabie (the Kasena population center) for the first missionary thrust among the Kasena—rather than Po (the French government center).

When I began missionary work at Corabie, the Kasena of that area were all animists, and attributed conscious life to nature and natural objects. Roman Catholics were working among the Kasena of Navrongo, Gold Coast (12 miles away). But neither Catholics nor Mohammedans had attempted to work among the Kasena of Corabie.

On November 5, 1946, missionary Harold Jones (accompanied by missionary Raymond Sanders) pulled my old Ford from Ouagadougou to Corabie with his pickup truck. My Ford was running good but was pulled to save a little gasoline—still a very scarce item in Upper Volta. Both vehicles were loaded with equipment and materials which I began immediately to use in constructing the mudbrick and straw mission station at Corabie. Jones and Sanders went back up country to their respective tasks the next day—leaving me alone with the Corabie project.

It was my plan to get the Corabie building started and continue with it for about 2 or 3 weeks then return to Ouagadougou for more equipment and materials to continue the project. I hired about 125 Kasena men to make mudbricks for the building and prepare straw for its roof. On November 22, I needed more materials from Ouagadougou. That night when I was preparing to pay my 125 men for what they had done thus far, I noticed that through a mistake of my own, I had brought with me only about two-thirds of the sum of money I needed to pay them.

As I impartially paid each man the same percentage of what I owed him, each one (from first to last) screamed at me as though he was going to do bodily harm to me. It was a dark night and my only illumination for my money table was a small kerosene lantern. I thought some of them might back away into the darkness, pick up some of the plentiful big rocks, and hurl them at me. An angel of God must have protected me because no rock was thrown at me. And I was not injured by the indignant men in any way.

I knew that "all things work together for good to them that love God" (Romans 8:28, KJV). And I knew that I loved God! But, as I drove away from Corabie the next morning, I was wondering how my failing to bring enough money with me was going to work for the good of our effort to win these people to Christ. Although I had promised each man as I paid him in part that I would come back and pay him in full, I felt that probably all of the workers thought, as they saw me drive away, that I might not come back, and that if I did I probably would not fulfill my promise to them.

Two weeks later, on December 6, I returned to Corabie with Stella, Warren, George, and more building materials. The first thing I did was gather together the men to whom I owed money for work. Each man knew exactly what I owed him. When I paid each one exactly what I owed him, it produced in him more faith in me—and in Christ whom I was exalting—than my paying him the full amount to begin with could have produced!

The first time I went to Corabie, I stayed in its French rest house (just a large round mud hut with a veranda all the way around it, all covered with the same large conical straw roof). My family and I stayed in the same place when I returned with them.

French rest house at Corabie where the Flatterys lived while building the mission house there

One day Stella was playing her accordion beside our rest house, and singing in Kasem "Yes, Jesus Loves Me" for a Kasena woman who had approached her. The woman left—causing Stella to wonder if she had frightened her—but came back soon with six other Kasena women. These primitive, nearly nude women approached Stella and her music by hiding first behind one tree then another (each tree a little closer to her than the preceding one). Then the Kasena women started dancing to Stella's music. This was not dancing in the Holy Spirit. But I believe her gospel music was the first step toward making Christ real to them.

The mud block walls of our mission house at Corabie were completed while I was there alone between November 5 and 23. Next, while I was back in Ouagadougou between November 23 and December 6, I had an African carpenter make mahogany shutters and doors for it. Then back in Corabie with my family, I supervised the completion of the house, which consisted of gathering poles and making straw mats for the roof of it; putting the thatched roof on it; setting the shutters and doors in it; putting the hard, glazed, native-style mud floor in it, and white washing with lime all its walls—inside and out.

Early in the mornings and late in the afternoons, Warren 11 and 1/2 and George 10 helped me with the building of the Corabie house, but we sheltered them from the strong midday sun. All through our time in Africa we worked and played games together as a family unit—first with our sons and, in later years, with our daughters. I think our togetherness helped to illustrate Christ's teachings on family life to Africans among whom we worked. We needed to "walk circumspectly" (Ephesians 5:15, KJV) before the Africans, for they copied our weaknesses as well as our strengths. One day one of us impatiently yelled "shut up" at one of our sons. Then we heard our cook impatiently yell the same thing at his children!

Kasena workers in front of the Corabie mission house, Warren seated and George standing on the roof

I first paid my Kasena workers by the hour, but couldn't get them to work as hard for me as they worked for their chief or for themselves. When working for himself a Kasena man would carry 2 or 3 16x8x4 dried mud blocks at a time on his head. But he would try to get by with carrying one at a time for me. He wanted to make his job last as long as possible! Then when I started paying by piece-work (so much per block carried) rather than by the hour, each man started carrying too many blocks at a time on his head, to earn as much as possible before the job ended.

We finished building the first stage of the Corabie mission house on Saturday, December 21. Then, beside the house, we held a church service the next morning for the Kasena, and drove that afternoon back to Ouagadougou.

On January 23, 1947, Harold Jones used his truck to move much of our baggage from Ouagadougou to Corabie. We followed him in our Ford which was heavily loaded with more baggage. That day, we began living at our new mission station at Corabie. Right away, we set up our equipment as best we could in and around our little house. About February 1, Yago, a Kasena Christian preacher, voluntarily came to us at Corabie to help us start the new mission work. He was a native of Corabie who had gone to Wale Wale, Gold Coast, and found Christ as his Savior. As native pastor, Yago greatly helped our work among the Kasena.

Stella had to do her own cooking for several weeks, an extra difficult job for her because we had no kitchen. We set up our wood-burning stove out in the yard, just north of the house. Then we laid a wall of mud blocks without mortar around the stove to protect it from the high winds—and to shield Stella, the cook, from the gaze of curious onlookers. She depended on her thick cork helmet while cooking under the midday African sun. Baking bread, boiling milk and water, heating water for laundry, pressure-cooking meat, and testing eggs in water were some of her kitchen tasks which having no kitchen made more difficult.

My first manual task after we moved to Corabie was to build an addition to our house for a shower room, store room, kitchen, and office (in that order northward from the attached, straw-thatched, first stage of the house). It took me about two months to build this rectangular addition of mud blocks with mud-and-pole roof. Having no block mason, I had to lay all the blocks myself. There was mutual sympathy between Stella and me as we worked in close proximity to each other under the midday African sun—she cooking and I laying mud blocks.

When the mud-block walls of this addition to our house were completed, and the flat mud-and-pole roof structure was in place on top of them, it was time to call Kasena women to pound the roof's glazed finishing coat of cow manure and boiled tree sap. I pointed out earlier in this chapter how Stella taught the girls in the school at Ouagadougou to wear more than skirts. Well, she had to continue this teaching on an increased scale among the Kasena women who wore no clothes at all. When they came naked to pound, she told them to go clothe themselves with skirts of tree leaves before getting up on the roof of our house. They complied and came back wearing such thick skirts that they looked like walking bushes!

The following picture of our completed Corabie house (built at a cost of about eight hundred dollars—mostly wages paid to African laborers) was made during the rainy season of 1947, about 4 months after the mud-and-pole roofed part was finished.

First Kasena Convert

Nasia, a witch doctor, was our first convert among the Kasena. He was converted at Corabie in February, three months after we began missionary work there in November, 1946. He was a well-known subsistence farmer in that area. During our three months of acquaintance with him before his conversion, he attended all of our regular church services and came to our house on many other evenings to question us about Jesus.

In front of the Corabie mission house, George Flattery is presenting native pastor Yago with a copy of his translation in Kasem of the Gospel of Mark.

Shortly after his conversion, Nasia brought us a large dried python skin. He told us that the snake which had lived in that skin had gone to his yard many times during the four years before we had opened the mission in Corabie. The snake had eaten many of Nasia's chickens and eggs during that time, in which Nasia was afraid to try to kill the snake—or even drive it away. Satan had caused Nasia to think that if he resisted the snake, it would bring leprosy upon him. But when Nasia repented of his sins and received God's forgiveness of them, the love of Christ entered his heart and removed satanic fear of the snake from him. In such love "there is no fear" (1 John 4:18). The next time the snake entered his yard, Nasia clubbed it to death!

We taught John 3:16 in Kasem to Kasena people who attended our regular church services. I notice in Stella's letter to her parents of March 5, 1947, that two or three dozen of them could repeat from memory "John 3:16 . . . in their own language." In that letter she added: "Next Sunday we will start them on another verse."

Nasia in his yard displaying skin of a destructive python that he had feared until he was converted to Christ, but killed after he was converted

Conception of Our Third Child

This conception happened in February, 1947. (God had chosen that time for it since before the foundation of the world.) Stella wrote her parents on April 9, that "it was planned" on our part too. When we had been married only 28 months we already had our two sons, but it was over 11 years between the births of our second and third children. After becoming A. G. secretary for missions in Africa, H. B. Garlock told us (while we were still in Leavenworth) that prospective missionaries to

Africa should prayerfully and carefully try to avoid having a large number of children before being appointed to Africa.

Then when the Garlocks visited us in Ouagadougou in the spring of 1946, Stella discussed our desire for a third child with Mrs. Garlock, and she told her the equivalent of: "If you and George desire another child, ask God for it and try to have it." It was about August, 1946, when we prayerfully began our own part in trying to produce the conception of our third child. We were unsuccessful for six months and Stella's letter of April 9, 1947, to her parents indicates how she (and I) felt about our lack of success just before the conception took place: "I went 6 months thinking I couldn't have any more."

There are things about God's production of the conception of our third child that "now I know in part; then I shall know fully" (1 Corinthians 13:12, NIV). From the first time I saw Corabie in November, 1946 (and even for a few months before that), I definitely felt that God had chosen my family to not only build a mission station at Corabie but also to go there to live and do missionary work. Warren and George wanted to move to Corabie from the time they first saw the area in early December, 1946.

But, understandably, Stella had some doubts about the advisability of taking our family to live in such a primitive area as Corabie was. Her first written expression of her decision to go to Corabie to live was in a letter of December 29 to her parents. Man never receives anything from God without doing what God has foreordained that he must do to receive it. Could it be that God foreordained that Stella and I go to Corabie to live and do missionary work—as a condition for His producing the conception of our third child? I hope to learn more fully about this when I get to heaven!

Back to Ouagadougou Temporarily

The Fred Glaser family came from Kaya to visit us in Corabie on May 12, 1947, and stayed with us three days. The first rain of the season came during the first night after they arrived. It was a very hard, blowing rain that came through the new straw roof of our house—like water through a sieve! (It usually takes a year or two for a new thatched roof to mat together and do a good job of shedding water.) Fred had attached his cot and mosquito net to a small tree at the east end of the house. He came into the house with his cot when the rain started—but got almost as wet inside as he would have outside!

That leaky roof was very inconvenient—but not the cause of our moving temporarily to Ouagadougou. We moved there about May 23, because we had no supply of drinking water available to us at Corabie. During the months of dry season that we had lived at Corabie since January, we obtained water from a swimming hole which we filtered and boiled for drinking. But the rains had washed surface filth into this hole to an extent that we could no longer filter the dirt out of its water.

Both of our efforts to dig a well at Corabie had failed. We struck granite rock in both wells. We had no anvil and tried to sharpen our digging bar on another granite rock. Progress through granite was very slow! We never even struck water at the first site, but did strike it at the second site at a depth of about 20 feet. The rains caused the sides of this second well to cave in before we were able to stabilize them with concrete.

When moving to Ouagadougou we told our Corabie Christians that we fully intended to move back among them as soon as we were able to provide a source of drinking water for our use at Corabie. Furthermore I told them that I intended to visit them frequently while my family would have to be at Ouagadougou. But they were deeply saddened by our temporary departure because they felt that we might not be able to get back to them. They knew they would suffer more persecution from heathen Kasena while we were away than they had suffered during the months we had been among them.

We lived at Ouagadougou again for over 10 months (through the rainy season of 1947 and the dry season of 1947-

1948). During those 10 months, my main missionary work was still for (and sometimes among) the Kasena at Corabie. On October 4, 1947, I wrote my mother: "Since moving back to Ouagadougou last May, I have made four trips back to Corabie, preaching to the people while there." I did not hold a revival campaign of daily preaching to them because I was busy each day with my studies and writings in Kasem—a considerably more difficult language for me than More.

A crew of Kasena well-diggers with some onlookers at the site of a well at Corabie

At the completion of one of those four preaching missions in Corabie, I took two Kasena Christians back to Ouagadougou with me to help me finish the translation of the gospel of Mark in Kasem. Stella said in her letter to her parents of August 16, 1947, that:

George completed the beginners reading book in the Kasena language just yesterday . . . he will get 200 copies multigraphed of it soon and take some to Yago . . . who is teaching a class of boys every night . . . the book is made up of 12 lessons. The first lessons introduce all the letters and syllables in their language. The last few lessons have the Scriptures . . . that George translated last month while he was in Corabie after many months of collecting words.

George with Kasena congregation on a Sunday morning where he preached to them under a tree near the mission house at Corabie

The rains of 1947 were over and we were in November—the month that we were expecting our new baby. On Saturday the 22nd, Stella entered the Ouagadougou hospital and was in labor until about 2:00 a. m. November 23, when our child was born. I had remained constantly at her side through the entire ordeal. It had been over 11 years since she had given birth, and this was almost as difficult for her as the birth of her first child had been.

Missionary Murray Brown, Sr., was in Ouagadougou the day before our child was born. He visited Stella and me at the hospital for several hours during the late evening and into the night of that day. His prayer for her greatly encouraged us. He wanted to stay until our child was born, but had to leave on his motorcycle about 11:00 p. m. for Dapongo, Togo (about 140 miles away), in order to preach in his mission church the next morning. Stella, Warren, George, and I were extremely happy that our new baby was a beautiful, blonde, blue-eyed girl. We named her Doris Ann.

There was manual labor for me to accomplish at Corabie during the dry early months of 1948 while my family completed its 10-month stay at Ouagadougou. First, with the help of missionary field superintendent John Hall and a crew of African dynamiters, I was able in January, 1948, to complete the well at Corabie which had caved in at the beginning of the 1947 rainy season. When completed, it provided us with a sufficient amount of good water—even in dry seasons.

I went down to Corabie early in March and built double doors in the south side of the thatched part of the house, so we could (after having moved back to Corabie a little later on) roll our beds out onto a veranda (which I built during the same trip) for some cooler air at night.

Missionary Russell Schirman of Yako (whose wife Ruth had supervised the cooking for our family while Stella was in the hospital for the birth of Doris) went to Corabie with me on March 17. Schirman helped me with supervision of putting cement floors in our Corabie house, whitewashing its walls, and cementing the sides of our newly completed well.

Back to Corabie

Stella, Warren, George, baby Doris, and I moved back to Corabie at the beginning of the new rainy season. I have described car trouble which I experienced on other trips in Africa, but the car trouble I experienced on this trip makes it stand out as a more difficult trip than any of those I've already described. Not more difficult because the car trouble itself was worse, but because my family was with me—especially because of the presence of our baby.

When we arrived at a point about two thirds of the way to Po from Ouagadougou, one of our old Ford's tires blew out, and its spare tire was flat. Our tire pump was broken and there was no shade tree near. We could not expect another car from either direction. The strong midday sun was bearing down on us as I, wondering what to do, looked into the face of our baby who was already getting too much sun.

I just prayed God to help us to get to Po on the rim. And He did! We went about 25 miles before stopping at a little settlement six miles north of Po. Unbeknown to me, my Ford (pulling a trailer) had gotten so hot during those miles that its fan belt burned in two. It was a miracle of God that we made it on that hot day to that settlement—on the rim and without a fan belt! After the motor cooled we drove on to Po (about 20 miles northwest of Corabie) where we stayed with the French government official that night. Then the next day (April 1, 1948) the French official first took our family to Corabie in his vehicle, then helped me to get our car and trailer there.

None of the Kasena, except our church people, expected us to arrive back in Corabie at the beginning of a rainy season. Because, apparently, no white person had ever lived there through a rainy season. We found around 100 attending the church services at Corabie, each one bringing his Kasem primer that I had compiled. Regarding our first Sunday morning service at Corabie after we moved back, Warren wrote in his letters, to my mother and Stella's parents, of April 4, 1948:

This morning after church had started, I took Doris out so the people could see her. They stopped the service and watched her. She laughed at them and had a good time, as did the natives. This was the first time that most of the people of this section had seen a white baby.

The fact that we had a baby helped the Kasena Christians

to identify themselves and their babies more completely with us as part of the same Family of God. In April, 1948, I built an open-ended, mud-block garage onto the west side of the mud-and-pole roofed part of our Corabie house. Then we started rolling the car out on Sunday mornings and using this garage for church services. Between November, 1946 (when we started the Kasena mission) and May 1, 1948, there were 82 converts at Corabie, 12 of them had been baptized in water, and two in the Holy Spirit.

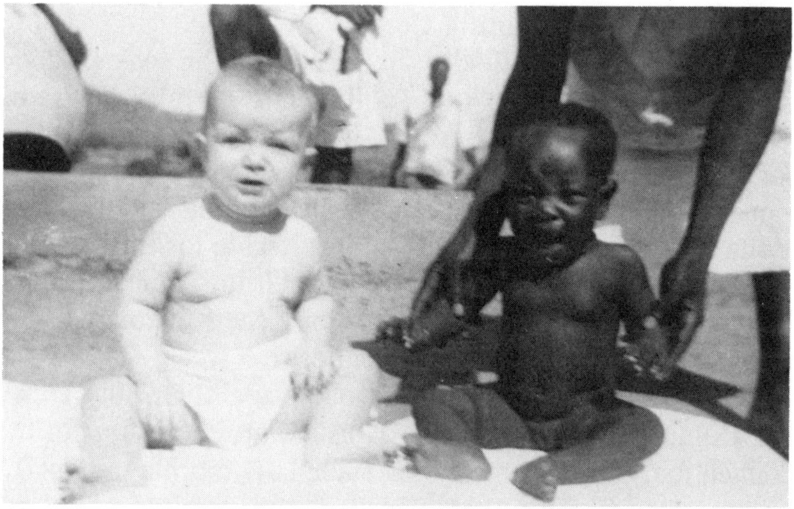

On the veranda of the Corabie mission house, Doris (left) and preacher Mankania Kasena's baby at 8 months (born the same day)

Since we had not had a vacation for 18 months, We took one in May, 1948. We went to Gold Coast again for this vacation trip. Of course, as before, it was a combination of business and vacation which we thoroughly enjoyed. We left Corabie on May 1, and got back on May 31. We enjoyed uplifting spiritual and social fellowship on this trip with A. G. missionaries: the Franklin McCorkles at Wale Wale, the Mel McNutt's at Kumasi, the Earnest Friends at Takoradi, and the Hal Lehmann's at Accra.

We took our Mossi house boy with us on this trip, and I've never forgotten how startled this African, from the interior, became upon seeing an ocean for the first time! On our way back to Corabie, Franklin McCorkle took Warren, George, and me hunting with him in the Wale Wale area. Our Upper Volta A. G. missionary, Henry Dahlberg, was at our house in Corabie when we returned. We were pleased to have a week's visit at Corabie, between June 8 and 15, from A. G. Upper Volta missionaries, Ed and Elise Simmons. We went with them (in the Jeep which the Field had lent us for the rainy season) on a picnic in the beautiful Corabie area.

The Upper Volta field's annual convention took place at Koubri, July 20-23, 1948 (about 3 months early), because its superintendent, John Hall, was to go during the next month on furlough with his family. The direct distance from Corabie to Koubri is about 90 miles. But since heavy rains had made the Volta river crossing (north of Po) impassable for cars, we had to travel about 225 miles to get to Koubri from Corabie. On this long route we had to go through Po, Leo, Koudougou, and Ouagadougou to get to the convention.

Our old Ford gave us much trouble again. On July 16 we left Corabie (pulling a trailer, as usual) at 5:00 a. m. for the convention. First, our car was stalled all morning about 15 miles west of Corabie. Then it stalled again about 15 miles east of Leo. A Pentecostal missionary family from Canada (Phil and Lucille Davies, whom we had met in Montreal in 1945) were missionaries at Leo. And Phil pulled our stalled car into Leo, where we stayed over night with the Davies.

The next morning we started out for Koudougou and our car stalled again, but we made it there that day through extremely flooded, small, back roads. At Koudougou we met, for the first time, A. G. missionaries Howard and Charlotte Fox. They were staying at the Koudougou mission station with Harold and Margaret Jones. After staying over night at Koudougou, we drove the next day to Koubri via Ouagadougou, arriving a day before the convention began. After the convention (on July 24) we heard that the Volta crossing north of Po was open so, leaving our trailer in Koubri, we started home to Corabie by the direct route.

The Volta river was still running quite a stream across our road, and our Ford flooded out and stalled right in the middle of the stream. By the time we could get some native men to pull our car up out of the river by hand, it was dark. Then we made it home to Corabie in our Ford that night. The next day, I went back to Koubri, got our trailer, and took it home to Corabie—a 180-mile round trip on which I, for once, had no car trouble!

John Hall, his wife Cuba, and their four children stayed with us at Corabie for a week, at the beginning of August, 1948. John, having completed his term as superintendent of our mission field, was going (with his family) to the United States for furlough. Missionary Edna Peterson also stayed with us that week. She too was on her way to the U. S. for furlough, and was with the Halls. We enjoyed fellowship with them all!

Edna Peterson (left), John Hall family, and George Flattery family; in front of the Corabie mission house, in August, 1948

Lack of enough household help (at Corabie, and later at Po) was one of the hardships that we frequently had to endure, during all of our seven years (1946-1953) of Pentecostal pioneering among the Kasena. For a while during the rains of 1948, both the jeep (lent to us by the Field) and our Ford were broken down, and we had to send native pastor Yago weekly by bicycle to Po (20 miles away) to get our mail. Missionary Henry Dahlberg was with us at the time, and went to Gold Coast to get parts for our cars. Our garden was doing well, and here is a picture of baby Doris holding one of our tomatoes!

Doris, 9 months, holding a tomato in our garden at Corabie, in August, 1948

Story of Adwa

Adwa (a Kasena Christian boy of about 12) was attending our church services at Corabie during the rainy season of 1948. His father had died about 6 months before we went to Corabie to establish the mission. The time arrived for the festival to be held in Adwa's yard in memory of his father. This was a festival which would last several days, and during which there would be much drinking and sinful merrymaking.

Adwa refused to take part in the festival because his Christian conscience would not permit him to do so. His uncles threatened to punish him because of his refusal. He ran away from the festival, and came the two miles to our mission compound for protection and advice. Mokura (one of Adwa's older brothers) came after him immediately, and when I would not let Mokura have Adwa, he became very angry and started back to his home.

When Mokura had gotten about 100 feet from Adwa and me, he gathered dust in his two fists and threw it back over his shoulders toward me. Then he turned around and, facing me, clapped his hands together, shaking off the dust from them at me. This was Mokura's manner of expressing disgust and hatred toward me for refusing to let him have Adwa.

The basic purposes for which Mokura flung dust at me were the same ones that caused "flinging dust into the air" (Acts 22:23, NIV) by hostile Jews when Paul told them of God's sending him "to the Gentiles" (v. 21, NIV). But I don't think Mokura knew anything about what the Scriptures say about the act of *throwing dust in disgust.* His act of throwing it at me was probably motivated by instinct, rather than learning.

We gave Adwa work in our garden for about 3 months, while the anger of his elders subsided. Then we were able to reason with them in the presence of the paramount chief of the tribe. They accepted Adwa back into their yard and were deeply moved by his faithfulness to Christ.

Anyan was paramount chief of the Kasena of Corabie, when we first went there in November, 1946. He was then a middle-aged man and had been both their political leader and religious leader (fetish high priest) for some time already. He was kind outwardly toward us and made favorable decisions toward our mission (as in the case of Adwa), when public opinion forced him to do so, and when doing so did not seem to diminish his stature in the eyes of his subjects. We, of course, tried to help him when we could: for example, when he saw the brilliant light of our pressure gasoline lantern (the only one in Corabie), he wanted one for his home. We bought one in Gold Coast for him; he was very pleased to get it!

Inwardly, Anyan feared the work of our Christian mission at Corabie, because he knew that its growth would diminish his power among his people. The greatest hindrance that our mission faced, during our first term there, was Anyan's secret persecution of it. Anyan remained paramount chief of the Kasena of Corabie throughout our first term. Then he died during our furlough, between our first and second terms at Corabie. His death had great significance for Christian missionary work among the Kasena. In the 1964 third quarter of the A. G. Junior Teacher's Sunday School Quarterly, I published the story of his death under the title "The End of Anyan." I will include this story at the beginning of the next chapter of this autobiography.

Conclusion

We moved once more from Corabie to Ouagadougou (after the end of the 1948 rainy season), where we spent the few remaining weeks of our first term in Africa. A big, rectangular, cement-block building (with wooden roof trusses and metal roof sheets) was built on the Ouagadougou mission compound during those weeks. Several missionaries worked with Harold Jones who coordinated its construction. I supervised the making of its roof trusses.

The east end of this large new building served as the dining room for missionaries who attended the West Africa-wide convention at Ouagadougou in December, 1948, for A. G. missionaries. A few days before Christmas, we flew from Ouagadougou to Springfield, Missouri (via South America), on the Ambassador (A. G. transatlantic passenger plane). When we arrived in Springfield, it lacked only a week of being four years since we had left the Queen City of the Ozarks for Africa via New York, Montreal, New York, Bermuda, Azores, and Lisbon.

(Because of the close relationship between our first furlough and our second term in Africa, I will write of furlough activities at the beginning of the next chapter.)

Flattery Missionary Card of 1950. Back: Warren (left), George, Sr., Stella, and George, Jr. Front: Doris (left), and Sharon

CHAPTER 6: SECOND TERM, UPPER VOLTA

Furlough Activities and Events

Our first furlough began when we arrived in the United States just before Christmas, 1948, from our first term in Africa. We lived during most of this furlough at 820 W. Calhoun street in Springfield, Missouri. It was a 22-month period which included 21 busy months in the United States, and 1 month of travel from New York back to French West Africa for our second term.

Before writing more about that first furlough, let me say that times have changed considerably in the last 25 years, or so, regarding a missionary's trips back to his homeland from his mission field: now, many missionaries frequently go to their homeland during a term on their mission field to attend funerals, weddings, and other significant events. During our twelve years actually in French West Africa (4 terms which averaged 3 years each), we made trips back to our homeland only at furlough times. And we seldom made even a phone call from Africa to the United States.

On a primitive mission field with difficult climate (extremely hot or cold) an important general reason for a missionary furlough, under former circumstances (described above), was to give the missionary a revitalizing change from his surroundings. Another important reason in foreign missions societies such as the A. G. (wherein missionaries raise their own finances) was to give the missionary opportunity to itinerate among churches and bolster his budget.

Christian missionary work has often been the preaching of the gospel of Christ to those who had never heard it. Read Romans 10:13-15 to be reminded that in this kind of missionary work, sending the preachers is just as important as the preachers' preaching: "How can they preach unless they are sent" (v. 15, NIV)? During their itineraries, missionaries should often tell their donors that those who send the missionaries will be rewarded along with the missionaries for what is accomplished on the mission fields.

Most of my time during our first furlough was spent in itinerating among churches to raise funds for our missionary work among the Kasena of Upper Volta. When I had itinerated among churches of Kansas (my home district) and Missouri in 1944, I was only a prospective missionary with no firsthand actual experience in Africa to describe. But during this furlough, I was a returned missionary with many stories of our work in Africa to tell about! I had no movie camera during our first term in Africa, but did take numerous black and white snapshots of our missionary work during that time. I had many of these snapshots made into 2x2 slides which helped me to promote missions in the churches I visited in 1949-1950.

My 1949-1950 itinerary included meetings in Kansas, Missouri, Arkansas, Nebraska, Wisconsin, Northern Michigan, Oklahoma, and a few other places. When this furlough began, I had never owned a new automobile (nor had I yet had the use of a new A. G. Speed-the-Light car). But I knew that I needed to buy a new car for all the itinerating that I would have to do before going back to Africa. So, I bought a new 1949 Dodge sedan which served me well during about 36,000 miles of travel in that itineration.

George (left) and Warren beside our 1949 Dodge in the spring of 1949

Our fourth and last child was conceived at Ouagadougou about one month before we left on the A. G. airplane for furlough in the United States. This child was the beautiful, brunette, brown-eyed baby girl who was born to us on August 29, 1949, in the old St. John's Hospital at Scott and Main in Springfield, Missouri. We named her Sharon Rose. I returned to Springfield from Fort Scott, Kansas (where I held a missionary service the day before Sharon was born), to be present at her birth. We were all extremely happy to have another girl to grow up with Doris!

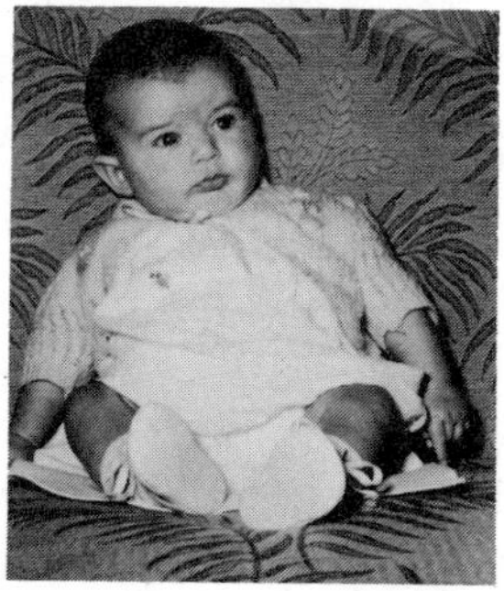

Sharon Rose Flattery at 3 months of age

In the summer of 1950, we moved temporarily from Springfield to the campus of the University of Oklahoma at Norman, where I studied at the Wycliffe Summer Institute of Linguistics. I completed their 10-week course for missionaries who are engaged in (or will engage in) translation of portions of the Bible into a tribal language.

Wycliffe Bible Translators have long excelled in translation of the Bible (or portions of it) into tribal languages of primitive peoples. On page 10 of the Jan/Feb 1990 issue of their periodical *In Other Words* is a report of their translation and publishing of the entire New Testament in Kasem, the language of the Kasena of Navrongo, and nearby towns in northern Gold Coast (now Ghana). I am very glad to know that they have accomplished this. I hope that some of the Kasena people of nearby Corabie and Po, Upper Volta (now Burkina Faso), will procure and benefit from copies of this Kasem New Testament.

Near the end of my preceding chapter, I referred briefly to Anyan, the heathen high priest and political head of the Kasena at Corabie. During his reign, Anyan was probably more powerful than any other Kasena leader in the entire Kasena tribe which extended over a considerable portion of southern Upper Volta and northern Gold Coast. Even the Kasena of Gold Coast came to his fetish altar. Anyan died an unusual death while we were in the United states on our first furlough.

To begin with, Anyan gave us a little hill about a mile from the center of the village of Corabie upon which to build our mission house. We had built our house there before we learned why he gave us this particular piece of land upon which to build. In their animism, the people of Corabie believed that this hill was the abode of evil spirits. They thought they had seen those evil spirits in the form of balls of fire rolling about on top of the hill. They feared those spirits and, therefore, had built no houses near it.

Anyan thought that those evil spirits would scare us away and keep us from establishing a Christian mission among his people. But he knew nothing about Psalm 91! Its verse 11 assures God's people that God will "command his angels" (NIV) to protect them against all evil. From the time we started building, our mission site was no longer (if indeed it had ever been) the dwelling place of evil spirits. God's angels scared them away! We finally learned, through some of the Corabie Christians, why no one had built a house near our location: after they were saved, they told us that before we had begun to build, they thought they had seen evil spirits on the mission site in the form of flames of fire dancing in the tree tops.

It was good for us that we did not learn how the natives had felt about our location until after we had built our house. To everyone of us (as well as to the Corinthian Christians) Paul says: "God . . . will not let you be tempted beyond what you can bear. But . . . will . . . provide a way out so that you can stand up under it" (1 Corinthians 10:13, NIV). It is enough that God has complete foreknowledge of our trials. If we had such foreknowledge, it might hinder our progress through (or even cause our defeat in) some of those trials.

I've already explained that when we had to temporarily leave Corabie at the beginning of the rains in 1947, Anyan told his subjects that the spirit of the rains had permanently chased us away—accomplishing what the spirits of fire had failed to do! French government officials had customarily spent considerable time in Corabie during the dry season while collecting taxes from the people, supervising the construction of a dam, and establishing a dispensary for lepers. However the roads had not been passable during the rains, and no white people had tried to live at Corabie throughout a six-month rainy season.

I've told (in the preceding chapter) how we returned 10 months later to live in Corabie during the entire rainy season of 1948. So, Anyan was the loser regarding the spirit of the rains as he had been regarding the spirits of fire! But Anyan continued as long as he lived to persecute Christianity. When we went to the United States on furlough after the rains of 1948, he did something that he felt would keep us from going to Corabie again, and would put an end to Christianity among his people: he gathered other priests and the Corabie people together for a ceremony in which he sacrificed a cow to his fetish. Then he pronounced curses upon us and upon the local Christians among whom we were planning to work again.

But his curses acted like a boomerang: instead of hurting either us or the local Christians, they fell upon Anyan's own head! A few days after he pronounced those curses, he suffered a mysterious death which no heathen could explain. The Christians of Corabie wrote to us in America and told us that Anyan was dead. They knew that it was God who had delivered them from his persecution. A few months after we heard that Anyan had died (when our preparations for going back to Africa were completed), we returned to Corabie.

Living Again at Corabie

At the beginning of this chapter, I briefly mentioned our return trip to French West Africa for our second term there. It was the only one of our four trips to Africa which included all six of our family. (Doris and Sharon were not yet born when we made the first one, and our boys were already beginning their own careers when we made the last two.) We sailed aboard Britain's big "Queen Mary" passenger ship from New York for England on September 29, 1950. And we arrived at Southampton after 5 days of the smoothest sailing the great ship had had in three months.

Then after a few days in London (where we found people still subject to austere post World War II rationing), we traveled to Liverpool by train and sailed on the MV Accra for Takoradi. We had rough sailing as we proceeded southward out of the Irish Sea into the open ocean. The ship rocked and many dishes were broken. Our 13-month-old Sharon vomited from sea sickness, but the rest of us made it fine. The remainder of the voyage was smooth.

Stewardess with Doris (right) and Sharon on Queen Mary ship in October, 1950

Warren with jerry can of gasoline on trip through the Gold Coast in November, 1950

The MV Accra made a brief stop at Freetown, Sierra Leone, where we enjoyed a brief visit with A. G. missionaries George and Helga Hemminger. We arrived at Takoradi on October 24, where missionary Eric Johnson and his wife met our ship. We enjoyed fellowship with them and attended their mission church. After one week in Takoradi we went on to Accra, Gold Coast, in our Jeep Speed-the-Light station wagon (pulling a trailer), where we stayed with missionaries Paul and Virginia Weidman. We had to wait on our French visas in Accra.

While in Accra I bought a small motorcycle for our use in the Corabie and Po areas. I had intended to buy 10 tons of cement at Accra for building our new mission house in Po, but had to go over to Lome, Togo, to buy it. We stayed about two weeks in Accra—visiting with the Weidmans, swimming occasionally at the ocean beach, and buying other items for our mission work among the Kasena in Upper Volta.

When we left Accra, John Weidman (about Warren's age) accompanied us on our trip home (up through Kumasi and Tamale) to Corabie. John, Warren, George, and I took turns driving our jeep, which was pulling a heavily loaded trailer. The trailer turned over while John was driving. He felt bad about that, but we cheered him up by telling him that the accident could just as easily have happened while any one of us was driving. Then we ran out of gasoline, and Warren rode a bicycle (which had been tied on top of the trailer's load) to the nearest filling station and bought a jerry can (5-gallon American army can) of gasoline. After putting the gasoline in the Jeep, we made it on to Tamale on November 24—then to Corabie a few days later.

While we had been in Springfield, Missouri (on furlough in 1949-1950), Thomas F. Zimmerman, then director of the A. G. radio department, supervised phonographic recording of my sermons in Kasem on "The crucifixion of Christ" and "The Good Samaritan," and of my family's singing hymns in Kasem. I played those records for our Kasena Christians at Corabie on the first Sunday morning that we were back there.

They clearly understood each word as the records were played, and were greatly blessed by the playing of them. I wish you could have seen the joy on their faces as they listened to those recordings in their own language! That evening I accompanied our national pastors, Yago and Belco, to the home of the paramount Kasena chief (son of the deceased Anyan) and played the Kasem records for a large group of heathen Kasena gathered in his yard.

The animistic, heathen Kasena may have attributed conscious life to the records—as they were doing to rain, fire, etc. But the Christians showed no such animistic reaction to the recorded speaking and singing. This new Corabie chief visited with Stella at our home in Corabie (while I was working in Po) on February 13, 1951—about two months after I played those phonographic gospel recordings for him in his yard. .

Stella wrote in her letter of February 14: "I helped the big chief of our tribe yesterday to pray through to salvation." Then on February 27 she wrote: "The big chief came a couple of weeks ago and got saved. I don't know how much he is going to be willing to give up. It'll mean several wives and the altar for sacrifices, etc. He is a young man and has been educated in the French school at Ouagadougou." Those gospel recordings in Kasem helped to cause this chief to visit our mission.

When we arrived at Po, from Gold Coast (on our way back to Corabie), we found that the French government had given us a choice site (100 meters by 100 meters, with nice shade trees), just a few hundred yards north of Po for our new mission house. Since there was no suitable place for us to live temporarily in Po, I had to drive the round trip between Corabie and Po (40 miles) each weekday, while building the Po mission house. We began those daily trips about December 15, 1950, when we began digging the trenches for the foundation of the house.

Just before I began to make the cement blocks for the Po house, our family was praying about not only finding proper sand (fine—not coarse) for making them, but also about a way to haul that sand to our mission concession. At Po, there was no one from whom I could buy sand—nor was there any one whom I could hire to haul it. Stella wrote in her letter of December 26, 1950: "George found a swell place by a little river that has plenty of good sand for the cement blocks . . . the big mission truck will be at Po tomorrow to haul sand." So, you see how the Lord answered our prayers concerning sand!

The Po house was the first A. G. missionary residence in the Upper Volta to be built of cement blocks with metal roof sheets. We first thought we might be able to move from Corabie into it about May 15, 1951, but it was on June 13, that we made that move. The rains had begun a few weeks before we could move, and our mud house at Corabie was beginning to cave in on us!

Left to right: John Weidman, George, Warren, and George Sr. beside the Upper Volta A. G. mission truck

For about 35 years after we first moved into this Po house, it served as a receiving station for incoming Upper Volta A. G. missionaries and their equipment. Missionaries (after me) who were receiving agents while living in this house with their families included: Maurice Peterson, Eugene Bascue, Del Tarr, Paul Chastagner, and Raymond Zents, Jr. When Stella and I visited Po in 1987, the house had been given over to the National Church. And Adwa Kasena (whom we had set free from fetish worship in 1948) was living in it with his family. In 1987 Adwa was the director of a government school at Po, and had 83 pupils.

It was about our second Sunday back in Corabie in December, 1950, when I officiated at Corabie's first Christian wedding. The bridegroom was Alia, the second convert among the Kasena of Corabie, and the bride was Kodana, a convert from a small Kasena village about ten miles from Corabie.

On January 17, 1951, I wrote the dear people whose love

gifts were keeping us on the mission field the following note about the Christmas-day celebration held by the Corabie Christians in the side-by-side yards of our native pastors and their families—just a few yards down the hill from our Corabie mission house:

Dear Friends, we bring you greetings from the church in Corabie . . . on Christmas day a love feast was held among the Christians. Some of them brought food such as goats, chickens, guinea fowl, rice, peanuts, and grain. The men killed and prepared the animals for cooking then the women cooked the meal. Those who had nothing to bring were privileged to partake of the feast also. How different was this Christmas festival from the pagan festivals of this tribe . . . characterized by drunkenness, adultery, and many other sins. Fear and bondage follow in their wake . . . the church here joins with you all in giving thanks to God for peace and joy through our Lord Jesus Christ.

Alia Kasena (next to left) and Kodana Kasena (next to right) with best man and bridesmaid

At that time, a practical indication that Kasena Christians were in much less bondage to ungodly fear than the heathen was the fact that they did not scream and yell—as did the latter—when a family member died. Christ had taught them not "to grieve like the rest of men, who have no hope" (1 Thessalonians 4:13, NIV).

From left to right: Belco's wife, Belco, Yago, Yago's wife

On that Christmas day of 1950 (in Corabie), Warren, George, and John Weidman supervised races and high-jumping contests among the Kasena boys and young men. After the games a large group of the Kasena came to our front veranda to see Doris Ann's Christmas doll open and shut its eyes. Stella wrote to her parents: "Some were afraid. Others just wondered how the doll could do it." Our own Christmas was made more enjoyable by the barrel of fruit and other things that the A. G. Women's Missionary Councils of the Oregon district had sent us for our missionary outfit.

I took the first Sunday in January, 1951, to emphasize (as I had done before in Corabie) that the Kasena Christians tithe their harvest of grain to the native pastors. Then I set the following Sunday as *Harvest Day* on which they were to bring their tithe of grain to the church service for them. Sharon (16 months) was just old enough to repeat all of our names at this point!

Before I began each day's work on the house at Po, I taught my Kasena workers a Bible lesson from the Gospel of Mark in Kasem, and prayed for them. This was something I could not do when I started to build Corabie four years earlier, because I could not yet speak Kasem. Stella (with the help of Warren one day, and George the next) supervised all the house work at Corabie—and taught the people there a Bible lesson in More (through an interpreter) each morning at 8:00 a. m.

When I first began to have my workers make 8x8x16 cement blocks for the Po house, they cracked because we had not put enough water in them. Then we put too much water in them and they slumped. Finally, when we put the right amount of water in the blocks, they came out strong! In addition to having the correct elements in the blocks (sand, gravel, cement, and water), we had to have the correct amount of each element in them. Each necessary element in its proper proportion is necessary to any successful synthesis of those elements. Let's apply what we've said about strong cement blocks to the making of a strong Christian.

In 2 Peter 1:5-7 is a list of eight elements that are necessary to make up a strong Christian. Read this list which begins with faith and ends with love. Strong Christians (like strong cement blocks) must be made up of the proper proportions of all the necessary elements. Of some of the Old Testament Israelites, we read that "the word preached did not profit them, not being mixed with faith in them that heard it" (Hebrews 4:2, KJV). Those Israelites had enough knowledge to follow God but not enough faith.

You saw in the preceding chapter how important a good well of water was to our mission station at Corabie. Again at Po, we failed to find water at the first location where we tried to dig a well. And as had been the case at Corabie, we did find water at the second location where we dug for it. Regarding our effort to produce a well of water at Po, Stella wrote to my mother on January 16, 1951: "As yet George hasn't got water on the concession. He is having the second well dug and hopes the men will find water. If we don't get water we won't go ahead and pour the foundation."

Now, some good news about the well and building at Po: "The well diggers are digging wet dirt now" (January 23). "George is pouring the foundation this week" (January 30). "George has started to lay the cement blocks. We have found water in the well but it has to be dug deeper" (February 6). Skipping ahead just a little, I notice in our letters that missionary Vivan Smith twice used dynamite to blast out granite rock from the bottom of our well at Po: first in mid-February, then in mid-March. These blastings helped greatly to give us the good well we had at Po.

About February 25, 1951, John Weidman, Warren, and I left Corabie for Kumasi, Gold Coast, with our mission truck to get building supplies and food supplies. When we reached Kumasi, John went on home to Accra. Our entire family had thoroughly enjoyed his three-month visit with us in Corabie. It was two weeks before Warren and I got back home to Stella, George, and the little girls. We brought with us all the mahogany lumber for the house, the metal roof sheets for it, and a Gold Coast block mason to help us build its walls.

George (then 14) was the guardian of our home while Warren and I were gone. While we were away, he shot and killed a crocodile in the water hole near our house, and kept its skin as a trophy. Then one bright moonlight night Stella, George, and the girls had gone to bed on our veranda (tucked under separate mosquito nets). And Stella thought she saw a wild animal crouched several yards east of the veranda. So she whispered to George about it. He had his gun with him under his netting (as he did each night that Warren and I were away). Taking his gun he got out of bed and advanced toward what Stella thought was a wild animal. But as he approached it, he saw that it was only a tree stump!

When Warren and I returned from Gold Coast, we brought

with us four big gunnysacks full of oranges. Stella had her cook extract the juice from the oranges, then after adding a little sugar to it, brought it to a boil and canned it in glass jars. The juice was delicious and helped to make up for our lack of fresh fruit and vegetables at Corabie.

The Flatterys: Stella (left) and George beside the Corabie mission house about March 1951

On a Saturday evening, near the end of March 1951, after Warren, George, and I had worked all day on our house at Po, our entire family drove to Ouagadougou to see Raymond, Lucille, and Charles Sanders off on the plane for America the next day. But, since their time of departure had been moved up a day, we did not get to see them. The illness of Raymond made it necessary for them to leave Africa before their furlough was due. He died in a New York hospital on April 16—just two weeks after his arrival in the United States.

I was happy with our progress in building the Po house from the time we started building it about December 15, 1950, up to the time Warren and I went to Gold Coast for building supplies about February 25, 1951. The work that Warren and George did on the house on alternate days made it like two missionaries were building it instead of one! (While receiving only the small allowance of missionaries' children, our boys were doing the work of missionaries.) After Warren and I returned with the Gold Coast mason, we made even greater progress on the building than before. And soon our progress was increased again through the help of a Gold Coast carpenter.

The added burden of 40 miles of daily driving caused our construction at Po to be the most difficult building job that I had ever engaged in. But the driving home to Corabie each evening was often a pleasure to us (Warren or George, and me) as we (even though quite tired from our work) took time along the way to do some hunting. During the six months of those daily trips we bagged about 85 wild guinea fowl and partridge, as well as some larger pieces of game. Each evening Warren, or George, would ride on the right flat front fender of the Jeep, with gun ready, and if the fowl were quite a ways from the road, we would leave the road (when suitable) to get a better shot at them.

Our missionary work was hard but never dull! On April 1 (no fooling) Stella was the midwife for the birth of Belco's wife's baby girl at Corabie. She tied and cut the cord, and performed other duties of midwifery. The baby's parents named her Nongelem, and Stella named her Esther. What a joy it was for Stella to visit with Nongelem Esther at Po in April, 1987. By then she had become a fine, healthy 36-year-old lady.

By April 10, 1951, the walls of our Po house were completed, and the big, 32-foot-long, self-supporting mahogany trusses were raised in place on top of the walls.

Household help for Stella continued to be a greater problem among the Kasena than it had been among the Mossi. In early April her work at Corabie had become almost more than she could do. She wrote on April 10, 1951: "My houseboy had to quit. The cook had to quit. The wash boy left for another place to go to school. The yard boy who waters the fruit trees quit." When she told the native pastor that she had to have help or move somewhere else, he intervened for her and got the cook and house boy to help her three days each per week, and the wash boy to help her twice a week.

Here are some things I remember about our life and work among the Upper Volta Kasena during the latter part of April, 1951 (before the rains began), when the weather was as hot as it gets throughout the year: our little girls, Doris and Sharon, were over the malaria which they had been afflicted with. We hadn't had a potato to eat for a long time and were using rice as a substitute! It was an excellent time for hunting wild animals that were gathered around the few remaining water holes. From 2:00 to 5:00 a. m. Warren and George went hunting several times at a water hole (about a mile from our Corabie house), where large eland antelopes (almost the size of a horse) were gathered. George shot one but he got away, crying and leaping as he went.

Back: Warren (left) and George (right), front: Doris (left) and Sharon (right) beside our Corabie mission house

From Gold Coast, Warren and I were able to bring fittings for a cesspool for our Po house. I built an underground cesspool for it of reinforced concrete—on the north side of the house. By about April 24, I had a second mason working. The work of building the partition walls, plastering them, and putting in the cement floors was progressing rapidly. According to Stella's letter of May 8, 1951, an A. G. missionary from Gold Coast saw our Po house when its exterior was nearly finished, and said, "it's going to be the nicest mission house in this part of Africa."

Also on May 8 Stella wrote: "The rains have started and we are very anxious to move . . . the . . . Corabie . . . roof leaks . . . if we have to move soon on account of rains . . . we can move into the front room and kitchen, then work on the rest of the Po house until it's finished." George and I had gone to Tamale about May 1, and bought 5 tons of cement with which to completely finish our Po house. And while there, we bought also the one item that we still needed to make our house completely modern: a toilet stool!

On June 6, A. G. missionaries Gene and Betty Bascue arrived at Corabie from America, with their daughters Pat and Judy, for their first term of service in the Upper Volta. We enjoyed fellowship with them until they went on up to Ouagadougou on June 12. Then the next day we moved into our new house at Po. Stella wrote on June 20: "We have moved into our new house . . . into the front room, dining room, kitchen, and bath room . . . the two bedrooms and the office are not finished."

Living at Po

On June 27, George and I were working on the roof of our house over the office, and Warren was using the jeep to haul sand in our trailer. We had poured the cement floor of one bedroom and would pour the floor of the other one the next day. Warren and I left early on the morning of July 9, for Kumasi to get supplies. Later that same day Stella wrote: "I haven't been away from home in 5 months . . . we can't all leave this house at once because we don't have the shutters all on." Each member of our isolated family greatly enjoyed the fellowship of each other member of it.

The unfinished, unpainted Po mission house into which the Flatterys moved from Corabie on June 13, 1951

Our Sharon of 22 months was talking more and more, was so expressive and entertaining, and loved to sing. And our Doris of 43 months had an unusually attractive positive attitude: One day Warren sent her into the bedroom to look for something, and she returned to him and told him it wasn't there. When he told her to go look again, Doris said: "O. K. but I betcha I'll come back and tell you it isn't in there."

We had enjoyable visits from missionaries Howard and Charlotte Fox, and Vivan and Florence Smith, during our first month in our house at Po. Smith killed a 350-pound male lion at sundown, just 8 miles north of Po. Warren and George went with Smith and me to get it. The female lion is more dangerous than the male when bereft of its mate. So, we watched in every direction for her as we loaded the dead male onto the trailer. We didn't see her. Sharon pulled my little motorcycle over on her, bruising the knee and instep of her left leg. But she was not seriously injured.

We had excellent village meetings around Po during our first month in our new house: on one Sunday night there were 17 conversions, and on another, there were 11. As I thought in July, 1951, of how much more time I had had during our first term in Africa to translate Scripture into Kasem than I had had thus far during that second term, I realized (perhaps more fully than ever) how greatly God had blessed me and my Kasena informants in that earlier translation work.

I longed to devote time immediately to more Bible translation into Kasem and wrote my mother on July 23: "I will be glad when we can let up on the building work so there will be more time for study and Bible translation for the African Christians." But I knew that I would have to continue at the same pace on the building for a few more months!

Near the end of July I was occupied with: 1) Attaching the sewer pipe to the cesspool (our cook and houseboy got a big pack rat out of the cesspool and killed and ate it), 2) transplanting our Corabie grapefruit and lime trees on our Po concession, and 3) finishing the cement floor of the big 8-foot veranda around the front of the house.

Warren went to Corabie with me to get the fruit trees and, on the way, killed a monkey for the natives to eat. When he killed it, other monkeys yelled and stood right there and scolded him. He said he would never kill another monkey because their reaction was too much like that of people! For some time, Warren and George had postponed their high school correspondence work because of the urgency of building. But on July 30, the house was near enough to completion that they took up their school work again.

About two months after we moved to Po, I used Vivan Smith's instructions in building a large, effective water filter as follows: 1) I punched small close-together holes all over the bottom of a 55-gallon steel drum. 2) After washing enough sand, 1-inch charcoal, and 1-inch white hard rock to fill the drum 2/3 full, I placed two thicknesses of household wire screening inside the drum over the holes in the bottom of it. 3) I placed this water-filtering 55 gallon drum on top of a 55-gallon water receiving drum into the side of which I had placed a faucet about 2 inches up from its bottom (to allow for settlings in it). 4) I placed successive 3-inch layers of sand, charcoal, and rock over the screening in the top drum, and repeated those layers (in the same order) until the drum was 2/3 full. 5) I washed more of the rock and filled the top drum almost full with it.

In pruning our citrus trees, I pricked the inside of my right hand between my index finger and thumb. Then I continued to work with cement. A serious infection resulted and I sought medical help at the Ouagadougou hospital. When I reached the hospital, my hand and arm (almost to the elbow) had swollen. The doctors put me to sleep to lance the infection. Just before I lost consciousness, I heard one of them say to the other: "Our surgery on this may be too late!" Four days and 16 penicillin shots later, I was dismissed from the hospital. The surgery was successful and I've suffered no ill aftereffects. But I still have a scar from that incision of 41 years ago.

Our whole family accompanied me (in our Jeep, pulling a trailer) on that trip to the Ouagadougou hospital. Warren was driving when about 35 miles north of Po, he and Stella saw a lion run across the road ahead of us. When Warren stopped the car right by the lion, it had stopped running and was sitting prettily (as if for a picture) as it looked at him. Warren then struck the lion down with one shot.

As it fell, it toppled into a shallow hole. Then Warren and I approached it. I, thinking the lion was dead, reached toward it to pull it out of the hole. But the mortally wounded lion jumped up a few inches and roared loudly! So, I grabbed our 12-gauge shotgun and put a ball into its head from close range.

George (with gun in hand) was sitting on the fender of the Jeep when that lion (which Warren killed) was crossing the road ahead of us. But he did not see it cross the road. Just before Warren shot the lion, two more lions appeared beside it. When he shot, those two ran a hundred yards or more away. George shot at and hit one of them, but it got away. Warren saw two more lions at that place, making five altogether!

After my four days in the hospital, I went to Koubri to help the Mossiland language committee with some translation in More. The rest of our family returned immediately in our Jeep to Po. When my language committee work was finished at Koubri, Warren and George started (in the Jeep) on the trip from Po to Koubri to get me. About 30 miles north of Po Warren hit a big hole in the muddy road and punched a hole in the gas tank. George said in his letter of September 10, 1951 (his 15th birthday):

> *I held my hand over the hole while Warren walked to the first village . . . to get a can to drain the gas into. The villagers lent us a siphon hose and a ten gallon drum. The drum leaked so we melted a piece of inner tube over the holes to stop the leaks. Then we poured the gas into the drum and put the hose in it. After that we connected the other end of the hose to the fuel pump and drove on in to Koubri.*

While they were teenagers, Warren and George had several experiences on the mission field which were valuable preparation for their own successful missionary careers later on. Their ingenious solution for this leaking gasoline tank is an outstanding example of that preparation.

In October, we were working hard (with the help of my electric table circular saw, powered by my gasoline-fueled Kohler electric plant) to finish our house's mahogany shutters and doors, so we could lock the house up, and all go to Ouagadougou Thanksgiving week for the yearly convention. About mid-October, George and I went to Gold Coast for a few days to get food supplies and 4 new tires for our Jeep.

When our well caved in during the 1951 rainy season, we

had to haul water from the Po French Government official's supply. It caved in because I had no time to get it lined with cement. During the dry season of November 1951-March 1952, I had our well cleaned out and dug even deeper than before. We struck water again at 45 feet and dug on down to 53 feet. I wanted to line the well with cement casings. But how would I accomplish the task?

George M. Flattery at Po on his 15th birthday

No kind of forms (metallic, wooden, or other) for making cement well casings were for sale. And I couldn't find any such forms that I wanted to rent or borrow! Once again it took some improvising: I made a metallic form from a couple of 55-gallon steel drums which was only half the height of a 55-gallon steel drum. But if the form had been any taller, each cement casing made in it would have been too heavy for my African well-diggers to let down into the well by hand! I spliced both the outer and inner walls of the form together in a manner that I could pour a 3-inch thick cement casing into the form. The cement was poured around reinforcing iron that I had placed in the form.

We had a nice 1951 Christmas with a duck dinner and an electrically lighted native thorn bush for a Christmas tree. Our 4-year old Doris wanted a new doll for Christmas. A Kansas A. G. church had sent her one, but it was stolen from the mail. So, without even telling Doris that her doll had been stolen, we got her one in Gold Coast and gave it to her on Christmas day. The stolen doll was probably better, but the doll from Gold Coast made not only Doris but all our family happy.

A. G. missionaries Herb and Margy Butler came about January 15, 1952, to our house in Po. During the following three weeks, while Margy stayed with us, Herb was getting their baggage from Gold Coast. We enjoyed fellowship with the Butlers. They had just arrived in Upper Volta for their first term.

Then on March 1-2, we enjoyed fellowship with Raymond and Katherine Zents and their two children, while they were in Po—on their way from Gold Coast to Ouagadougou, and then to Tenkodogo to begin their second term. As we visited with the Zents, Raymond recalled that exactly 5 years before (on March 1, 1947), he and his family had arrived at our house in Corabie on their way to Tenkodogo for their first term. Quite coincidental—and even more so when we realize that March 1 is Raymond's birthday!

I helped both Butler and Zents in their dealings with the French customs office. As missionary receiving agent for Upper Volta A. G. missionaries, it was my responsibility (while living in Po) to help them all through customs.

On February 12, I left Po with Harold and Margaret Jones on an 800-mile trip (one way) to the coastal city of Lome, Togo, for a meeting of the Federation of Protestant Missions of French West Africa. We went in a Plymouth station wagon, pulling a trailer. The trip took two days. The first day was trouble-free, and we stayed overnight with David and Claudia Wakefield at Bassari, Togo. The second day we had both car and trailer trouble. I wrote from Lome on February 16, 1952 regarding those troubles:

> *First the trailer hitch broke, and we had to tie the trailer on . . . and go slow . . . finally we put the trailer on the train and were making good time until the oil pan struck a rock . . . the pan was pierced and oil was shooting out in a small stream . . . we had to be towed in by a truck.*

The A. G. field secretary for Africa, H. B. Garlock, attended this Federation meeting along with many delegate-missionaries of the A. G. and other Protestant missions. It was a helpful meeting.

In March, 1952 our whole family was feeling better than at the height of our work a year before. I had made a healthful gain in weight from 142 to 157 pounds. Stella, too, had made a healthful weight gain. But she was still feeling occasional pains, from her then subsided case of dengue fever. Doris and Sharon were feeling much better, after having had malaria during the preceding year. Warren and George were feeling better physically, and studying from 8 to 10 hours daily on their high school correspondences courses. They were optimistic concerning realization of their hope to begin their college work at Central Bible Institute in Springfield, Missouri, the following September.

Henry Dahlberg got married on his furlough. He and his wife were missionaries at Dapongo, Togo. About March 1, H. B. Garlock, his brother-in-law A. N. Trotter, and Trotter's 16-year-old son Tom came to us in Po for a few days of hunting. Warren and Tom were together when Warren shot 5 times at two big roan antelopes that weighed perhaps 600 pounds each. Then Tom shot once at one of them. Two of the antelopes fell mortally wounded, a second or two later, several yards apart. Warren might have killed both of them, but they credited each other with having killed an antelope.

Soon after this episode, I had to go to Ouagadougou in our Jeep (pulling a trailer), and George accompanied me to try to *catch up with Warren* by shooting a big roan antelope. He shot and killed one just north of Po. I wrote on March 10, 1952 that "Georgie . . . hit it at 100 yards through the heart. It weighed about 400 pounds." We loaded it on the trailer and hauled it to Koubri for the Bible school students to eat. It provided many a delicious meal of beeflike meat for them!

Left to right: Sharon, George Sr., Warren, George Jr., and Tom Trotter behind a dead roan antelope, which Warren or Tom killed near Po

A little later in March, an elderly Kasena man called us and all of the Christians to his home (near Po) for a witchcraft paraphernalia-burning ceremony. This was an open testimony to all that he was then determined to break away from idolatry and follow God!

Stella wrote on March 22, 1952: "One day Sharon ran to the well . . . and stood looking down in it. She looked back to see if we were looking and she was really proud of herself. She leaned over again and George ran across the yard . . . up behind her and grabbed her. We were all scared to death!" (It was me,

George Sr., who grabbed her.) When Sharon did this the well was about 45 feet deep and we, as yet, had no protecting wall above the ground around it. This was another of the memorable experiences that filled our lives at Po.

We were eating breakfast on April 6, and got to talking about a trip we had planned to take to Dahomey in November, 1951, but never did take. We decided to go to Dahomey that day. We would first stop and visit with Lehmanns in Bawku, Gold Coast (90 miles away). But just as we were ready to get in the car and go, Lehmanns drove into our yard (unannounced) from Bawku. We all visited at our house for a day, then all drove to Bawku where we stayed two nights with Lehmanns. Next, we drove on 40 miles to Dapongo, Togo—stayed one night and had a nice visit with Henry Dahlberg and his wife. After that we drove on 135 miles to Tanguieta, Dahomey, where we thought Greenaways were still living.

When we arrived in Tanguieta at noon, we met Vernon and Marjorie Metz, and Ted Schultz, who told us that Greenaways had just left on their move to Natitingou. Metz and Schultz had gone to Tanguieta to see Greenaways just before they left, and they also were just ready to leave. (The Metzes moved to Tanguieta a few days later to live.) During our cordial greetings with them, they showed us the new mission house and church at Tanguieta. Then we drove the 30 miles to Natitingou and had a late lunch with the Greenaways.

After an enjoyable two-day visit with the Greenaways, we went 30 miles to Ted and Laura Schultz' mission station at Boukombe, Dahomey. After enjoying lunch with them, we drove 135 miles to Yendi, Gold Coast, where we enjoyed a brief visit with the George Andersons. After one night in Yendi we drove the 60 miles to Tamale, Gold Coast, and stayed two nights. After shopping for food supplies in Tamale, we drove the 60 miles to Wale Wale, Gold Coast. We stayed one night in Wale Wale, and drove the 70 miles home to Po the next morning.

Left to right: Mary, Sandra, and Charles Greenaway, standing in front of the A. G. mission house in Natitingou, Dahomey (Benin since 1976)

We arrived home from this 10-day vacation trip on April 16. "The trip was tiring but refreshing to our spirits" according to Stella's letter of April 18. In that letter she added: "The boys have always wanted to see Dahomey, so we took them."

I have already described my making of cement casings to line our well at Po. It took 45 of those casings to do the job. And the rains of 1952 were about to begin when I finished the job of placing them in the well, and building a 3-foot high protecting wall around the well above the ground. As we put the casings in place we filled all space around the outside of them with rock.

The *caving in* of the preceding rainy season had left quite a large hole at the bottom of the well, which we filled in with rock when we began to place the casings in it. All this rock around the casings helped to cleanse the water in our well and made it a better well than it was before it caved in. The *caving in* brought tribulation when it happened, but it resulted in a blessing which beautifully illustrated the fact that "in all things God works for the good of those who love him, who have been called according to his purpose" (Romans 8:28, NIV).

About May 1, we went to a village near Po to hold a gospel

meeting. Just as we arrived, an old man died. The chief was in his hut with him. He came out to tell us the man was dying, so we went in but the man had already died. The old fellow had been in some of our meetings but had never outwardly accepted Christ. We offered condolences to the village people but did not hold a service. About 55 had been saved in that village.

We took Warren and George to Ouagadougou, in our Jeep, to leave for the United States via Europe. They were eager to get back to America, where they could be among other young Americans and attend Bible school. But when we left Po that morning, they were glad for one more opportunity to do what they had enjoyed doing so many times during the 20 months of our second term in Africa that they had been with us: shoot at wild animals from the hood of the Jeep!

George (left) and Warren, at Po, ready to cross through wild-game country during the first part of their journey to America in June, 1952

On June 25, 1952, all A. G. missionaries who were at Ouagadougou, many national Christians, and other people who knew Warren and George gathered with Stella, Doris, Sharon, and me, to say goodbye to Warren, George, and the Foxes, as they left together for Europe on an Air France DC-3 plane.

None of we Flatterys broke down and cried as we saw Warren and George off, but it was quite an emotional strain on all of us, except perhaps Sharon who was a little too young to know just what was going on. Stella had a real good cry that night after they left.

Warren and George sailed on a Holland boat from Le Havre, France, on July 17, for New York, and arrived in New York on July 24. They then went to Tulsa, Oklahoma, where Stella's brother Manford Engel and his wife Lucille received them, and helped them in many ways to get back into American life again.

Doris (almost in tears) and Sharon (right), telling Warren and George goodbye on June 25, 1952, when they left Ouagadougou for Europe, on their way to America

We left Ouagadougou early the next morning (after Warren and George had gone) for Ouahigouya, Upper Volta, where we visited the Halls and Mattoxes (John and Audrey) for a few days. On Saturday evening we enjoyed a picnic with them, then started home to Po on Monday. While enroute home, we purchased a number of shrubs in Ouagadougou for planting in our yard at Po.

Left to right: Warren, Charlotte Fox, Howard Fox, and George—ready to leave Ouagadougou for Europe, on their way to America

After returning to Po, I began spending considerable time in translating portions of lessons from Myer Pearlman's Adult Teacher's Quarterly, first from English into More, then (with the help of Kasena preachers, Mankania and Nasia) from More into Kasem. During the last part of our second term in Africa (while at Po), I translated 52 of Pearlman's lessons into both Kasem and More. Early in July, I finished the translation of the first quarterly of Bible lessons in Kasem. On the first Monday and Tuesday of July, I gave each of our Kasena preachers a copy of that quarterly, when they came to Po for the preachers' conference.

From the French official's yard, we got mango trees to set out in our back yard, and a small Flamboyant tree to plant in the center of the large circle of rocks in our front yard. Also, we hired a couple of men to clear out stumps from the road between our house and the main road.

Before Warren and George went to America, George carefully studied a wiring diagram. Then, he wired our house for lights. One day after George had gone, our light plant failed to produce lights (even while its gasoline motor was running). Not having George to consult, I got out the instruction manual, and it said that "an open circuit in the automatic switch in coil 'J' would cause trouble." Then I noticed that a muddobber had built his house in that switch. When I cleared away the little *mud house* that had stuck the circuit open, we had lights!

Tomatoes did well in our rainy-season garden of 1952. When I was using our seeder to plant beans, lettuce, radishes, beets, and carrots in it, I remembered (with a sense of accomplishment) that we hadn't even had time during our first year at Po to learn how to use the seeder. There was still never a dull moment for us at Po!

Toward the end of July, Pierre and Blanche Dupret, with their children and Miss Annie Franca, came from Ouagadougou (where they were operating a French elementary and secondary school for African children and young people) to visit with us in Po for three days. We four Flatterys greatly enjoyed their visit! Doris and Sharon let the Dupret boys, Joel and Yve, play with their tricycle, most of the time. Duprets really liked Stella's homemade bread. We took them hunting a couple of times in that hunter's paradise. We got some partridge and wild guinea fowl—but the big game escaped us!

About August 10, I went to Ouagadougou for a meeting of the administrative committee of the A. G. Upper Volta mission field. I, together with all the other committee members, helped the director of the French missionary school (Pierre Dupret) to select the location (on the concession which the school already had) for the school's chapel. During my 70-mile night-trip home (Koubri to Po), after the committee meeting, I experienced what I had often experienced during our first term in Africa with our old Ford, but had seldom experienced with our Speed-the-Light Jeep: car trouble!

The Jeep had already had almost 2 years of hard use when, on the trip that night, it ran too hot because of a leaking radiator.

When necessary, I added radiator water along the way, but the Jeep's motor refused to function after I arrived at Peyiri (6 miles from home). I arrived at Peyiri at 10:00 p. m., then tried until midnight to get its motor to function. When my efforts failed, I tried to get some sleep in the car, but the mosquitos wouldn't allow that. So, at 2:15 a. m. I began a 6-mile walk home to Po—carrying my lantern and loaded shotgun through pitch darkness—and arrived at 3:40 a. m. To top it all off, the last 3 miles was through a drizzling rain!

The driver of a radio-telephone equipment car went out with me the next morning in his car and towed my car the six miles home. He thought I might have burned out a bearing. But all my car needed was a new distributor cap and rotor arm (parts which I had brought with me at the beginning of that second term).

Marie Johnsrud came and stayed with us at Po for about 10 days during the first half of August. While with us, she and Stella washed and prepared a lot of cucumbers for pickling. Those delicious sweet pickles filled a 3-gallon crock and half of a large icebox pan. (The cucumbers were given to me by the Simmons at Ouagadougou and the Butlers at Koubri.)

When Abassoure's wife died early in August, I witnessed for Christ, at her graveside service, to the many heathen Africans who attended her funeral. Late in August, I painted the front of the cement-block Po house white with Bondex cement paint.

We transplanted 8 large (about 12-feet tall) trees in our Po yard for shade. They were a cross between cedar and mahogany, and grew very slowly. On September 3, 1952, I wrote: "We probably will not get to enjoy them but then we have enjoyed . . . shade from trees that other missionaries planted over 30 years ago!" About that time (to help save Stella's strength), I took over a large part of our cooking and dish washing because we had no African household help. And Doris (still not quite 5) helped me with dish drying! The Henry

Dahlbergs had moved by September 1, to Bassari, Togo, from Dapongo. They had visited us in Po for a couple of days just before Warren and George left for America.

Russell and Ruth Schirman visited us in Po for a few days around September 1. They went with me to Corabie for a Sunday morning service, where Russell preached in More, and I interpreted his message into Kasem. Then that night at Konkwian (near Po), I translated Ruth's message in More into Kasem.

Warren and George realized their most important goal of the past 15 months, when Central Bible Institute of Springfield, Missouri, accepted them as students for the fall semester of 1952. (Perhaps the CBI registrar was guided by 1 Timothy 4:12 when he accepted George who turned only 16 the week he was accepted!) Both of our sons followed in my footsteps in finding employment as bookbinders. Eleanor Parry, CBI librarian, directed their bookbinding at the school.

A little later Warren found additional employment as a helper at A. G. headquarters in the Division of Foreign Missions. And George (with an eye for business) added to his employment by establishing his own bookbinding operation with fellow-student Phil Jones (in the latter's basement). In my letter of November 21, 1952, I wrote regarding George's private bookbinding: "He bought himself some iron pipe and boards and built his own press and work benches." That's just what I had done in Wellington, Kansas (with the help of Stella's father), 15 years earlier!

It always seemed to Stella and me that there was an unusual mutual closeness between our two sets of children—especially in view of the 11 years between our youngest boy and oldest girl. Naturally, our 4-year-old Doris missed our boys more than our 2-year-old Sharon when they went to America. One day Doris said, so seriously: "When I get to America, I really mean I'll set between Warren and Georgie and I really mean I will love them."

The French government sent a customs official to Po with his wife and two small daughters about the ages of Doris and Sharon. Stella and I were intending to invite those little girls to come visit our girls, but we just hadn't done it yet. Then one day after Doris cried because she couldn't play with them, we invited them. When they came all four girls played admirably together.

This helped to eliminate the loneliness our girls were having. After all four girls had visited back and forth for about 8 months, Stella wrote, just before we went on furlough: "Our girls . . . understand quite a bit of French. They have learned it from the customs official's little girls." We have forgotten the last name of those little girls, and remember the first name of only one of them: her name was Claudie.

Left to right: Claudie, Claudie's sister, Sharon, and Doris

About October 1, we received a telegram from Harold Jones at Ouagadougou that missionary Florence Smith had died. And the same day we received another telegram from him that Yago, our first native pastor at Corabie, had died. Yago (then no longer a young man) had entered the Mossiland Bible school at Koubri as a student. Both of them died "in the Lord" and because good "works do follow" such people, both of them are not only resting in heaven "from their labor" on earth but will also be rewarded for their labor (see Revelation 14:13).

The building of a woven wire fence with iron-reinforced concrete posts around our Po concession (100 meters square) was the last major building project that we undertook during our two years of living at Po. On October 10, 1952, I wrote: "I am beginning to work on the fence . . . have men grubbing out stumps in the fence rows." I started, at the same time, to make iron reinforcings for the posts. Timnyimna (the grubbing foreman) and his gang completed their job on October 17.

The first part of the old Corabie mud mission house had completely caved in (after two unattended rainy seasons on it). So, I used some of its old doors and shutters for forming the concrete fence posts. The making of heavy concrete-reinforced corner posts, gate posts, and braces for them, was a rather time-consuming part of the fencing job. These heavy posts were all set in concrete foundations. There was a large number of individual fence posts to be cast, of them I wrote on November 14: "I am still working on the fence posts (will be for some time)."

Native pastor Belco's wife Datounsamye with her children, in front of the caved-in Corabie mud mission house, after the rainy season of 1952

Then I wrote on December 12: "I am still making fence posts. Have about 25 more to make. I make 7 a day." Finally on December 19, I "poured the last fence post!" But I had not yet begun to install any of the fence. All this preparatory work for installation of it was accomplished, along with "the care of all the churches" (2 Corinthians 11:28, KJV), in 70 days. On October 17, I wrote: "I had good services at Kampala and Konkwian last week. Two men ask pardon at Kampala and two boys at Konkwian." Then I had a longer than usual monthly conference with the Kasena preachers which ended on October 30. I had to prepare them for teaching 5 Sunday lessons at their churches during the following month.

About October 20, we made a trip to Tamale to have our Jeep valves ground. As the months went by, Sharon was realizing more and more that Warren and George would not return to us at Po. As we were leaving for Tamale, She asked her mama if we were going home to see Warren and Georgie. Her mama replied: "No, we're going to Tamale." Then Sharon asked: "Won't the ar-pane come?" By that we knew that our 3-year-old was mentally visualizing the departure of our sons 4 months earlier!

We cleared the grass away from our fruit trees so the 1952-53 dry season brush fires could not reach them. We dug up about 25 wild fruit trees from our yard to make room for more domestic development of it. By November 7, we had eaten fruit from the guava trees of our own planting. On Armistice day (November 11—even more reverently celebrated in France than in the United States), I took Doris and Sharon to the Flag raising ceremony in Po. I parked by the town's east front gate, where they enjoyed watching the ceremony and the big crowd, from the hood of the Jeep.

The annual convention of the Upper Volta mission field took place at Ouagadougou on November 27-28, 1952. Harold and Margaret Jones did an excellent job of preparing for this convention. They had written all of the missionaries in advance and told each of them what food to bring. They had also informed them just where they would be lodged during the convention. Forty-seven (missionaries and their children) attended this convention. A. G. missionary Harold S. Lehmann of Gold Coast delivered two uplifting spiritual messages each day of the convention. Paul Moore was elected field superintendent for the coming year.

Daniel, the Simmons' former houseboy at Koubri, attended the Ouagadougou convention, and heard that we needed household help at Po. The Lord prompted him to go home with us and do house work for us. John, Cuba, David, Jim, and Betty Ann Hall visited us from November 29 to December 4. I went hunting with John and the Hall boys a few times. David killed a monkey perched on a rock. We also killed some wild guinea fowl and partridge which we and the Halls enjoyed eating together.

Back (left to right): John Hall, Cuba Hall, David Hall, Stella. Front (left to right): Betty Hall, Jim Hall, Doris, Sharon. Po mission house in the background

With Yuletide approaching, Stella and I translated the Christmas song "O Come All Ye Faithful" into Kasem. At that time we already had about 15 gospel songs in Kasem, and were adding about 4 each month. Before our term at Po ended, we compiled our Kasem songs into a booklet and had them mimeographed. It was difficult to find suitable Christmas gifts for our daughters, so I decided to repair their broken toys for Christmas 1952. How could I do that noisy work without them finding out about it?

My work bench, drill, vice, etc. were still out under the tree at the east side of the concession, where I had made the well casings the year before. I made a temporary shelter around the bench with 8-feet-tall aluminum roof sheets, and hid myself from the girls while I repaired and repainted a doll bed, doll buggy, and ironing board for Doris. And a doll cradle and doll buggy for Sharon. The girls did not find out about this in advance. They really enjoyed getting the repaired toys for Christmas!

Paul and Lillian Moore (back in Africa for another term of missionary service) arrived in Po just in time for Christmas with us. On December 26, Stella wrote Warren and George: "Brother and Sister Moore are here . . . their presence surely helped us over the loneliness of Christmas." Our house boy, Daniel, brought in a fine looking thorn bush for a Christmas tree. Stella thought she would run out of cotton in decorating it. In stretching the cotton more than in previous years, her decoration produced the prettiest, airiest, thorn-bush Christmas tree that we had yet had.

The Schirmans had chosen Stella and me to help them with their native convention in Koudougou (December 29, 1952 to January 5, 1953). We worked with them during those eight days of that convention, which was also a short-term, dry-season Bible school. Stella taught the women twice during the convention, and I taught the people three times each day.

About three months before this convention, I had sent my translations in More of Myer Pearlman's quarterlies to Schirman, so he could mimeograph them in large enough quantities for me to distribute them to all the people at the convention. This was the time when Koudougou began having separate conventions for the Mossi and Lele peoples. It was significant that this first all-Mossi convention had more people attend it than had attended any preceding combined convention! The attendance reached 300 on the final Sunday of the convention. On January 8, we enjoyed the overnight visit at Po of Dahomey missionaries Ted and Laura Schultz and Mademoiselle Helene Iselin.

Back (left to right): Ted Schultz, Laura Schultz, Helene Iselin. Front: Sharon Flattery. Po mission house in the background

The first Sunday after we returned to Po from Koudougou, I held services in Corabie, and brought back some men to help Belco and Batako with the construction of a large round hut in Belco's yard to house our first area-wide Kasena native convention. After the convention, the big hut served as a temporary church building at Po. We held this convention at Po during the last week in January. Fifty-one people attended (all from Corabie except Belco's and Batako's families).

I taught all the people daily during the convention. Stella held question-and-answer sessions in More for the women each morning, and I served as her interpreter into Kasem. Three people received the Baptism of the Holy Spirit and one was refilled with the Spirit. The people feasted on a hog that Belco killed for them at the end of the convention. On the Sunday following the convention, I held a water baptismal service at the dam by the government garden in Po.

My biggest construction task at Po, in 1953, was the installation of the 400-meter-long fence around the concession. This installation consumed nearly all of my time for manual labor between February 6 and March 6, when I finished the job—except for the front gate. (Looking ahead in the chronology of 1953 work, I notice that I was completing the installation of the front gate on May 2.)

I wrote on March 6, 1953: "The fence is all up now. Iron reinforced cement posts with woven wire stock fence 4-feet high and one strand of barbed wire above it . . . white washed . . . posts with Bondex cement paint . . . the fence decorates the yard so nicely." We gleefully watched neighborhood goats try (but fail) to get in and ruin our fruit trees!

After the election of Paul Moore as field superintendent in November, 1952, Harold and Margaret Jones were thinking that it might be time for them to start building a church in downtown Ouagadougou. But sufficient funds were not available. The field committee (of which I was a member), knowing that the moving of the Mossiland Bible school from Koubri to Nagabagere was a more urgent need at the moment than the building of a church in Ouagadougou, suggested that the Joneses supervise construction at Nagabagere.

Jones complied with the committee's suggestion and began the Nagabagere project about February 1. I wrote on March 6, 1953: "Brother Jones is going ahead well with the new Bible school project . . . he is building a small missionary residence, a large classroom building, and native student quarters."

At Po, we enjoyed visits of several missionaries during the dry season of 1953. Some of them were: Hermie and Vi

Engelgau, Ward and Twila Woods, Phil and Lucille Davies from Leo, Pauline Smith and Adeline Wickman from Gold Coast, Herb and Margy Butler with baby Sandra, Paul and Virginia Weidman.

My last major 1953 task (before we left Po to go on furlough) was writing rather than manual labor—it was my translation of the book of Acts from More into Kasem. (Of course, while translating Acts I had to continue to do what I had been doing since about July, 1952: translate More Sunday School lessons into Kasem for the month immediately ahead.)

Harold Jones in front of the temporary shelter from which he directed the building of the Bible school at Nagabagere

I started translating Acts into Kasem on March 16, and worked through the first 5 chapters the first week. I had almost finished 10 chapters by March 28. I had reached Chapter 23 by April 10. And by May 2, I had completed the translation of Acts. At various times I had Nasia, Mankania, and Alia as informants while translating it.

It made me sad when thieves stole from our furlough baggage the only copy I had of my translation of Acts in Kasem. I was glad, however, that no other part of the considerable amount of translation work that I had done in French, More, and Kasem—while in Africa—was stolen. My informants and I received heavenly "treasures" in spiritual blessings (from our translation of Acts into Kasem) which thieves did not and could not "break in and steal" from us (Matthew 6:20, NIV)!

Conclusion

We spent four months more than three years in Africa

during our first term. Then (with permission from the A. G. Division of Foreign Missions), we returned to the United States in June, 1953, after our second term: four months ahead of the originally scheduled October, 1953.

We had felt that the Kasena work would progress very slowly (or might even die) if we did not go back to it for a second term. At the end of that second term, the excellent progress of the Kasena work (especially with reference to preparation for the ministry by young Kasena men who were converted at Corabie during our first term) encouraged us greatly: three of the eight who graduated from the Upper Volta Bible School in Koubri, about March 1, 1953, were Kasena young men who had been converted at Corabie during our first term.

Those three were Alia, Apouri (Job), and Agwouleweno. In addition, Sedan finished his first year at Koubri in March, 1953. Alia began preaching at Konkwian, Job went to help Sidabe at Kampala, and Agwouleweno stayed at home to help the elderly Corabie pastor, Mankania. The Maurice Petersons were chosen to succeed us. They took our place at Po.

We began packing for furlough on May 3 (separating what we would take with us from what we would not) and completed it on May 17. Then on May 18, we went to Ouagadougou, where we got our shots and signed out of the Upper Volta. We left Ouagadougou for Takoradi about June 1. We had already said our "goodbyes" at Po and only stopped briefly there.

Paul and Lillian Moore took us in their car from Ouagadougou to Takoradi. On June 15, at Takoradi, we boarded the MV Taurus (a freighter) for New York City. At about 9:00 a. m. on June 29, the Taurus landed us at New York. Robert T. McGlasson, of the A. G. Foreign Missions New York Office, met us at the dock. We left New York that day by train at 6:45 p. m. for Springfield, Missouri, where we arrived the next day at 10:30 p. m.

Flattery Missionary Card of 1955. Left to right: Doris, George, Sr., Stella, and Sharon

CHAPTER 7: THIRD TERM, UPPER VOLTA AND SENEGAL

Furlough Activities and Events

Our second furlough began when we arrived in New York from our second term in Africa on June 29, 1953. It was a 29-month furlough (the longest of our furloughs). At the beginning of it I went to Newton, Kansas, and purchased my furlough Dodge Meadowbrook sedan, through Harry Baker who gave me a good discount on it. I went to Detroit on July 6, and took delivery on it the next day. Warren and George were working in Michigan and went to Detroit to see me (and our new car). I hadn't seen them since they left Africa on June 25, 1952. What a happy time we had together!

My whole family was pleased with the dark red color of our new Dodge. But we were wondering (back in 1953) whether some of the church people of my missionary itinerary might think its color was too bright! Usually, the first thing I would do after entering a town where I was to have a missionary service was to visit the pastor who would be in charge of that service. One day, after parking my dark red Dodge in front of the home of an Iowa pastor, he asked me how I could itinerate with a red car.

I don't remember the exact wording of my reply. But having found nothing in Scripture which seemed to imply that a particular color of an automobile would be among the "things that offend" God which His angels would "gather out of his kingdom" (Matthew 13:41, KJV); I answered, in effect, that God's people should not be offended by anything which does not offend God, and that I did not think the color of my car offended Him. Then, that pastor and I got along fine together the rest of the day, and I had a good missionary service in his church that night.

Before I began my missionary itinerary, I separated all of the 16 mm. color movie scenes that I had taken during our second term in Africa into two groups: this was a separation of scenes for my missionary film from the remainder of the scenes. All the scenes which I did not use in the 15-minute missionary film have been very valuable through these many years as home movies. I used the missionary film as a supplement to—but not as a replacement for—missionary preaching.

On August 25, 1953, Stella and I drove (with Doris and Sharon) to Milwaukee, Wisconsin, to attend the General Council of the Assemblies of God. Up to that time, Warren and George had continued to work in nearby Michigan. Having finished their work there, they joined us in Milwaukee to attend the General council during the last week of August. All six of us participated in the colorful Sunday-afternoon missionary service during the Council. Then Warren and George returned home to Springfield, Missouri, with us immediately after the Council meeting concluded. A few days later they entered C. B. I. for their second year of study.

My second furlough itinerary (1953-1955) was considerably more extensive than my first furlough itinerary (1949-1950) had been. The 18 states where I held missionary meetings during my second furlough were (alphabetically): Arizona, Arkansas, California, Illinois, Iowa, Kansas, Michigan,

Minnesota, Missouri, Montana, North Carolina, Oklahoma, Oregon, Pennsylvania, Tennessee, Texas, Washington, and Wisconsin. About half of all those meetings were in Kansas (my home district). A considerable number of them were in Missouri and Iowa. My itinerary in Iowa in the fall of 1953 had been planned for Mrs. W. R. Steelberg but, when she broke her leg, I was asked to take it.

Back (left to right): George Jr., George Sr., Stella, Warren. Front (left to right): Sharon, Doris. At Milwaukee General Council of the Assemblies of God in 1953

I had completed 10 semester hours of college work (in the Wycliffe Summer Institute of Linguistics at the University of Oklahoma) during my first furlough. Then, during this second furlough, I continued my education by completing 15 semester hours of classroom work at Southwest Missouri State College, and 10 semester hours of French through the Missouri University school of correspondence. I accomplished this correspondence work little-by-little throughout the long weeks and months of my missionary itinerary.

This college work was an important part of my preparation

for helping (during the last 18 years) with the Pentecostal pioneering that the A. G. International Correspondence Institute has accomplished.

It was my privilege to teach French at C. B. I. during the academic school year of 1954-1955. A number of my students have had successful careers in various vocations: examples of them are John Weidman (whom I had known well as a teenager at Corabie) in missionary work, William Eastlake in A. G. administrative work, and Ginger (Carlson) Martin as a pastor's wife.

During this furlough the Upper Volta field committee sent word to me that they wanted me to raise funds for a downtown church in Ouagadougou, return to Ouagadougou, and supervise the building of that church. In February 1954, Noel Perkin, director of A. G. Foreign Missions, asked me to join the Foreign Missions staff at headquarters on a temporary basis. I worked as one of J. Philip Hogan's helpers in the promotions division for 16 months. This work, my teaching at C. B. I., and my raising of funds with which to build a church in downtown Ouagadougou required an extension of our furlough.

One of my assignments at the missions department was given to me by DFM committeeman Maynard Ketcham: it was to write on "Americanisms Abroad" for the missionary seminar (forerunner of the school of missions) of 1954. I wrote a 6000-word paper. In it are 19 illustrative incidents from my first two terms of Pentecostal pioneering in Upper Volta. Letters from missionary leaders and Melvin Hodges' book *The Indigenous Church* were among other sources for my paper. I enjoyed writing this paper and reading it to the seminar. The missionaries (some with experience beyond mine on its subject) received it well.

We thoroughly enjoyed our 29 months in Cottage 11 at Mission village during this furlough. In 1954, I put up swings and teeterboards (in cement foundations) by our cottage for Doris 7, Sharon 5, and other village children. Stella and I were then about 40, and thinking ahead (perhaps more than previously) about our lives later on. We were impressed that a good beginning toward the fulfillment of our hope to own our own home in retirement would be to immediately have a small rental residence built and begin payments on it.

I chose 2915 North Grant in Springfield, Missouri, for this project. John Dill, my builder, hired Warren and George to help him build this house. The project supplied our sons with some needed finance for their third year in C. B. I. On July 8, 1954, Stella wrote her parents: "Our house will be finished in another week . . . we'll rent it to make it pay for itself." We did just that, and when we returned to Africa, we placed the renting of it in the hands of George Sample who did a good job of keeping it rented.

The marriage of our son, George Manford Flattery, to Esther Ruth Scheuerman on May 29, 1955, in Windsor, Ontario, Canada, was an event as important to Stella and me as was the birth of each of our four children. What a joy it was to me to participate in their wedding ceremony and, following it, to fellowship with them and all who witnessed their vows!

Back to Ouagadougou

We completed our scheduled furlough missionary services with meetings in the Sheffield Assembly of God Church on Sunday, August 28, 1955. C. W. Quattlebaum was pastor of that church. It had just begun to send (through the Foreign Missions Department) $235.00 monthly (almost half of our personal budget at the time) for our missionary support. And it continued to send that amount monthly for the next nine years (until we retired from missionary work in Africa). This was several times as much as any other church ever gave in monthly support for our missionary ministry.

Stella and I participated in the great Foreign Missions Rally of the General Council of the Assemblies of God in Oklahoma City on Sunday afternoon September 4, 1955. After that, at our cottage in Mission Village, we packed for Africa in September and early October before leaving October 12 in our Speed-the-Light Plymouth station wagon for New York City. Esther rode with Stella, Doris, Sharon and me. Warren and George drove the Upper Volta mission truck (loaded with our equipment) to New York. Esther had only one day to see New York City for the first time. Then Warren, George, and Esther went back to Springfield: the boys to their classes at C. B. I. and Esther to her work at the Gospel Publishing House.

Concerning our return to Africa for our third term, I wrote my mother from New York City on October 27, 1955: "We will sail tomorrow morning on the 'SS United States' of the United States Lines." Just before we sailed, Stella and I received this telegram from Noel Perkin and his staff: "BON VOYAGE GREETINGS TO YOU THE MCCULLEYS AND MISS WINTERS. GOD BLESS YOU AS YOU RETURN TO AFRICA."

Left to right: Stella, Doris, Janice McCulley, Sharon (in front of Janice). On the "SS United States"

The "SS United States" landed Stella, Doris, Sharon, and me at Le Havre, France, during the morning of November 2. We immediately took a train to Paris and were there only a day and a half. We enjoyed a brief excursion throughout Paris, then took a night train to Marseilles, where we boarded the French passenger ship "General Mangin" for Abidjan, Ivory Coast, French West Africa.

We enjoyed our brief excursion on the Mediterreanean island of Majorca, where we saw 1000-year-old olive trees which had been planted by the Moors. While we were viewing Chopin's piano, a lady caretaker slightly reprimanded our 6-year-old Sharon, when she ducked under its protecting rope and touched it! Next we stopped briefly at Algers, Algeria. After we stopped at Casablanca, Morocco, we went on an excursion to Rabat (the Moroccan capital), where we examined old Roman and Moorish ruins. Then we had brief stops at Dakar and Conakrey, before reaching Abidjan on November 15, where Paul and Virgina Weidman met us, and took us in their station wagon to Takoradi, Gold Coast (Ghana since 1957).

Doris and Sharon spent quite a bit of time in the water at the Takoradi beach with Faith Weidman (a few years older than Doris). After learning to swim, Doris enjoyed the deep water, while Sharon was enjoying the shallow water. After clearing our baggage at Takoradi harbor, we made the 700-mile inland trip to Ouagadougou in our 1955 Plymouth station wagon. We arrived in Ouagadougou on December 3, 1955.

Left to right: Sharon, Faith Weidman, Doris

George Flattery, Sr., checking his drums of baggage at the Takoradi harbor in November, 1955

We arrived in Ouagadougou on the first day of the Upper Volta mission field's annual convention. We had a good convention with crowds reaching at least 1000 in the nightly mass meetings. I had been the field's secretary during the preceding term, and was chosen as its treasurer at this convention. The treasurer had to spend more time at being treasurer than the secretary did at being secretary. One day, while I was devoting many hours to my task as treasurer, Stella remarked, good naturedly, that the choosing of me as treasurer was an example of "let George do it!"

Our 1955 mandate from the Upper Volta Mission field to supervise missionary work in downtown Ouagadougou included the spiritual aspect of the work as well as the building of the church building. As soon as we got back to Ouagadougou, I began holding gospel services downtown—four nights a week and on Sunday.

I held these meetings in various yards of people who lived

in Ouagadougou. After about 15 weeks of these yard meetings, I wrote on March 25, 1956: "Our . . . services have been well attended. There have been a number of conversions . . . in the services which I have held in native yards in the city. We are going to a new yard, which has not had a service yet, next Tuesday night." Then on May 11, I wrote: "Last night I went to an African male nurse's yard . . . and held an evangelistic meeting. Four women and one girl were converted."

Missionaries at the Upper Volta convention at Ouagadougou in December, 1955. Center front: E. L. Phillips, secretary for Africa

Remodeling Our Residence

I could not start building the downtown church in Ouagadougou until May, 1956. I was occupied until then with extensive remodeling of the eastern half of the large adobe residence on the Ouagadougou mission compound. That residence was a duplex and the eastern part of it was our living quarters when we got to Ouagadougou in December, 1955. About 5 weeks before I completed this remodeling, I wrote on March 25, 1956:

We have done considerable remodeling on the east section of the large adobe duplex. I made a convenient kitchen and adjoining dining room. I put in a water system (mud tower with a barrel on it) and kitchen sink with tile drain board. Then I began construction of a flush toilet system, making the underground septic container (4 feet wide by 7 feet long by 6 and 1/3 feet deep) of poured, iron-reinforced concrete. This has been quite a job but it should be ready for use in about a week. I am also installing a lavatory and shower in the remodeled bathroom.

It was not our main object to make that old mud house pretty, but to make it as convenient as possible. Each physical convenience that we had in Africa strengthened our spiritual service there, because it helped us to accomplish our physical activities with less expenditure of strength. There is no better example of the point I am making than our missionaries' use of the Speed-the-Light vehicles that were supplied to them by friends of foreign missions.

I've been emphasizing what I did during the first six months of our third term in Africa. During these months Stella was doing (as always) her part in our missionary work and, in some ways, doing it in more trying circumstances than ever before: During the two years of our furlough, relationship between Africans and foreigners became much more strained than it had been. Africans' understandable effort to better their standard of living (through institution of labor unions) required us to pay a higher percentage of our missionary budget for household help. But that was only a minor aspect of our more trying circumstances.

After we had been in Ouagadougou 27 days, Stella wrote on December 30, 1955: "Doris and Sharon didn't like it here at all for a few days. When we started a couple of days ago to do our own cooking, they seemed to feel more at home." My remodeling of our living quarters had to start with the kitchen. Remodeling it disrupted normal living for our whole family.

However, the main thing which caused more trying circumstances for Stella and me (and our daughters) at the beginning of this third term was something more demoralizing than disruption of our kitchen: it was a spirit of disdain for foreigners on the part of Africans. This spirit had crept into the relationship between African Christians and supervising missionaries. Stella and I did not allow it to curb our missionary work. Doris and Sharon quickly adjusted to this new spirit and lovingly socialized with the African children.

Our 6 and 8 year old daughters' adjustment exemplified the childlike trait which prompted Paul's advice: "In malice be ye children" (1 Corinthians 14:20, KJV). Their love included even a stray dog, about to have puppies, which showed up in our yard! At their insistence, we took this dog into our home. We called her "Queenie." Needless to say, Doris and Sharon enjoyed playing with Queenie's puppies.

Sharon (left) and Doris with two of Queenie's puppies at Ouagadougou in 1956

As in preceding years in Africa, Stella's work included both the teaching of African women and our own children. She taught Doris and Sharon at the same packing-case school desks that I had made in Ouagadougou a decade earlier for Warren and George. I wrote on March 25, 1956: "Stella is teaching Doris and Sharon the Calvert courses. They are doing real well in school and she enjoys teaching them. Stella also has a Sunday School class of about 30 Mossi women to teach."

Stella by front steps of Ouagadougou adobe mission duplex in 1956

On February 22, 1956, I left Ouagadougou by plane for Bamako with Howard Fox to attend the three-day meeting of the Federation of Protestant Missions of French West Africa. It was a good meeting, and was attended by two representatives from each of the Protestant missions. Some of the representatives came 3000 miles (one way) to attend the meeting! For several years Pierre Benignus, a Frenchman, had been executive secretary of the Federation. He resigned at this Bamako meeting—with the understanding that he would fulfill his year before leaving office.

George, ready to leave Ouagadougou airport for Bamako Federation meeting in February, 1956

On May 11, 1956, I wrote (from Ouagadougou):

We went to Boromo—110 miles west of here—to visit Hermie and Vi Engelgau and their two children, Carlyle 8 and Charlene 6, on Stella's birthday, April 27. This is the Engelgaus' first term, and they are due for a furlough some time this year. They have done a good work in the newly opened station.

Right after we returned to Ouagadougou from Boromo, I devoted an entire week to drawing plans for the new church in downtown Ouagadougou. I was its architect as well as its builder. I calculated the window and door openings to fit in with the cement blocks in such manner as to eliminate much unnecessary block cutting which makes the masons' work slower and increases the cost of the building. (I had calculated in this manner when drawing plans for the Po mission house about 5 years earlier and it helped a lot!)

During the second week in May, 1956, the missionary members of the Upper Volta language committee (Eva Radanovsky, Howard Fox, and myself) met for a few days at Ouagadougou with four Mossi informants to revise the Gospel of Mark in More. During those days, we had Eva and Marie Johnsrud eat dinner with us one evening. Then (with their day's work finished), they played some table games with Stella, Doris, Sharon, and me after dinner. Such "cheerful" relaxation (when not overdone) was a "good medicine" (Proverbs 17:22, NIV) for missionaries that helped them to do better work the next day!

Language committee missionaries (left to right): Eva Radanovsky, George Flattery, and Howard Fox, working with four African informants at revision of the Gospel of Mark in May, 1956, at Ouagadougou

Building the Downtown Church

On May 16, I began to build the church. My job that day was to supervise the French surveyor's marking of the positions of the corners of the building. I worked very steadily on the new church for about five and one half months (mid-May to about November 1), finishing less than half of the job costwise but about half of it timewise before I ran out of funds, and had to wait until May, 1957 to begin the remainder of the job.

Before describing our progress through the first half of the building of the church in Ouagadougou, I will go back to February and tell you about the prefabricated British building which I purchased for shipment to Takoradi when we arrived there from the United States in November, 1955. By February, our prefab had arrived in Takoradi. On February 5, 1956, I wrote from Takoradi:

> *Brother Bascue and I came down here to supervise the loading of an Aracon prefabricated building with metal trussing and supporting posts. This will be the framework of our church in Ouagadougou. A roof of corrugated asbestos sheets is included in the purchase. We will fill in the walls with cement blocks, making a nice built up front with glass block cross design. The structure is . . . 14 feet 6 inches to the eaves and about 30 feet ground to gable cone. The weight of the steel framework is 9 tons and the asbestos sheets 11 tons. We will start tomorrow to load it on two 10-ton trucks which will carry it through to Ouagadougou.*

This prefabricated building was 100 feet long and 50 feet wide. It had seven metal trusses (including a truss for each gable end). Each of the six spans between the trusses was sixteen and two thirds feet. By cutting the length of our church down from 100 feet to 84 feet, and building concrete block gable ends, we used only four of the seven metal trusses that we had purchased. We sold the three extra trusses, the six metal posts, and the part of the asbestos sheets that we did not use to the national Mossi church at Koudougou for its new church building.

The cost of this prefab and the hauling of it to Ouagadougou was about $8,000. When we went to America for furlough in 1953, there was about $3,000 in the downtown Ouagadougou church fund which had been raised by Harold and Margaret Jones in 1945. I raised approximately $5,000 more for it while on furlough. After paying for the prefab, the fund had nothing left in it. All we had to work with when we started building in May, 1956, was what the Koudougou church paid us for their part of the prefab.

Two semitrailers on the Ouagadougou mission compound in February, 1956, loaded with prefabricated framing and roofing for the downtown Ouagadougou church

Right after this picture was taken, these building materials were deposited on the downtown church lot. The new church would accommodate about one thousand people (seated on its floor). I had been trying for some time to get the official French government stamp on my drawings for the new church building, and I was receiving government assurance that I would get it. Then on June 22, I received the government stamp of approval—after I had already poured seven of the eight large iron-reinforced concrete footings for the building's pilasters.

Perhaps the government just wanted to see a little action on my part before it stamped my drawings. I had waited (because of the good reasons, explained above) five months to begin building the new church. On the day I began to build it, I told a missionary colleague that I was finally ready to start building the church. This colleague replied, good naturedly: "Well, it's about time!" And I, just as good naturedly, heartily agreed with that colleague.

On June 30, 1956, I wrote my son Warren: "Each building job is easier from the standpoint of 'know-how' . . . each one gets a little tougher from the standpoint of 'climbing the ladders.' If a young man could have the experience of an old man and an old man the strength of a young man, what two wonderful combinations that would be!"

Then I wrote my mother this summary of what I had done on the building up to July 17:

> *I think good progress has been made . . . the bases (2-feet square and 3 and 1/2 feet high) of iron reinforcd concrete have been made for the 8 steel vertical beams. We have finished leveling cement in all of the wall foundation trenches. This week we will begin raising the prefabricated tubular steel trusses (fifty-foot span). I am also making the forms in which to pour the foundation on the sub-foundations. This foundation will reach up to floor level, thirty inches above the ground.*

Before I started raising the steel trusses, I noticed that the wrong length of asbestos roof sheets had been sent to Ouagadougou. The positioning of steel fasteners on the trusses would not fit with those sheets. We solved the problem by removing the fasteners and welding them on at proper positions. Gene Bascue lent me his welding equipment and Howard Fox, an experienced welder, did the welding. I was grateful for this help from my two missionary colleagues.

By August 18, the steel framework (including trusses) was all raised in place, and the above-ground foundations were all poured on the sub-foundations (except a section left open for trucks to enter the building with fill dirt). The following, written by me on September 16, tells about all this more fully (and adds some information about what we did between August 18 and September 16):

We had to erect a gin pole about 34 feet high for lifting the steel trusses. Then we formed lumber to a height of about thirty inches above ground and poured the foundation (except for the section for fill-dirt trucks). Since September 1, we have been laying the cement block walls and are now to the tops of the doors . . . I hired a big construction company here to fill the building with dirt and rock to floor level . . . they have worked four days already and have about three more days to work . . . the rains are still falling . . . they pack the fill dirt and make a better foundation for the cement floor.

A French builder in Ouagadougou lent me his gin pole and its pulley for the raising of the trusses, and also sent me some African workers who knew how to use the pole and pulley. It would have taken our mission truck about two months to accomplish the fill-dirt job that the French *Draggage* accomplished in a week with three dump trucks. By about November 1, I had supervised the pouring of the iron-reinforced course at the top of the side walls and around the entire building. And the Ouagadougou downtown church building fund was empty!

Back: Stella. Front: Doris (left) and Sharon. Half-completed downtown Ouagadougou church building in background

By June 4, 1956, Bill and Margaret Lovick had arrived in Ouagadougou for missionary service, and Bill was due back from Ghana that evening with their baggage. We went to visit Bascues at Yako on Saturday June 9. I relaxed from the building work by going hunting with Gene that day. Then the next day we were with Bascues and the Yako people in their Sunday church services.

On Sunday, June 17, Howard Fox, Bill and Margaret Lovick, Gene and Betty Bascue, Paul Moore, Marie Johnsrud, Eva Radanovsky, Stella, and I went to Po to be with Maurice Peterson in the dedication service for the church building that he had built in Po. Peterson was to leave Po for his furlough immediately after the dedication service, and join his wife and children who were already in America on furlough.

But when we arrived in Po, Peterson had already gone on furlough without telling any of us about his departure. He had not been able to finish the building, but we were grateful for what he had accomplished. We had the dedication service without him. God blessed the service and all those who attended it. On June 18, 1956, Stella wrote: "The Po yard is beautiful . . . the trees we transplanted . . . all grew. And all the flower bushes. Its a beautiful compound now. The white fence is so pretty . . . the airport is directly across the road from our house."

I took each Saturday off from building the church. On Saturday June 30, we four and the Lovicks went to Nagabagere for hunting and a picnic somewhere in the bush with the Moores. During the first week in July, the Mossi church on the Ouagadougou mission compound elected Gwomtanga as their pastor. Almost eleven years had elapsed since Stella had taken him directly from the bush, trained him to be our wash boy, and also gave him his first lessons in reading and writing. Right after Gwomtanga became pastor of that church, I remarked in my letter of July 17, regarding it: "We are having some very good meetings in our old mud church on the compound."

Back (left to right): Stella, Margaret Lovick, Lillian Moore, Paul Moore, Bill Lovick. Front: Doris (left) and Sharon

On July 22, Charles Greenaway and Sandra, with Chaney and David Wakefield, arrived in Ouagadougou with truck, car, jeep, and trailer all loaded with baggage. Charles was on his way from Dahomey to Tambacounda, Senegal, to open the Senegal mission field. He put all vehicles and baggage on the train at Bamako and accompanied them by train to Tambacounda.

In her letter of July 29, 1956, Stella wrote of her Mossi cook Gwombila: "He is the best cook I've ever had. He's smart and likes to work. I do very little work in the kitchen." What a welcome change from our almost constant problem with household help among the Kasena of Corabie and Po for seven years (1946-1953)!

On August 3, 1956, we received a telegram from Fort Worth, Texas, from George and Esther announcing the birth on August 2 of their son (our first grandchild) George Warren Flattery. Now, at 36 (in 1992), he is a highly respected ordained A. G. minister of varied experience who has accomplished (among other things) four years (with his family) of successful missionary work as an A. G. missionary in France. He is currently pastoring a strong A. G. church in Painesville, Ohio.

Bascues moved from Yako to Po in August, where they hoped to do considerable bush work in the starting of new preaching points. Herb and Margy Butler began building in Zabere, in August. In my letter from Ouagadougou of August 18, 1956, I wrote:

> *Yesterday morning at 6:00 a. m. Brother Fox and I left in his pickup for Zabere between Tenkodogo and Po . . . Herb Butler is starting to build a mission station there. We went down to mark off the concession corners and locate the position for the future residence on the lot. We arrived at Zabere about 11:00 a. m., finished our work at 4:30 p. m., drove back to Ouagadougou, and arrived there about 10:00 p. m.*

Herb Butler (left) and Howard Fox on the mission concession at Zabere, Upper Volta, in August, 1956

On Sunday evening, September 23, in the church on the Ouagadougou mission compound, I was handed a note just before I was to start preaching. The note was a call for help from Mossi pastor Bourema at Ipala (20 miles west of Ouagadougou) for someone to go to Ipala to get a Mossi woman who was about to have a baby, and take her to the Ouagadougou hospital. Stella immediately left our church service in our car, went to Ipala, got the woman, and took her to the hospital. The woman got along fine while giving birth to healthy twin girls!

The 6-year-old daughter, Katherine, of Lebende Miningou (president of the national Mossi church) fell in the open well at her home (ajacent to the Ouagadougou mission compound) in October, 1956, and drowned. A certain pattern in the beating of drums signaled to everyone within hearing distance that a person had drowned in a well.

This precious little girl had brought to us a lovely gift of boiled peanuts the day before she drowned. It was an extremely grevious loss to Lebende and Katherine's mother, Rachel. Rachel was out of her mind with grief to the point that Stella had to restrain her from jumping into the well, even after Katherine's body had been retrieved.

Lebende and Rachel had buried their son Nathan (about 2) just two months before Katherine drowned. With my tools downtown (at our building site) I made forms for concrete grave markers for both Nathan and Katherine, poured them, etched their names into them, and gave them to Lebende and Rachel. It was a small gift of love from me to them for which they expressed great gratitude.

Lebende Miningou and his wife Rachel with their children

Doris and Sharon had to postpone their studies at the beginning of this third term. But they made up for lost time when they got started on their lessons. On October 13, 1956, Stella wrote: "I've got the girls caught up in their school work. They are right where they would be at home. Doris has finished two months in the fourth grade, and Sharon two months in the second grade."

In Tamale, Gold Coast, on October 30, 1956, Stella received a letter from Esther by which she learned that her father, Reverend George Engel, had died. His death at 78 was hardly unexpected for he had been quite ill for some time. Esther wrote that all the relatives were so glad "the boys could be at grandpa's funeral." All four of us wished we had been in America so we could have attended it. No person (outside our own four children) was ever dearer to Stella and me than her father.

In beautiful application to her own circumstances of the principle of sorrowing taught by Paul in 1 Thessalonians 4:13, Stella wrote her Sister Roma from Tamale, on November 7, regarding the death of her father: "I'm happy he has made his entry into the presence of the Lord. Bless his heart." Although the death of a dear loved one is always disquieting to a child of God, sorrow over it can be mitigated by hope in Christ.

When we left Ouagadougou On October 30, we had planned a vacation to Accra, but our Plymouth motor burned out just 52 miles south of Tamale. A truck pulled us back to Tamale. The crankshaft had to be ground for one bearing, so I took the car's motor to Accra by truck and train to have the work done. While the motor was apart, the garage in Accra put new piston rings in it, and changed the clutch disc. The car ran fine after that, but all four of us missed out on the vacation we were planning—Stella, Doris, and Sharon had to remain in Tamale until we returned to Upper Volta on November 17.

The annual Upper Volta missionary convention began in Ouagadougou on December 3, 1956. I was elected by the missionaries to be their field superintendent during the following year. On December 9, Bill Lovick was loading a truck with his baggage in preparation for moving from Ouagadougou to Bassari, Togo, with his wife Margaret, to take over the mission work that David and Claudia Wakefield had founded.

Late in November we had started holding an open air evangelistic meeting each Sunday evening beside our partially completed church building in downtown Ouagadougou. From the beginning, good crowds of people attended these meetings. After more than three months, Stella wrote on March 9, 1957: "Every Sunday evening the crowds are getting bigger at the open air services . . . we use the loud speaker . . . from five to seven hundred people stand about us, and several hundred more hear over the loud speaker."

We had an early morning 6 o'clock service on Christmas day in the adobe church on the mission compound for the Ouagadougou Mossi church people. After the service we passed out treats of candy and fruit to them. Then in the afternoon they (especially the young men and boys) enjoyed the games and races we had organized for them. Marie Johnsrud ate Christmas dinner with us, and we all enjoyed our traditional native thorn tree decorated with cotton! The French often celebrate Christmas with fireworks—so I shot off some for our daughters on Christmas night.

Ouagadougou Mossi church congregation on Christmas day, 1956

Early in January, 1957, I installed another cesspool for the Ouagadougou compound. (A year before, I installed one for the eastern part of the adobe duplex.) The second cesspool was for the western part of it and other apartments on the compound. I had installed only one toilet with the first pool, then installed two with this second one—a toilet in the western apartment of the duplex, and another one outside the duplex for the other apartments.

By January 3, 1957, Howard and Charlotte Fox had moved to Nagabagere to take care of the Mossi Bible School until John and Cuba Hall would arrive from furlough (probably in late summer of the same year) to take care of it. Then before February 7, we had moved from the eastern part of the duplex at Ouagadougou into the western part of it (where Foxes were living until they moved to the Bible School).

George Flattery, Sr., praying the ordination prayer for Mankania Kasena on the Ouagadougou mission compound in March, 1957

We had a convention of the A. G. Upper Volta national church pastors on the Ouagadougou mission compound. It began on February 22, and closed on March 5. All the Upper Volta missionaries and 115 national pastors attended this convention. National pastors, not yet ordained but ready for ordination, were ordained during the convention. Mankania Kasena had been the leading pastor of the Kasena works of Corabie and Po for several years, but had not yet been ordained. He chose me to pray the ordination prayer for him in this convention.

Stella wrote on March 9, 1957, regarding a service which we held in the partially completed downtown Ouagadougou church building during that convention for national church pastors: "One night we held a service in the unfinished church building and showed Roberts' T. V. film. We had a thousand people or more. No chairs. Just dirt floor. It was a thrilling experience for them to see the film and its miracles of healing."

Doris and Sharon were continuing to do well in their Calvert school work. On February 25, Stella wrote: "This morning I intend to order out Doris' fifth grade books and Sharon's work books for the third grade." We were glad that the Duprets were bringing their children over to our house each Thursday afternoon to play with Doris and Sharon. It was an association through which our girls made some progress in French. Their happy association with the Dupret children had begun back in our second term when Duprets visited us at Po.

Foreman Karim of window-ventilator, block-making crew on Ouagadougou mission compound in April, 1957

On April 1, my African crew began making window-ventilator concrete blocks for the windows of the partially-completed Ouagadougou church building. They made them in the east part (garage part) of the large metal-roofed building on the mission compound that I had helped to build, back in 1948. Then we hauled the blocks the two miles to the downtown building site.

Little Sharon's liveliness gave us many a happy moment. But one day it brought us some sadness: On April 2, she (then 7) rode her bicycle right into the church on the mission compound, swerved to avoid hitting some people, hit the platform, fell from the bike, and broke her arm! When the cast was taken off, her arm looked a little crooked at first. But it straightened out and she suffered no permanent damage from the break.

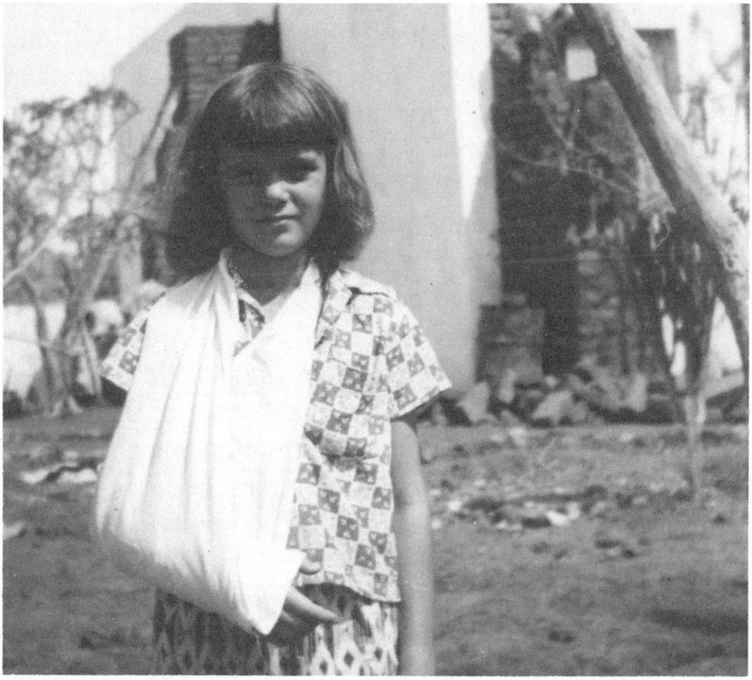

Sharon with broken arm at Ouahigouya about May 1, 1957

M. A. Daoud and his wife, Jane (Collins) Daoud, of Dallas, Texas, flew into Ouagadougou unannounced on April 3, 1957, to hold a campaign of nightly healing meetings that lasted about a week. The first three meetings were held in the Ouagadougou soccer stadium. But persecution by the Ouagadougou Roman Catholic church organization was so strong against this campaign that French government officials ordered us to hold the remaining meetings on our lot beside our partially completed church building. As I was leaving the stadium on the 3rd night with the evangelists in my car, stones were thrown at us, but none entered the car.

The first night at the stadium, about 3000 people attended. When we had to go to our church lot, the crowds were much smaller, but many hundreds of people continued to attend. Many people were healed, and I believe the overall influence of the campaign on the Mossi work was positive. If we had known the Daouds were coming, and could have gathered Christians to Ouagadougou from other mission stations for the campaign, it would probably have had an even greater positive influence on God's work in Upper Volta. I think that the outrageous Catholic persecution of the campaign embarrassed some of the Catholic church leaders in a manner that caused them to show a better attitude toward our Protestant mission than they had ever shown before.

During the last week in April, the committee of the Federation of Protestant Missions in French West Africa met in Ouagadougou. Stella and I provided some of the meals for those committeemen while they were attending the meeting. When it was over she, Doris, Sharon, and I spent five days at Ouahigouya, Upper Volta. According to my letter of May 19, 1957: I "spent April 29 to May 3, at Ouahigouya building two large abutments against the sides of the house to keep the rains from causing it to fall." I also had the low ground around those abutments filled in and pounded. We held gospel meetings in the Ouahigouya church while there.

Repairing Ouahigouya mission residence about May 1, 1957

I pointed out (some pages back) that our first day of work on the downtown Ouagadougou church was May 16, 1956. A year later (on May 8), I wrote our supporting churches in America: "We are starting work on the church again tomorrow. Some finances have come in." (The largest single offering that had come in while we were held up because of lack of finances, was an offering of $500 from a former Upper Volta missionary, Fred Glaser. Raymond Zents, Sr., a current Upper Volta missionary, also sent in a substantial offering.) My first job on the church in May, 1957, was to pour the nineteen window sills, then lay in place the window-ventilator blocks (made previously on the mission compound). We began laying those blocks on May 20.

On Sunday, May 12, Doris, Sharon, and I attended the water baptismal service which was held at the dam near the Duprets' French school. Stella needed some rest and did not attend it. I remarked in my letter of May 19, 1957: "Herb and Margy Butler have shown real courage in opening up Zabere. They moved into their new house (not finished) about a week ago. He wants to learn Bousanse and get Mark translated this term."

In their December, 1956, convention the Upper Volta missionaries asked Harold and Margaret Jones to return to Upper Volta to establish a print shop and book room on the downtown church lot. The Joneses arrived in Ouagadougou on June 11, 1957, with offset printing equipment to begin that work. When they returned to Po for baggage, Doris went with them to visit the Bascue girls, and Bascues were ready to go on a trip to Accra. So, at their invitation, she went with them and all the girls enjoyed swimming in the ocean together!

Our social interaction with missionary colleagues continued to be (as it always had been in Africa) a source of blessing to us. Doris wrote in her letter of June 27 to George and Esther: "We are going to go over and eat with the Duprets tonight." Our fellowship that evening was enlivened through the fun enjoyed by the Dupret children and our girls as they played together.

By June 27, I had completed the building of the concrete-block back gable end of the downtown Ouagadougou church and, also, had about one fourth of the asbestos roof sheets on. Then on June 28, I began pouring a cement cap over the sides of those sheets which were resting on top of the western slope of that gable end. Too much sun from that day's work caused me to have a fever that night. The fever caused me to lose a few days work, but I suffered no permanent ill aftereffects from it.

This is a good time for me to express gratitude unto the Lord that no one was seriously injured in any part of the building of the church!

Before beginning to build up the front facade of the church (above the height of side walls), I had my masons plaster all concrete-block construction (inside and outside) clear around the entire church. On July 7, I wrote: "A few more days of plastering and we will be going up with the front." Other men were putting on the roof sheets while masons were plastering. I personally supervised the positioning of every roof sheet before my helpers fastened it in place. When the roof was completed the French *Draggage* asked me, seriously, if I would build roofs for them. I replied "no, I must continue with my missionary work."

On July 19, John and Cuba Hall (with their children: David, Jim, and Betty Ann) arrived from furlough for their work at the Nagabagere Bible School. Howard Fox built a chapel for the school during the months that he and Charlotte were in charge of it, before the arrival of the Halls. I supplied asbestos roof sheets for this chapel from a surplus of them in my supply for the Ouagadougou church. The design which I had drawn for the front facade of the Ouagadougou church was used first for the Nagabagere chapel, then for the Koudougou church, and later by many other churches in Upper Volta.

I observed during my years in Africa that tragedy prevails more often among primitive heathen people than it does among civilized heathen people. I've already referred to one example of this in the frequent killing of primitive people by wild animals. One day we were seated with the Halls' at their table in Nagabagere, and ready to begin the evening meal with them. Word came that a student's wife had started to have a baby but couldn't deliver it.

Stella went with Cuba Hall to the woman in her hut. They decided immediately that I must take the woman in our car to the Ouagadougou hospital. So, the four of us left with her (without our supper). The tragedy here was that the doctor and his helpers had to remove the baby in pieces. But they did save the life of the mother! In writing of this incident, our Doris, 9, wrote: "We were really hungry when we got home, Aunty Jones fixed our supper for us."

By August 5, I was installing the glass-block cross in the front facade. After finishing the front, I had masons pour and trowel the cement floor in the entire church. On September 15, Stella wrote: "George got a big part of the floor in last week." Our capable masons achieved a good floor over the solid 30-inch fill of dirt and rock that the French *Draggage* had provided. (When I visited Ouagadougou 30 years later—in 1987—this cement floor was still in good condition.)

On September 27, I was putting in outside steps, and the church was being painted. All the work of building and painting it was completed on October 5, 1957. By adding two masons from Senegal to the two which I already had, I was able to complete the downtown Ouagadougou church earlier than I had expected.

Downtown A. G. Ouagadougou church building in October, 1957

The photographic company *Editions de Luxe* of Abidjan was so impressed by the appearance of our new Ouagadougou church that it made a pictoral postcard in color of the church. We knew nothing about the project to produce that postcard until we saw it already printed!

We finished the church just in time to have the biennial convention of Evangelical Missions of French West Africa and French Togoland in it. So, the 40 delegates to this convention (from all over French West Africa) were among the approximately 700 people who attended the first service in the completed new church building on Sunday morning October 6. At this convention of Evangelical Missions, I was elected as a member of its five-man administrative committee.

On Sunday morning, October 27, I preached in French in the new downtown church building. Pastor Gwomtanga interpreted my message for those who understood More only, and Stella taught a Sunday School class of 57 Mossi women who had 40 babies with them. More people attended this service than had attended the first service on October 6.

The dedication of the new downtown Ouagadougou church included a service in front of the building on Saturday afternoon, November 30, and two services inside it on Sunday morning, December 1. Of this dedication, my article on page 10 of the February 16, 1958 *Pentecostal Evangel* says:

> *Dedication ceremonies commenced on November 30 with the unveiling of the grey marble dedication stone with black lettering etched on it. The stone was a gift of the Sheffield Assembly of God, Kansas City, Mo. (C. W. Quattlebaum, Pastor). Missionary Howard Fox brought a sermon at the Sunday morning dedicatory service in the More language. Another service followed which was conducted in French. The district commander and a personal representative of the Governor of Upper Volta attended. The message was given by Andre Brisset of the French Assemblies of God. The program planning com-*

mittee asked that I give a resume of the project in both services. National pastors from all of the major districts of the Assemblies of God work in Upper Volta attended and helped make the time a season of refreshing. Graduates of the Bible School had their graduation exercises following the dedication. John Hall, the director of the school, conducted the service for the twelve graduates. Harold Jones gave an exhortation to the graduates using Acts 26:19 as his text.

George Flattery, Sr., giving a resume on December 1, 1957, of the building of the downtown Ouagadougou church. Seated (left to right): John Olay, Andre Brisset, Harold Jones, Pierre Dupret, and Lebende Miningou

I built the downtown Ouagadougou church entirely on the pay-as-you-go plan. In building it, I used almost all of the funds that were available for it. The cost of it was approximately

$13,000. It would have cost twice that amount if it had been built by a local contracting firm.

Crowd of about 1000 people that filled the downtown Ouagadougou church building for its dedication service on December 1, 1957

On to Tambacounda

By an exploratory trip of an A. G. committee in 1949, all of our Upper Volta missionaries were made aware of the need for Pentecostal pioneering in Senegal. Excluding closed North Africa, it was among the most prominent areas in Africa which was yet without the full gospel witness. Charles and Mary Greenaway proved to be a good choice by the A. G. Missions Department to open the Senegal work at Tambacounda (about 1200 miles west of Ouagadougou), in 1956. Stella and I had thought of ourselves as among those who might some day follow them in the Senegal work. But when we returned to Africa in 1955 for our third term, we were committed to spending all of it at Ouagadougou, if the downtown church project needed us that long.

During our 58 years in the ministry together, God has often spoken to each of us directly (at the same time) concerning what He wanted us to do. But at times God has worked through me to convince Stella: that was true of our going from Ouagadougou to Corabie, in 1946, to pioneer Pentecost among the Kasena. At other times He has worked through Stella to convince me: this was true of our going from Ouagadougou, in 1957, to continue the Greenaways' pioneering of Pentecost in Tambacounda, Senegal.

Hebrews 1:1-2 (NIV) refers first to God's indirectness then to His directness in speaking to people: "In the past God spoke to our forefathers through the prophets . . . in these last days he has spoken to us by his Son." When God speaks to a human through a prophet, He speaks to him indirectly (through another human), but when God speaks to a human through the Son, He speaks to him directly (through Himself).

Because of the excellent progress we had made toward finishing the building of the Ouagadougou church, God had convinced me (largely through Stella) by about mid-August, 1957, that we would be free to transfer to Tambacounda in December and, thus, release the Greenaways to go on a needed furlough. I had never even thought of being a long-term pastor of the new church in Ouagadougou. But I must admit that there was in my heart a natural longing to enjoy worship and fellowship a little longer in our new Ouagadougou church before going to Senegal.

Yielding to the Spirit, I wrote our Division of Foreign Missions in August that we would like their permission to move to Tambacounda the following December. About mid-September we received a lovely letter from Donald G. Foote which conveyed the Mission Department's approval of our transfer to Senegal. Foote's letter, after expressing his surprise that we would be free so soon to pioneer Pentecost in Senegal, stated (to our surprise) that the Missions Department would pay our moving expenses.

Not wanting any of our missionary colleagues in Upper Volta to think that we might leave Ouagadougou before we finished the church, we did not tell any of them about our move until we had finished it on October 5.

Before moving my family to Tambacounda in December, I went there (by plane to Bamako and by train the rest of the way) on October 28-29, so that Charles Greenaway could transfer the chairmanship of the Senegal A. G. Mission work to me before going on furlough to America with his family in November. Then on November 4, I participated in the dedication of the Tambacounda church building that Greenaway had just completed. On November 5, I began my two-day journey back to Ouagadougou.

Assembly of God mission church built by Charles Greenaway at Tambacounda, Senegal, in 1957

After having put a few pieces of baggage on the train at Ouagadougou for Tambacounda, Stella, Doris, Sharon and I left Ouagadougou for the same destination at 2:00 p. m. on

Monday, December 10, 1957. The first day, we visited briefly with our missionaries and national Christians at Koudougou and Boromo, then drove on and reached Bobo-Dioulasso about 11:00 p. m. At Bobo, it took all day Tuesday to have the rear springs in our Plymouth station wagon changed. We left Bobo for Bamako Wednesday morning. Since we could not quite make it to the Bamako ferry on the Niger river by closing time, we stayed Wednesday night at the Sirakoro mission (near Bamako) where two single ladies were operating a dispensary.

Early Thursday morning, we crossed the Niger on the ferry and entered Bamako. We had planned on driving clear to Tambacounda. But Sharon had a bad cold and some fever. So, we thought it best to avoid the long, rough, dusty car trip between Bamako and Tambacounda. I put our car on a freight train for Tambacounda. Then we left the next day (Friday the 14th) on the passenger train. Both we and our car arrived in Tambacounda on Saturday, December 15. We arrived at 4:00 a. m. a little ahead of our car!

Mission residence at Tambacounda, Senegal (built by Charles Greenaway) which was the home of George, Stella, Doris, and Sharon Flattery for almost a year in 1957-1958

After only ten days at Tambacounda, we celebrated Christmas in a simple but adequate fashion. We had a small tree with electric lights on it, and invited three of the townspeople (strangers, of course) to our turkey dinner. Rather than ship our girls' old bicycles to Tambacounda, we had sold them in Ouagadougou, then bought new French-made, Christmas bicycles for the girls in Tamba. Our yard and all the roads around it were very dusty. On January 30, 1958, Doris wrote Warren: "Today Sharon and I washed our new bicycles that we got for Christmas."

We began having village gospel meetings right after we got to Tambacounda. Our gospel team included Kenga Zongo and Etienne Miningou (Mossi preachers who helped the Greenaways and us in Senegal) as well as Stella, Doris, Sharon, and me. In her letter of December 28, Stella wrote: "We have started our village work."

Stella Flattery and a village crowd gathered around her for a gospel meeting at Kotiara, Senegal, 17 miles east of Tambacounda

It was more difficult to get people to accept Christ in the almost entirely Mohammedan area of Tambacounda than it had been in Upper Volta. After three months of village meetings and regular meetings in the church, I wrote our supporting friends and churches in America: "So far we have only one definite convert. He is Samba Ngai of the Sarakole tribe . . . Kenga . . . has started to teach him to read . . . Samba did drink heavily and is still tempted to drink. Please pray that he will get complete victory in Christ."

At the beginning of our village work at Tambacounda, I had to preach in French and have an interpreter translate what I said into Bambara. I had to depend on government school boys (who knew little about spiritual truth) as interpreters. Later in our year at Tambacounda, when I preached in Bambara (in a very simple manner, of course) at the village meetings, I had better results in conveying the gospel message to the people.

Left to right: Gwombila (our cook), Etienne, Kenga, Hamidou (our houseboy), and me—ready to go on July 6, 1958, in the mission jeep to a village gospel meeting in the Tambacounda district

Charles Greenaway had nearly completed the Tambacounda mission residence before we got there, but there remained a few things to do. Since the door leading from the closed-in veranda was too narrow to allow a double bed through to the outside veranda, I made it the kitchen door and placed the double kitchen doors where it had been: such modification of wall openings was quite a job, but we wanted to sleep outside during the hot season in extremely hot Tambacounda! Then I finished up the screening of the house; installed a flush toilet, lavatory, and shower for the guest bedroom; and hooked the toilet to the cesspool which had been built for the house.

On January 18, Mr. Roussane, operator of the Tambacounda electric plant, sent men to our compound to install an electric water pump in our yard. (It was the first time in Africa that we had water at the touch of a button!) I built a small chicken house and some rabbit hutches (near the pump) for our few chickens and rabbits.

Sharon and our girls' pet rabbit by the chicken pen in our yard at Tambacounda

We wanted to send Doris and Sharon to the Mamou school in French Guinea (about 385 miles from Tambacounda) for the first halves of the 6th and 4th grades from August to December. We received permission from our Missions Department to do so, but the school was filled and could not take them. So Stella (with a little help from me) continued to teach them the Calvert correspondence courses during 1958. On February 19, Doris and Sharon started "sitting in" on reading classes at the Tambacounda French school. They did not earn any scholastic credit from this, but it did help them to improve in French.

About a week or two after we arrived in Tambacounda, I began editing, writing, mimeographing, and distributing a Sunday School lesson in French for each week. On March 31, 1958, I wrote my supporting friends and churches in America concerning these French lessons: "Our lessons are based upon the French translations (supervised by Assemblies of God missionary Richard Scotti in Belgium) of our Springfield G. P. H. Adult Student Quarterly. We . . . pick the quarterlies which we feel are best suited for the beginning of our work here."

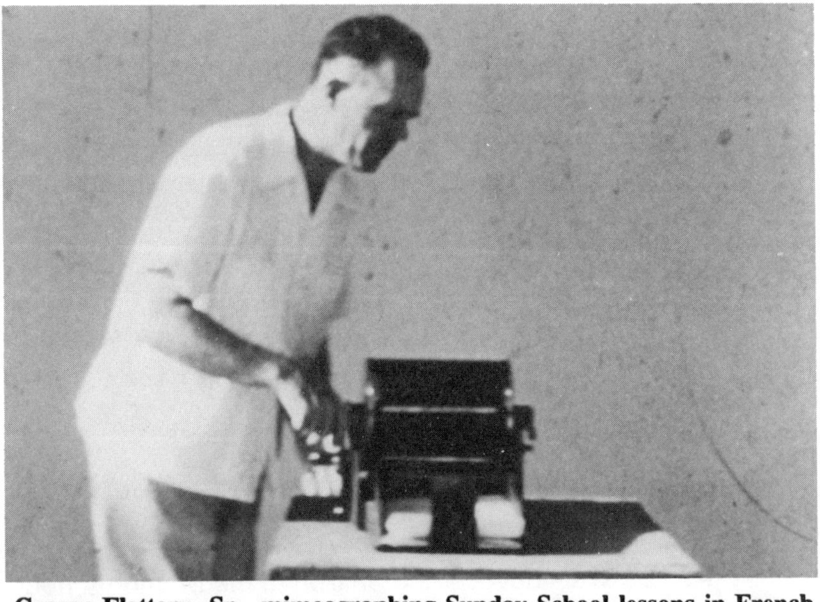

George Flattery, Sr., mimeographing Sunday School lessons in French at Tambacounda in 1958

My editions of these French lessons were shortened and simplified versions of Scotti's translations. In addition to giving a lesson to everyone who attended our church, I distributed one each week (free of charge) in each of the 56 boxes at the Tambacounda post office. Twice, a post office employee strike hindered this distribution: first a 9-day strike in early February, then a 14-day strike in late February and March.

My sister Helen's letter of February 21, 1958, from Wichita, Kansas, informed us in Tambacounda that my mother "was very low." Then our son Warren's letter of March 3 informed us of her death. Helen's letter had stated that mother (then 74) was not expected to recover from her paralytic stroke. So, we were expecting the news received in Warren's letter.

Concerning news of mother's death, I wrote Warren on March 13: "It was hard for me to take as I thought of the many sacrifices she had made to help me and my brothers and sisters and dad . . . her letters to us this term were usually 2 or 3 months apart or more . . . she did not feel up to writing so often as she had always done before." Mother's funeral was in Wichita on the day of a bad winter storm.

Warren, then living in California, sent flowers but did not go to Wichita for the funeral. Our son George, living much closer, went by bus from Fort Worth, Texas, and attended it. All four of us wished (as we had wished 16 months earlier concerning Stella's father's funeral) that we had been in America so we could have attended my mother's funeral.

Stella and I celebrated our 44th birthdays in 1958 at Tambacounda (mine in March and hers in April). She wrote regarding my birthday: "I fixed him a chicken and noodle dinner—black devil's food cake and ice cream. I made him some peanut brittle and Doris wrapped it up nice."

Each week during the year that we lived at Tambacounda, a refrigerated train car brought us a large basket of vegetables—wrapped in dampened banana leaves to help keep them fresh—from Dakar. And I made quarterly trips by jeep from Tambacounda to Gouloumbo (40 miles south of Tambacounda), to buy such staples as flour, sugar, margarine, and soap, at the border town in British Gambia just across the river from Gouloumbo.

These quarterly trips reminded me of the trips for food supplies we had made during our second term from Po to Tamale for food supplies—especially because in each case I was a missionary from a French colony who went to find food supplies in a British colony.

(Left to right): Gwombila the cook with Stella's 44th birthday cake, Stella, and Hamidou the houseboy. On April 27, at Tambacounda

George and the wild hog he killed July 16, 1958, about 10 miles south of Tambacounda

Many wild hogs roamed the district of Tambacounda. After peanut harvest, they would gather around peanut patches to glean what the harvesters had missed. I had gone hunting several times to try to shoot a wild hog, so we could have some fresh pork to eat, but had not succeeded in killing one. Then after having lived at Tambacounda about seven months, I shot and killed one on July 16 (about 10 miles south of Tambacounda), during my trip to Gouloumbo to buy groceries.

We went to Dalaba (about 350 miles, mostly south but some east, from Tambacounda) in the mountains of French Guinea for a 4-week vacation between May 13 and June 10, 1958. Before we went, Stella wrote on May 6:

> *"We thought we'd stick it out here but it's too long. Tamba is the hottest place in West Africa we've been told . . . we'll have a 2-day trip getting there . . . bad roads, one ferry and mountains the last part of the way. By the time we get back the rains should be started."*

After we'd made this long, hard, 2-day journey (while we were in Dalaba) Stella wrote again on May 27:

> *"We are having a real vacation. It is beautiful here . . . the temperature goes up to 78 . . . and down in the 60's at night . . . we appreciate the rains that come almost every day . . . this is the first real vacation we ever had out here."*

"Out here" includes both Upper Volta and Senegal. "Christian and Missionary Alliance" missionaries owned about 15 of the inexpensive mountain cottages in the center for vacationing missionaries at Dalaba. We talked of building one there for ourselves. If we had gone back to Tambacounda for our fourth term in Africa (instead of to pioneer a new mission station in Kaolack), we might have done that.

Most of the missionaries at Dalaba (while we were there) were of the Gospel Missionary Union of Bamako. We enjoyed playing volley ball and swimming with them and others. We went to see a beautiful waterfall about 6 miles from Dalaba, and went on a picnic in a pine grove. And we visited the Mamou school for missionaries' children (about 35 miles from Dalaba).

Sharon, Stella, Doris, George, in front of their mountain cottage on June 1, 1958, while vacationing in Dalaba

After we arrived back in Tambacounda from Dalaba on June 10, I taught daily afternoon classes in Bambara to Kenga and Etienne. On July 1, Stella wrote Warren to send her a copy of the song "How Great Thou Art." She had heard a little girl sing it at Dalaba and especially wanted to teach it to Sharon. On the same day I wrote him to send us some tomato seed. The Earl Downeys were scheduled to replace us at Tambacounda about mid-October.

Stella wrote Warren again on July 17: "We received the seeds and song yesterday . . . we were surprised. We thought they would take about 3 weeks and here they came in 15 days!" After planting the tomato seed, I, too, wrote Warren on July 17: "If the plants do well we should have tomatoes by mid-October . . . when Downeys are with us." The seed and the song were successful projects. We had plenty of delicious tomatoes from our garden while Downeys were with us. Both Doris and Sharon learned "How Great Thou Art" by heart. Let's be mindful of the spiritual values of seed and song: "Those who sow in tears will reap with songs of joy" (Psalm 126:5, NIV).

As a member of the committee of the Evangelical Missions of French West Africa and French Togoland, it was my responsibility to attend the meeting of this organization in Ferkessedougou, Ivory Coast, French West Africa, in September, 1958. I made the trip of about 675 miles from Tambacounda to Ferkessedougou by train.

I was so busy studying Bambara that I went a few hundred yards on by my destination, then asked the trainman to stop the train and let me off. He graciously complied. I walked back to the Ferkessedougou station. My colleagues on the committee got a good laugh out of that! And I just laughed with them. What else could I do? We had a real good Federation meeting.

The committee of the Evangelical Missions of French West Africa and French Togoland, at Ferkessedougou, Ivory Coast, in September, 1958. Extreme right is Georges Mabille, executive secretary of the committee. Next-to-right is me, George Flattery.

Conclusion

I've reached October, 1958 in the story of my life. This third 3-year term in Africa began with our sailing from New York on October 28, 1955. October, 1958 was the final scheduled month of it. The Earl Downeys arrived (as planned) in Tambacounda (with their two small daughters) in October to replace us, so we could go to America on furlough. Their oldest daughter Candy was about 2, and their daughter Cathleen was just a few weeks old. It was my privilege to dedicate baby Cathleen to the Lord, in the Tambacounda A. G. mission church On October 26, 1958.

George Flattery, Sr., holding baby Cathleen Downey, when he dedicated her to the Lord

Stella, Doris, Sharon, and I were hoping that a house could be found in which we; George, Esther, Georgie; and Warren could all live together during the approaching furlough. I had written George and Esther on August 14: "It might be a good idea to inquire about the rental cost of a big house that would do for us all." A house was found in Dallas, Texas where we did all live together during much of that furlough.

On November 3, we were in Dakar waiting to board the Bakala, a French freighter. We boarded it on the 6th, and were scheduled to arrive at New York on the 16th. But our ship stopped at Boston before going on to New York. We arrived at New York about November 18, and proceeded immediately to Springfield, Missouri, by train. After a day or two in Springfield, we went to Dallas for a happy reunion with George, Esther, and Warren. What great joy it was for Stella and me to see our first grandchild, Georgie (then 28 months old), for the first time!

A man, reading the Arabic Bible he has procured at a village gospel meeting near Kaolack, Senegal, in 1962, from a display on the windshield of the Flattery Speed-the-Light car

Flattery Missionary Card of 1960. Left to right: George, Sr., Doris, Sharon, and Stella

CHAPTER 8: FOURTH TERM, SENEGAL

Furlough Activities and Events

Our third furlough began when we arrived in the United States from our third term in Africa, in November, 1958. All of we Flatterys had decided (even before Stella and I and our daughters had arrived from Africa) that we would like to live together in one big house during this furlough. Our son George and his family were living in Dallas where he was minister of education at the Oak Cliff Assembly of God church. Therefore, any house where we could all live together would have to be in Dallas.

We found such a house at 3718B Penrod, in the Cockerell Hill section of west Dallas, rented it, and moved into it about January 1, 1959. It was commodious, even though it looked like something built onto! The partings from each other that we had experienced both in Africa and the United States had conditioned us to want to live for awhile under one roof again. We had 13 happy months together in that house.

Africans of all levels of life (among whom I had worked since 1945) were striving to become better educated in order to better their standards of living. Therefore, I knew that it would help me with my future missionary work among them if I could complete a fully recognized college degree before going back to Africa for a fourth term.

3718B Penrod, in Dallas, Texas, where the George Flattery Sr. family, the George Flattery Jr. family, and Warren Flattery lived from January 1, 1959, to about February 1, 1960

After receiving the approval of the A. G. Division of Foreign Missions, I chose Texas Wesleyan College of Fort Worth, Texas, as the place to earn my college degree. Texas Wesleyan allowed me (toward a Bachelor of Arts degree) a generous 66 semester hours of credit for my three years of schooling in Southwestern Bible School at Enid, Oklahoma, in the 1930's, plus the 34 and 1/2 hours of accredited college work that I had earned subsequently on my first and second furloughs from Africa.

For my Bachelor of Arts degree with a major in English, there were 38 of the required 138 and 1/2 hours left to earn at Texas Wesleyan. Dr. H. Howard Hughes was Texas Wesleyan's English Department head, and taught some of my classes. I appreciated all he did to help me with my education while I was at Texas Wesleyan. As a parting gift, Dr. Hughes gave me a copy of *Moby Dick* which was one of his favorite novels.

While earning this degree, I drove (with Warren who

completed his degree at Texas Wesleyan while I was completing mine) the 44-mile round trip (to the college and back) on school days of the 2nd semester 1958-1959, the entire summer session 1959, and the 1st semester 1959-1960. We enjoyed talking of earlier times and future years, as we made the daily trips together. Warren and I received our degrees together on May 22, 1960.

George Flattery, Sr. (left), and Warren Flattery, robed for reception of Bachelor of Arts degrees at Texas Wesleyan College in Fort Worth, Texas, on May 22, 1960

Stella had not taken any college courses during our first and second furloughs from Africa. But after we moved from Dallas to Mission Village in Springfield, Missouri, she enrolled at Evangel College for the second semester of 1959-1960. Evangel allowed her 20 semester hours of credit for her year of study at Southwestern Bible School in 1933-1934 (just before our marriage). Then, during this third furlough, she received 11 more hours of credit toward the Bachelor's degree which she earned later (after our 20 years of pioneering in and for French West Africa were completed).

I held missionary meetings frequently during the year that I studied at Texas Wesleyan. My entire third furlough itinerary (1958-1960) was a very busy one. Between December 14, 1958, and July 25, 1960, I held about 160 meetings. A third of them were in Texas where we lived for two thirds of our furlough, and another third were in Kansas (my home district). More than half of the remaining third of the meetings were in Missouri. The few others were held in Arkansas, Iowa, Louisiana, Nebraska, and South Dakota.

One of our most remembered Christmas seasons is that of 1959. Some of our Christmases between 1952 (when our teen-aged sons left us in Africa to go to college) and 1959 had been rather lonely. But in 1959 we had all of our immediate family, our son George and his family, Stella's sister Roma's family, and her brother Manford's family with us for Christmas at our commodious house on Penrod street in Dallas.

Back (left to right): Roma, Manford, Stella. Front: Grandson George. At 3718B Penrod in Dallas, Texas, for Christmas, 1959

The families of George Flattery, Sr., and George Flattery, Jr., celebrating Christmas together in 1959, at 3718B Penrod, Dallas, Texas

In 1960, as we were getting ready to return to Africa for our fourth term, we needed help from the A. G. Women's Missionary Councils of Kansas. They furnished much of the outfits needed by Kansas A. G. missionaries. On February 20, I wrote Vera Samuelson, their president:

> *We have made lists of our outfit needs for the coming three years in Africa . . . our needs are many . . . it is our responsibility to completely furnish the new station which we are planning to build at Diourbel, Senegal . . . we will be attending the District Council in Wichita and any of the articles which are . . . brought there will be taken by us on to Mission Village to pack.*

The place in Senegal where we opened a new mission station in 1960 turned out to be Kaolack—not Diourbel! But our outfit needs were the same in Kaolack as they would have been in Diourbel. Once again, the Kansas WMC's did a splendid job in supplying what we needed.

Just before Stella, Doris, Sharon and I boarded the freighter

Nopal Branco to return to Senegal, we were guests during the third and fourth weeks of July, 1960, at New Orleans, Louisiana, in the home of our longstanding friends, Charles and Florence Craighead. I've told in detail, near the beginning of my autobiography, of the summer of evangelistic work in Tennessee that Stella and I had with them at the beginning of our ministerial careers in 1934. We and the Craigheads enjoyed reminiscence of that long-past ministry together.

Vera Samuelson and a trailer for our items of outfit, at the 1960 Kansas District Council of the A. G. in Wichita

Left to right: Philip, Sammy, Florence, and Charles Craighead at their home in New Orleans in July, 1960

1960 in Senegal

The Nopal Branco had planned to take us on board in New Orleans for Africa, but forced us to travel overland the 333 miles to Houston, Texas, in order to get on board. The ship did this when it found out that Houston would be its last port of call before crossing the Atlantic Ocean. Our son George, grandson George, Warren, and Esther's brother Fred Scheuerman went shipside with us when we boarded the Nopal Branco on August 2, 1960. (Esther was expecting her second child, and her doctor would not let her make the trip from Dallas to Houston to bid us goodbye.) After 16 days on the ocean, we arrived in Monrovia, Liberia, on Thursday, August 18.

We were received by the A. G. missionary Crabaughs, and stayed in their home (10 miles outside Monrovia). While there we talked to George and Esther in Dallas over Crabaugh's short wave radio set. We tried to talk likewise to Warren in Denton, Texas, but couldn't get him. Sunday, August 21, we left Monrovia for Dakar on a log-hauling German freighter. Its logs had shifted so much to one side that we feared the ship might capsize. Our cabins were on the low side, but we remained afloat!

On August 24, we arrived in Dakar, and were met by our missionary colleagues, Talmadge and Marjorie Butler. They took us home with them for lunch. Margy had prepared a nice spaghetti meal for us. We ate it like we were hungry for it. (We never told her we'd had mostly spaghetti—even for breakfasts—for about three days on the German boat!)

Regarding our boat baggage, Stella wrote on August 25, from Dakar: "The German ship's agent in Monrovia decided he wouldn't let the ship wait over the extra 2 hours it would take to get our stuff off of the Nopal Branco . . . so we passed right by the Branco with our stuff still on it." We learned a few days later that our baggage had to go from Monrovia to Abidjan to be put on a French boat before being shipped to Senegal. We stayed at the Tambacounda A. G. mission station with our missionary colleagues, Bill and Peggy Lasley, while we were waiting for our boat baggage.

Talmadge and Marjorie Butler with son Stephen, at Kaolack

Left to right: Bill Lasley, Peggy Lasley, Talmadge Butler. At Kaolack

The annual convention of the A. G. Senegal mission took place in Tambacounda on August 30-31, 1960. I was elected as Field chairman for the following year, and was asked by the Senegal missionaries to write French Sunday School Literature for all of the A. G. mission stations in Senegal.

The A. G. Division of Foreign Missions asked us to pioneer

a new mission station in Kaolack, Senegal. Kaolack's population was about 75,000 in 1960. It was larger than any city in Senegal except Dakar, and without a Protestant church of any kind. Kaolack is about 120 miles inland from Dakar and 200 miles west of Tambacounda.

I was very glad to get our boat baggage through customs at Dakar for only $75.00, which was a charge to cover office expenses. As soon as it arrived there, I hauled it in the Senegal mission field's truck to Kaolack, where I placed it in the apartment that we had rented above the F. A. O. department store on September 1.

The grinding of the valves (at Tambacounda) of the white Ford sedan which we had bought from Talmadge Butler delayed our moving to Kaolack about 3 days. We finally got there at 9:00 p. m. on September 23. Within about a week we had finished about two thirds of our unpacking and getting settled. We had to make shelves and a store room for groceries in one corner of the girls' bedroom.

Our Kaolack apartment was well screened in; we slept there without mosquito nets. It was close to the Kaolack port where oceangoing freight boats (having come about 50 miles inland by way of a natural estuary) took on salt and peanuts. There was a 3-story building between our apartment and the boats which kept us from seeing them from our apartment windows.

Back on August 25, Talmadge Butler and I left Dakar in his small airplane for the Butlers' mission station in Kedougou, Senegal (about 400 miles inland from Dakar), where I helped him with some minor building repairs. Then on September 15, I flew with Butler and Lasley in Butler's plane to Ouagadougou, for a meeting in which matters pertaining to the printing of gospel literature for the three A. G. mission fields in French West Africa would be discussed.

It had been planned to hold the meeting in Ouagadougou. The representatives from Dahomey did not get to Ouagadougou. So, two Upper Volta representatives, Howard Fox and John

Mattox, joined us three from Senegal, and all five flew in Butler's plane to Natitingou, Dahomey. We then joined with Dahomey representatives for the meeting. The Upper Volta men asked the Dahomey men and the Senegal men if they would like to have their printing done by the Ouagadougou A. G. press. But because of the great mileage that separated the three fields and the uncertainty of the mails, Dahomey and Senegal thought it best to continue—for the time being—with their own printing.

Throughout all of our time in Africa, our missionary work included various aspects of spiritual and physical activity. Otherwise it could not have been well balanced. But, being mindful of Paul's teaching about "godliness" (1 Timothy 4:8), we always considered our spiritual activity with the Africans to be foremost in importance among all of our activities.

During the first two months of our term at Kaolack, the home in Kaolack of the Mossi preacher Etienne Miningou, who had helped us with village work in Tambacounda, served as our church meeting house. We were glad for it, but we needed a place that was bigger and better known throughout the city.

After spending several weeks in getting acquainted with Kaolack town authorities, I was able to procure the use of the Kaolack Youth Center (an area enclosed with a high solid wall but mainly without a roof) as a meeting place for our church services. On November 18, Stella wrote: "We will start services Sunday in the Youth Hall, hope to have larger attendance." Then eight days later she wrote: "We had good services this Sunday and last Sunday in the Youth Building. Its more encouraging to have a crowd. In Etienne's house, it was hard to get people to attend."

The Youth center was on a very busy street with many pedestrians passing by it at all hours of the day. A few minutes before church time, I would stand on the street in front of the center and invite passersby into our services, as I gave them a copy of the French Bible Lesson that would be studied that morning. Some of them were attracted to enter the center by the accordion music that my wife was playing inside. We always had a crowd!

Our main drawback at the Youth Center was our inability to get people to form a habit of coming to our meetings. On December 8, Stella wrote: "We are having good crowds in the Youth Building, but it is a different crowd each Sunday. We will be glad when some start coming back." The spirit of indifference to Christianity was a greater obstacle to our pioneering of Pentecost among the Mohammedans of Senegal than it had been among the people of Upper Volta. The Mohammedans of Upper Volta seemed to be less deeply rooted in Mohammedanism than those in Senegal.

Crowd in front of the Kaolack Youth Center that had just come out of it after attending a Sunday morning service in it

Within two or three weeks after we moved to Kaolack, I began preaching the gospel in the numerous Serere villages of the district. I went to several villages each week. I did not often return to a village for a second meeting, because I wanted to witness as soon as possible in as many villages as possible. Sometimes, Mossi preacher Etienne attended these meetings with me. Almost no one understood English or More, and not many understood French or Bambara. Upon entering a village and greeting its elders, I would ask someone to interpret into Serere what I had to say to the people in French.

Matthew 6:19 refers to "treasures on earth . . . where thieves break in and steal" (NIV) as though such theft is very frequent, and anyone may be a victim of it at any time. We all know from observation of life on earth that this biblical reference (like all biblical references) is accurate! From accounts we have heard of other missionaries' losses, we lost comparatively little through theft during our four terms in Africa. During our first three terms, our only major loss from it was our four drums of baggage at Po in 1953.

Then at Kaolack on Sunday morning, October 30, 1960 (just after we had gone to church), someone broke into our apartment and stole $450 in currency from us. We were pretty sure that the thief was a young African from Sierra Leone who had been riding to church with us, and had washed our car a few days before. The police found him in a theater the next day. He had spent a little over half of the money. We got back $200.

The A. G. Division of Foreign Missions sent Dr. Jerry Melilli and his wife Kitty (an R. N.) to Senegal to explore the feasibility of establishing medical missionary work in Senegal. I picked them up at the Dakar airport on Wednesday November 2, and drove Dr. Melilli around to see some medical installations in the Kaolack area. On November 5, I took him to visit the clinic at Nioro du Rip (35 miles south of Kaolack). I took the Melillis to Dakar for their departure to Liberia on Sunday, November 6. We enjoyed fellowship with them during the few days they were with us.

When we arrived in Kaolack, we found that it had a white population of about 2200. We enjoyed fellowship with many French and Lebanese people. Mr. Barnard, a Catholic banker, and his English Protestant wife were very friendly to us. They ate at our house, and we ate more than once at theirs. When they left about November 10, 1960, for furlough in France, they left their beautiful female dog, Pelouche, with us.

Doris and Pelouche on the sidewalk in front of our apartment in Kaolack

Just a few days after we moved to Kaolack, Doris and Sharon started their studies by correspondence again. Doris wrote Warren on December 30: "I have done 60 lessons in school. Sharon has done 57." At ages 13 and 11, school (and other things) were more difficult for them in Africa than before, because they were missing America more than they had in preceding terms.

But our girls enjoyed the beach (about 6 miles from our apartment) on Kaolack's salty estuary. All four of us swam together in it. Naturally, it was very easy to float in it. On November 26, Doris wrote Warren: "On my birthday . . . I floated out over the water deep enough for the boats and swam back several times. Dad has learned to float real good." We enjoyed the water by ourselves, by going once a week to this beach about 5:00 p. m. We were out of the water by the time the crowd got there around 6:15.

We four went out many evenings, for a little while, to get some refreshing air on the sands just across the estuary from our apartment. We played the game of boulles together, and with French and Lebanese people. Africans seldom cared for boulles! When our missionary colleagues were with us, we would sometimes have a game of softball with them at that place. Butlers went to Switzerland in December, 1960, to study French for a few months.

Christmas was on Sunday in 1960. It was approaching when Stella wrote: "We got a pine tree . . . here in Kaolack and . . . have decorated it . . . the lights are . . . like we had at Dallas." (Somewhat different from our many preceding thorn-bush Christmases in Africa!) Sharon and Doris did not get new bikes for Christmas but did get, among other things, some new parts for their old ones. We had a Christmas Sunday morning church service in the Kaolack Youth Center. A Kaolack banker and his family came to our house for the Christmas evening meal.

1961 in Senegal

The big Federation of Evangelical Missions in French West Africa had broken up. And an important event in 1961 for Evangelical Missions in Senegal was the January forming at our apartment in Kaolack of the "Senegal Federation of Evangelical Missions" to deal with some of the problems that the big Federation had dealt with.

I think that the French policy of allotting a given territory in French West Africa to one Evangelical mission only had sometimes hindered the progress of the gospel of Christ. We committeemen of the newly formed Senegal Federation of Evangelical Missions were glad that in our formational meeting of January, 1961, Pierre Cadier (the French committee member) agreed to have Dakar declared an open city to all missions then working in Senegal.

As I continued to hold village gospel meetings among the people of the Kaolack district, I think I became progressively more successful in actually reaching them both intellectually and spiritually. The crowds were probably averaging about 50 or 60 people per service. My letter of January 1, 1961, indicates that since September 1960, I had averaged about 10 village services per month.

Committeemen of the Senegal Federation of Evangelical Missions: (left to right) Flattery, Prince, Macindoe, Cadier, and Rabe

I usually preached in the Kaolack Youth Center early each Sunday morning. But on Sunday, January 1, the Youth Center was being used for a sports festival, so I went on out to the nearby village of Passy. There, I had opposition from Mohammedans. The service went well until it was nearly over, then one or two hot-headed young Moslems began to stir the crowd (of a 100 or more) against the message of Christ.

The majority of the crowd remained sympathetic to my message. But when my interpreter (a Moslem whom I had brought to Passy) got in my car to leave the service with me, one of the agitators pulled him out—falsely insinuating that to shun a Christian preacher would help a true person of God to "abstain from all appearance of evil" (1 Thessalonians 1:22, KJV)! It was the first outward opposition that I had experienced in the villages of the Kaolack district.

When God provided Abraham with a ram to offer as a burnt offering instead of his son, "Abraham called that place The Lord will provide" (Genesis 22:13, NIV). Our village meetings succeeded through the provision of God for them. God provided me with inspiration to speak His Word, and the villagers with incentive to listen. Just one week after the episode at Passy, I arrived in the village of Saremousso (16 kilometers from Kaolack on the Koutanga road), and there was no one to interpret for me.

Then, seemingly by chance (but actually by the provision of God), a man who knew both French and Serere rode into Saramousso on a motorcycle with no intention of stopping there. I flagged him and he consented to stay with us long enough to interpret my gospel message. Thus, the Lord did provide! And the people of Saremousso invited me back to preach again.

Let me reach ahead into June, 1961, for an indication that these villages services meant much to me. Warren had sent me in advance a Happy Father's Day note, and I wrote him this reply on the day after Father's Day: "Thanks for wishing me a happy Father's Day—it was, I had one of my best village services last night!"

About February 1 or 2, we received a telegram from George and Esther that announced the birth of their second son (our second grandson) Mark Douglas Flattery on January 30, 1961. Now, at age 31 (in 1992), Mark and his family are appointed A. G. missionaries to East Africa. Mark was a capable college basketball player, as was his brother George before him.

During the week between March 19 and March 26, we went to Dakar and traded our large white Ford station wagon in on an Arianne Simca—a French-built Ford sedan—which required only half as much gasoline. The following Sunday (April 2) was Easter, the day of our first Sunday morning public church service in our apartment above the F. A. O. Twenty-three (French, Lebanese,and Africans) attended that service in which we were all blessed of God as we took communion together.

On April 3, the U. S. Vice-President Lyndon Johnson and his wife went to Dakar to participate in the Independence Anniversary Celebrations of Senegal. We were invited by the American Ambassador to a reception in their honor. We greeted them and shook hands with them.

We held our Sunday morning service in our apartment each Sunday morning after we began holding it there on Easter Sunday. Some Portugese and Syrians attended it. Quite a mixture—when added to the French, Lebanese, and Africans! In these services Stella played the organ, Jacqueline Melon led the singing with her fine strong voice, and I preached in French. On a Sunday in May, a young Lebanese man said after attending about 4 of these services: "I felt a big blessing when I was singing." Stella said in her letter of Sunday, August 27: "We had a wonderful service in our home today. More Africans than usual were here."

Our field was honored by the visit of T. F. Zimmerman (General Superintendent of the Assemblies of God) and J. Philip Hogan (Executive Director of Foreign Missions). They spent May 5-7, 1961, in Senegal. They were flown in our mission plane by Talmadge Butler from Dakar to all three of our mission stations: Kaolack, Tambacounda, and Kedougou. It was my privilege to accompany them and Butler. Butler gathered a large crowd of people in Kedougou to hear gospel messages by Zimmerman and Hogan on Saturday night May 6. I served as their interpreter to translate their messages from English into French.

It was June 5, Tuesday, 1961, that I drove (with my family) down to visit the W. E. C. (World Evangelization Crusade) and New Tribes missionaries in Ziguinchor and other places of the

Casamance. We enjoyed fellowship with them. On the 6th, I preached a gospel message in French at their street meeting in Ziguinchor. Then on the 7th, I gave a short talk in French to Christians at Oussouye, Casamance.

Thomas F. Zimmerman (left) and J. Philip Hogan. At Kaolack on May 6, 1961

Our delightful trip to the Casamance included ferries over the Gambia and Casamance rivers. We (from barren Kaolack) thoroughly enjoyed the lush tropical flowers, shrubs, trees, and grass that were interspersed among the swamps of Casamance. We were glad to get back on June 8 to our home and work in Kaolack, but its terrain seemed even more barren than when we had left a few days earlier!

It was during the last week of September, 1961, that I, the A. G. Mission's empowered agent, signed the legal documents that gave to the Kaolack A. G. Mission its property in the center of the city. The acquisition of property for our Kaolack mission had been constantly on the heart and mind of myself and my family during the 13 months that we had lived in Kaolack. From the time we had arrived there, we had considered both vacant lots and buildings as possibilities for a church and missionary residence.

It was early in 1961, when we first heard that the property we eventually obtained from the NO SO CO NIGER (a French Commercial Company) might be for sale. We felt from the beginning that this property was the one for the Assemblies of God. E. L. Phillips, A. G. secretary for Africa, confirmed our feelings when he visited us, as did Thomas Zimmerman and J. Philip Hogan when they visited us a little later.

This property had a large concrete and steel two-story residence on it, and another large concrete and steel building, part of which could, with some interior alteration, serve as a church auditorium. The rest of this second building could be utilized for other needs of the church and mission station. As we prayed about how to finance the acquisition of this property, we solicited help from missionary-minded churches and other organizations that had helped us in our preceding terms in Africa—and from some new ones as well. Gordon Lindsay of Dallas, Texas, visited us in Kaolack, in 1961. Through his "Winning the Nations Crusade," Lindsay gave us $4,000 for this project, and two Assemblies of God churches gave us $1,000 each.

Kaolack property purchased about October 1, 1961, through George Flattery for the Kaolack A. G. Mission

We then had $8,000 (including the $2,000 I had raised during furlough) toward the sum of about $12,250 we would need to acquire the property. Our manner of conducting all of our business in Kaolack had spoken well enough to one of its banks that it lent us the balance of money we needed to acquire the property. We then paid cash for the property, and (in about a year) paid back all we owed the bank with money that we received from renting the first floor of the residence. Thus, we continued to adhere to the pay-as-you-go plan for property in Africa that we had followed in preceding terms at Corabie, Po, and Ouagadougou.

On Tuesday, July 4, we four flew with Talmadge Butler to his mission station in Kedougou, then he flew us back to Kaolack on July 7. We enjoyed a fine visit with the Butlers, and I helped with some roofing. Butler flew low over the wild game reserve of Niokolo-Koba so we could get a good look at the wild animals and the hippos in the Gambia river. Since we hadn't been to Dakar for almost 3 months, we went there early in August and enjoyed its change of air for a few days. Stella, Doris, and I were at our Kaolack beach with Sharon during the afternoon and evening of August 29, to celebrate her birthday.

Top, Talmadge Butler; below, George Flattery; and African workers

When, late in August, Warren conveyed the first information to us about a young lady who had won his heart, he did not reveal her name to us. Stella wrote him immediately, on August 27: "She must be something special! Has she broken down your resistance?" Before Warren got his mother's letter, his telegram came identifying this special, irresistible young lady as Willa Jean Hall, and announcing his engagement to her. Jean was a home economics teacher of the 7th and 8th grades in San Antonio, Texas. She had come to study in the *Texas Woman's University* at Denton.

Warren met Jean at the A. G. church in Denton which he had founded more than two years before, and was still pastoring. He wrote us that he loved her at first sight. But because of his policy of refusing to date any woman who attended his church, Warren did not ask Jean for a date until about ten days before her studies at the university would end. He proposed marriage to her on their third date, and received her acceptance of his proposal three days later on their sixth date.

They were married in San Antonio on November 24, 1961. When we received the announcement of their wedding date, Stella wrote her Sister Roma on November 6: "I would sure like to be there . . . everyone thinks a lot of Jean . . . I'm glad Warren is going to have his own home . . . Doris had always planned on being in Warren's wedding. Sharon was in George's wedding." I would like to have been there too! It was the only one of our four children's weddings that I was unable to participate in. Stella and I were glad that Reverend and Mrs. H. C. Ball stood in for us at Warren and Jean's wedding.

It was early in October, 1960, when Doris began her 8th grade studies in the Calvert correspondence school, and Sharon began her 6th grade studies in it. They worked very faithfully at their school desks during the ten months that it took for them to complete these grades. In early August, 1961, Doris successfully completed the 8th grade and Sharon the 6th grade.

On Tuesday, September 19, 1961, we flew with Butlers to Bathurst, Gambia (about 70 miles from Kaolack), where 16 years before we had spent our first night on the African continent. Stella wrote: "It was a thrill to see it again." We bought a radio there that day—first one we'd ever had in Africa!

The annual meeting of the Senegal field missionary fellowship was held in our apartment above the F. A. O. at Kaolack on September 27, 1961. The missionaries elected me for another year as their field chairman. They had voted a year before that I launch a French Sunday School literature program for all A. G. Senegal stations. I was glad to be able to read from my chairman's report for the preceding year: "The French Sunday School literature program, authorized by last year's convention, was launched in December, 1960. Lessons for all of 1961 have been printed—a total of approximately 15,000 lesson leaves in all." The arrival of my new office typewriter and multigraphing machine in May helped me with this task.

Multigraphing French Sunday School lessons in our F. A. O. apartment at Kaolack, about August, 1961. Left to right: Stella multigraphing, Doris displaying a lesson, George typing

We moved into our new Kaolack mission property on September 28-29, immediately after we had closed the deal with the NO SO CO NIGER for it. Before closing the deal with us, they waited about 75 days after we had made them our first and final offer for it. I think they felt immediately that it would be the best offer they would receive for it. When I told a Kaolack business man that I thought the NO SO CO NIGER might reject our offer, he replied: "Pastor, just be patient, you will get the property because you are the only foreigner who wants to stay in Kaolack!" He exaggerated some, but not much!

On about October 5, I flew with Butler and Lasley (in Butler's plane) to Ouagadougou for an LMC (Literature Management Committee) meeting of delegates from all three A. G. mission fields (Upper Volta, Dahomey, Senegal) in French West Africa. They decided to have the Ouagadougou A. G. press print my French Sunday School Lessons for all three fields. I wrote on October 15: "8,000 copies will be printed for each Sunday instead of the 300 which I have been multigraphing for our Senegal field during the past year." Ouagadougou press manager John Weidman was asked to draw an illustration for each lesson.

Back: Dolly Tarr (left) and Del Tarr. Front: Two of their children. At Po, Upper Volta, in October, 1961

Before returning to Senegal, Butler flew me down to Po, where missionary Del Tarr had me preach in Kasem on Sunday morning, October 8. Then Tarr took me out to Corabie where I preached again in Kasem that afternoon. It had been four years since I had seen the Christians of Po and Corabie. They rejoiced greatly in seeing me again and wished that they could have seen Stella, Warren, George, Doris, and Sharon.

We were unable to have our Sunday morning worship services in our newly acquired Kaolack residence on October 1 and 8. The turmoil of our moving prevented a service on the 1st, and I was in Upper Volta on the 8th. Our first Sunday morning service in our new home was on October 15. All of the faithful who had been attending the services before we moved were there, and continued to come each Sunday morning.

By November 4, I had made shutters and screens for three rooms of our *second* second-floor living quarters in Kaolack (we'd lived on the second floor of the F. A. O., also). Then it was sometime in December before I had finished the construction and installation of some large 4-sectioned screens or grids to protect our newly acquired living area from the entrance of thieves.

A large 4-sectioned grid of heavy expanded metal to be positioned in a second-floor opening to the A. G. mission residence at Kaolack

We decorated our house for Christmas by using strands of electric light bulbs to design a Christmas tree on one of my newly installed protective grids. We also had our electrically decorated Christmas tree inside. We enjoyed a delicious Christmas evening meal at the home of the Melons: Jacques, Jacqueline, and small son Didier. Stella wrote on December 28: "We had one of the nicest Christmases we ever had . . . and I've started a painting for a little diversion." Her painting of a snow scene (while living where it never snowed) was a refreshing diversion from her daily routine in the tropics!

1962 in Senegal

The annual meeting of the "Senegal Federation of Evangelical Missions" took place again in our home in Kaolack during the second week of January, 1962. A missionary representative of each of nine missions attended. On Tuesday night, January 9, our Sunday morning people attended a service in our living room with those missionaries. All told, there were 30 people in that service. Stella wrote on January 12: "Our people really enjoyed hearing the testimonies of all the missionaries." Mr. Macindoe, the chairman of the federation, was soon to go to Scotland on furlough. I was chosen as chairman to fill out his term.

During each January the period designated by the French as *La Traite* is at its height in Kaolack. Multitudes of farmers come to Kaolack to negotiate sale of their harvested peanuts. Knowing it will not rain until June, companies that buy the peanuts stack them up in mountainous piles outdoors. Then after the peanuts are shelled, they are shipped by boat to various parts of the world.

At the beginning of 1962, we noticed Kaolack's great influx much more than we had noticed it the year before, because our new residence was just across the street from the railroad station. Stella wrote on January 16: "There are about 16,000 natives in town from surrounding areas . . . we see the hundreds get off of each train . . . they spend their money . . . in one day a large French company sold 2,250 bicycles." Then on January 23, she wrote: "We hear the clattering of the horses drawing the taxi wagons night and day. At the end of February the town will be back to normal."

There was a continual interspersion of discouragements with encouragements for us throughout our time in Africa. To illustrate: on January 16, we hadn't had a household helper for three months, but Catholics (realizing that they needed Protestants' help in the struggle against Communism) were showing a markedly improved attitude toward Protestants. When discouragements seem to outweigh encouragements, just remember that "God . . . will . . . provide a way . . . so that you can stand up." (1 Corinthians 10:13, NIV).

A picnic lunch (like the one we had on February 19, with the Melons and Miss Thelma Wagner, a teacher at the school for missionaries' children in Dakar) was a refreshing encouragement when we needed a little change from routine activity.

Back (left to right): Sharon, Jacqueline Melon, and Doris. Front: Didier Melon. At Kaolack in 1962

During our first two terms in Africa our sons' correspondence schooling was always of major importance to us—even when it had to be postponed for a while. Then, during our last two terms, our daughters' correspondence schooling was just as important to us. It too had to be postponed sometimes.

With reference to her 9th grade work, Doris wrote on February 5, 1962: "In a couple of weeks I will be done with my first semester. I got behind when we had company." Regarding her 7th grade course, Sharon wrote on March 5: "I finished lesson 106 today. If I go right through, I will be done at the end of May." Then I wrote on July 26, to all our helping churches and friends: "Doris and Sharon have completed the 9th and 7th grades . . . they made good grades."

Doris and Sharon were like nearly all sisters in that while growing up they had disputes from time to time. But I don't think any of those disputes ever tended toward an extended lack of mutual appreciation between them. During earlier terms in Africa they nearly always accompanied each other in their visiting of other children. But they were both teenagers in 1962, and tended to have separate other friends more than before.

On February 5, Stella wrote of Sharon's special friendship with a 14 year old girl of French and Chinese extraction, whose parents were renting the first floor of our residence. Then on April 5, she wrote of our daughters' girl friends: "At 4 o'clock Sharon is to be at the home of Chantal de Montity for a birthday party, and Doris is going to Anique's place to visit . . . I'll be taking them both as it is too hot and too far to walk." Chantal's mother was American, her father French and Far Eastern. Anique was French.

A Literature Management Committee meeting of the A. G. fields in French West Africa and French Togoland was to be held on May 1, 1962, at Ouagadougou. The Senegal field's airplane was being repaired at Casablanca. So, Talmadge Butler secured the A. G. Dahomey field's small plane to take him and me to the meeting. On the morning of April 30, Butler and I, with Mossi preacher Kenga Zongo, left Kaolack in this plane for Ouagadougou.

The plane developed engine trouble which caused two

forced landings that day. The first was on an air strip, but the second was in a rough field at Toukoto, Mali (about 400 miles on our way from Kaolack but 600 miles short of Ouagadougou). As we approached that field, I noticed big rocks in it that could destroy our little plane and bring death to us.

Knowing that "the angel of the Lord encamps around those who fear him, and . . . delivers them" (Psalm 34:7, NIV), we three were calm as the plane struck a big rock, causing considerable damage to it but no physical harm to us. While descending in the plane, I had been sensing some protection in the thick, hard helmet I was wearing. But when I noticed that our pilot was bareheaded, I quickly placed my helmet on his head. He was best prepared (among we three) to try to keep the plane rightside up after it landed! A piece of plastic cloth had shut off air from the gasoline and caused the plane's engine trouble.

After the accident we went to Bamako by train then by commercial plane to Ouagadougou. The LMC meeting was postponed until we got there, and it was a good one with delegates of all four French-speaking A. G. fields (including Togo) present. The Ouagadougou press was instructed to continue to print 8,000 copies of my French Sunday lessons for the four fields. Harold Jones had become manager of the press, and John Weidman was still drawing illustrations for the French lessons. After the meeting, I had to wait several days for a commercial plane to Dakar. While waiting, it was my privilege to preach in the church I had built in Ouagadougou 5 years earlier. I was gone from Kaolack 11 days, instead of 4 as planned.

In this autobiography, I have written much about my study of the languages of the Mossi, the Kasena, and the Bambara, during my first three terms in French West Africa. During the first 13 months of this fourth term, my mind was so occupied with getting a property for the A. G. mission that I couldn't seem to settle down to intense language study—even though I knew that I needed to learn Wolof (spelled *Ouolof* in French). In October, 1961 (after we moved into the new mission residence) I began to study Wolof many hours a day.

Up until that time my village preaching had been to more Sereres than Wolofs, because the former were more open to the gospel of Christ. But I chose to learn Wolof rather than Serere because it was the most widely used language in Senegal. In 1962 it was estimated that Wolof was spoken by 85% of Senegal's 3,000,000 people. There were more Serere people who understood Wolof than Wolof people who understood Serere.

My notebook descriptions of village meetings I held in the Kaolack District from 1960 to 1963 indicate an increase of attendance and interest in the 1962 meetings—over the preceding ones. I think the greatest factor in those increases was my preaching in Wolof rather than French between May and December, 1962.

At Tchamentaiba on May 14, I tried to preach briefly in Wolof. My speech was filled with mistakes, but the villagers were pleased that I spoke some in their language. In Gossas on August 6, I preached a 20 minute sermonette in Wolof. Again the villagers were pleased with my effort in their language. My speech in Wolof was improving each week!

Free distribution of gospel tracts and sales of small gospel books and Bibles were increasing at the end of each village meeting, as people gathered around the display of literature on the windshield and engine hood of my Speed-the-Light car. In my letter to friends and churches who were supporting our missionary work, I wrote on October 31, 1962: "When we ministered as missionaries in the Upper Volta, we found more open-hearted response to the Gospel of Christ than we are finding in Senegal. But, the Senegal represents the greatest opportunity that we have had in Africa to spread the gospel by colportage." (At that time the percentage of literate people was greater in Senegal than in Upper Volta.)

Literature evangelism in a village of the Kaolack district, about May, 1962

In May, 1962, I began to translate the Gospel of Mark into Wolof with the help of my Wolof informant, Mr. Simon Sarr, who was an attendant at the Kaolack hospital. We had completed four chapters of the first draft of Mark by June 24. Then on July 26, we had completed about half of it. Stella wrote Warren and Jean on August 24, regarding this translation: "Dad thinks it will be done by tomorrow night . . . he's on the last chapter." I do not remember whether or not I completed it on August 25, but according to my quarterly circular letter of October 31, I did complete that first draft of my translation of Mark into Wolof in August.

We continued to have a large but different group at the Youth center each Sunday at 9:30 a. m., and a small group of individuals who came every Sunday at 11:00 a. m. for the worship service in our home. The average attendance in our home, between Easter Sunday, 1961, and the end of 1962, was only 16 per Sunday, but we reached 27 on Easter Sunday, 1962. My July 26, 1962, letter contains this encouraging note regarding the services in our home: "This month we had a 20% increase over last month in . . . church attendance."

John, Cuba, and Betty Ann Hall visited us in Kaolack for three weeks during the late summer and early fall of 1962. (You know of our earlier long time association with them in Upper Volta.) Stella wrote on October 5: "Doris, Betty, and Sharon really enjoyed each other. Betty hated to leave to go to Dapango, Togo, where they will be this term." John preached each Sunday in French at the meeting in our home, and went with me to the village services, where I interpreted his French into Wolof. About two weeks later Don Penney, his wife, and their 5 children (newly arrived Conservative Baptist missionaries to Thies, Senegal) visited us on Sunday and Monday. Penney preached in English at the Sunday morning meeting in our home, and I interpreted his message into French.

George Flattery, Sr. (left) and Simon Sarr translating the Gospel of Mark into Wolof in Kaolack

Jim Stanley, his wife, and their 5 small sons (aged 1 to 7) arrived in Senegal in June, 1962, to do missionary work, but without sponsorship of any mission society. They were a Canadian Pilgrim Holiness family that had sought missionary appointment but failed to receive it because they had 5 children. I was so favorably impressed with them that I sought and received permission from the A. G. Foreign Missions Committee in Springfield, Missouri, to place the Stanleys temporarily at our vacant Tambacounda station. They did good work there at that time, and for several years after that, with our mission in Senegal.

I had to go to Dakar on July 15, to take care of some mission business with French government officials regarding our mission's purchase of land in Dakar for an evangelistic center. I took my family with me so they could enjoy a break from the hot climate and routine work of Kaolack. Stella wrote on July 26: "We were in Dakar from the 15th to the 20th of this month. George had business to do, so we girls got in a little vacation. We went to the beach twice and visited the city zoo."

On July 31, 1962, at 11:45 a. m., there was an annular eclipse of the sun at the village of Keur-soce (about 10 miles from Kaolack). Astronomer Stoddard of California, another American astronomer, and an English astronomer formed the team of scientists that went to Keur-soce to film this event. I served as the interpreter into French of what Dr. Stoddard had to say to Mr. Benoit, the reporter from Radio Senegal who interviewed him.

Left to right: Mr. Benoit, George Flattery, Sr., and Dr. Stoddard. At Keur-soce at the time of the eclipse of the sun on July 31, 1962

Some things of personal interest to our family which took place between June and October, 1962 were:

1) Before June 15, Doris fell and cracked a bone in the side of her foot while at a picnic on the island of Goree near Dakar. She had to have that foot in a cast until June 28.

2) We four went to our Kaolack beach (six miles from home) on August 23, and discovered (when ready to go home) that we had locked the key to our car in the car trunk! I started my six-mile walk home to get our extra car key, and it started to pour down rain. Fortunately, I caught a ride home soon after the rain started.

3) Then about October 1, we were at the same beach, and when we left for home, Stella forgot her purse—leaving it on the ground where our car had been parked. I was back there looking for her purse within 25 minutes, but the thieves had not left it where I could find it, after they had taken what they wanted from it! In addition to losing valuable cards (which had to be replaced), she lost her best pair of Glasses which took about three weeks to replace.

On October 16, in my study at Kaolack (where I had completed the translation of Mark a few weeks before), I began a 9-month series of thrice weekly, night, Bible-study classes for 4 young men. In the picture below, the middle African is Pierre Keita then 27, a Soce native of French Guinea who had been an orphan all his life. I had known him for only 2 years, but he had been in Senegal for about 9 years when I started those classes.

The Lebanese man is Nahbi who was converted in an English mission just before he went to Senegal. (At the moment, I can't locate the record of the names of the other two Africans.) Our textbooks for this series of classes were the Bible and the French translation of *We Believe* by R. M. Riggs.

David and Claudia Wakefield arrived with their 4 children (Ruth 17, Jonathan 16, Becky 14, and Beth Ann 8) in Senegal on Monday, November 19, 1962, to begin their work of opening an evangelistic center in Dakar. The whole family stayed with us at Kaolack for 5 days. On November 22, the annual conference of the Senegal field fellowship took place again at our home in Kaolack. Knowing that we would be going on furlough in about 8 months, I asked the fellowship to elect someone else as field chairman during the coming year. They elected David Wakefield to that office. I worked with Wakefield as field secretary-treasurer until we went on furlough.

George Flattery, Sr., teaching a night Bible-study class at Kaolack in October, 1962

We went on Tuesday, December 11, to Thies and enjoyed an overnight visit with the Don Penney Conservative Baptist missionary family. Next morning, we went to the Dakar airport and saw the Butlers off on furlough. We shopped in Dakar for Christmas in the afternoon and stayed that night with the Wakefields. We shopped again Thursday in Dakar and went home to Kaolack that evening. We had a lovely Christmas with the Wakefields in our home. Then Doris and Sharon went home with them to Dakar for a couple of weeks, taking along their school books.

Left to right: Jonathan Wakefield, Doris Flattery, Ruth Wakefield, Sharon Flattery, Becky Wakefield, and Beth Ann Wakefield

1963 in Senegal

On Wednesday January 9, I returned home to Kaolack from Ziguinchor, where I had attended the annual meeting of the Senegal Federation of Evangelical Missions. It was commendable that the delegates to this meeting made further progress in the removal of constitutional clauses that would restrain helpful freedom of movement among Evangelical Mission Societies throughout Senegal. Eight other delegates to this meeting stopped briefly at our house (on the way to their homes in Thies and Dakar), to exchange friendly greetings the day I got home.

E. L. Phillips, secretary for A. G. Missions in Africa, visited us in Kaolack, and preached at our morning worship service in our home on Sunday, February 10. Doris went with me that afternoon when I took Brother Phillips to the Dakar airport to board a plane for his next place of ministry. Then we went to the Wakefield home, and picked up Becky who went with us for a visit when we returned home to Kaolack.

Much of my time between Christmas, 1962, and February

20, 1963, was spent with Simon Sarr in the final preparation of the Gospel of Mark in Wolof for printing at the Ouagadougou A. G. press. On February 20, I sent the typed final copy of it (50 pages) to that press for printing.

Our two teen-aged daughters and the Wakefield teen-aged daughters were anxious to get acquainted with the six American young men who were working in the Kaolack district with the Peace Corps, an American organization that seeks to improve conditions in underdeveloped countries. Four of the six were Catholics—including the youngest, Mike Yanasak, 20. Mike went with me on Sunday afternoon, March 4, to help with my village gospel meetings at Niahar and Toucar.

At the end of each meeting he helped with distribution of literature. As he gladly and willingly passed out tracts, I contrasted (mentally and silently) his helpful effort with the effort of some Catholics to stone me and my evangelistic party at Ouagadougou six years before!

George Flattery, Sr., preaching in Wolof at Kaolack Youth Center on March 31, 1963

In February, 1963, we were continuing with the regular Sunday morning services at the Kaolack Youth Center, which we had been having for 27 months—since November, 1960. On February 10, I made my first effort to preach in Wolof at the

Youth Center. I began my preaching in Wolof in the villages, then preached in it at the Center, only after I had learned more of it. My preaching in Wolof at the Youth Center was always right in front of the Center—as close to the street as the city ordinance would allow!

According to my notebook, there was: "excellent interest as I preached in Wolof" at the Kaolack Youth Center on February 10, and "a real good crowd and interest to hear my Wolof message" on February 17. We continued through Sunday, July 21 (five days before leaving Kaolack on furlough), to hold Youth Center meetings. My week-to-week improvement in speaking Wolof helped to produce more interest among the townspeople in those meetings.

In addition to continuing our Kaolack Youth Center meetings until we went on furlough, we continued, likewise, our Sunday morning worship services in our Kaolack residence. Our farewell worship service, on July 21, was attended by 31 Kaolack people (the largest number of Kaolack people in any of the worship services since we started having them in our apartment at the F. A. O. on Easter Sunday in 1961).

Stella wrote on March 25th: "Doris is teaching a Sunday School class in French and she is really happy about it. She has a little French boy, some Lebanese and Mulattos and African children." Sharon's singing in our services was an inspiration to those who heard her. In Senegal, our daughters followed in the footsteps of their brothers, who had been a benediction upon our missionary work in Upper Volta more than a decade earlier. Doris was getting top grades in her correspondence high school work through Nebraska University. And Sharon was doing real well in her 8th grade Calvert correspondence school work.

On April 12, I wrote our homeland friends: "Traveling by auto in the hinterland of Senegal is not easy . . . but . . . necessary . . .on this mission field: between March 18 and 22, we made a 650 mile trip (over sections of very bad road) in our Speed-the-Light car; and conducted gospel services in our mission churches in Tambacounda and Kedougou. We rejoiced in God's blessing upon these services." The Tambacounda station was vacant because Stanleys had moved to Kedougou to occupy Butlers' station before we made that trip. However, Jim Stanley had gone to Tambacounda to receive us there. He then made the trip to Kedougou with us.

We had great fun in making that trip with the Wakefields in our two cars. Jonathan, Ruth, Becky, Doris, and Sharon (all teenagers) rode in our car with me. Stella joined David and Claudia Wakefield, their 8-year-old daughter Beth Ann, and Jim Stanley in the Wakefields' car. All of us enjoyed the scenery at the large Gambia river, a picnic lunch beside the rustic Sementi hotel, and the sight of wild animals all around us as we traveled in the expansive Niokolo-Koba game reserve. Along the way, we had to cross over many rather precarious looking (but usually dependable) native-style pole bridges over small streams.

Flatterys' Speed-the-Light car between two pole bridges in the hinterland of Senegal

The Wakefields' car was nearly new but ours was well worn. We had used it for two years. In addition to our car's normal wear from its mileage, parts of it had corroded considerably in the atmosphere produced by Kaolack's salty estuary—an atmosphere that was even more corrosive than seaside air.

When our muffler fell off on this trip, I thought "oh no!" Because I knew that we would have to listen to the car's extreme noise until we got back to a garage in Kaolack. But all the teenagers with me took it hilariously, saying: "Now, we sound like an airplane!" They were helpful as well as hilarious on the trip: when I had a flat tire in lion country, they jumped out of the car to help me change it. We were back at our Tambacounda mission station when the two families celebrated my 49th birthday with a nice meal on March 21. The next day we arrived home in Kaolack and Wakefields, after having supper with us, went on home to Dakar.

In my three years of Pentecostal pioneering at Kaolack, I had few people to baptize, few weddings to solemnize, few babies to dedicate, and few people to bury. I baptized two, solemnized two weddings, dedicated three babies, and had three funerals. At 3:00 p. m. on Sunday, June 16, 1963, our church congregation of about 40 went to the Saloum river in Kaolack to watch me baptize Pierre Keita and Maria Andrade (a Portuguese woman from the Cape Verde Islands). No one before them had ever been baptized by immersion in the Kaolack district.

Left to right: Pierre Keita, Maria Andrade, and George Flattery, Sr., giving Pierre and Maria instructions for baptism in water

Pierre Keita had been sprinkled as an infant by an Anglican missionary and, for some time, refused to be baptized by immersion. But near the end of our 9-month series of Bible-study classes, he told me the Lord had shown him he should be baptized by immersion. After I baptized him, he told me he wanted to remain a member of the Anglican church, but he became more friendly to the Pentecostal way as he learned more about it. He listened with real interest each time I talked to him about the Baptism of the Holy Spirit.

During the last week of April, David Wakefield and I went to Ouagadougou for an LMC meeting, and found that the Ouagadougou press had just completed the printing of 5,000 copies of my translation of Mark in Wolof. (John Weidman did the art work and Harold Jones managed the production.) Wakefield and I took 300 copies of it (150 each) back to Senegal in our plane luggage.

LMC committeemen at Ouagadougou in April, 1963. Left to right: George Flattery, Sr., Vernon Metz, John Weidman, Harold Jones, David Wakefield, Raymond Zents, Sr., and Herman Engelgau

The first time I showed my Wolof translation of *Marc* (French spelling) in a Kaolack service was in the early Sunday morning meeting on May 5, at the Youth Center, after I had preached in Wolof. About an hour later I showed it to the people at the worship service in our residence. The people in both services expressed gratitude to me for having made the effort to learn Wolof, and translate the Gospel of Mark into it.

On May 19, I sold several copies of Mark in Wolof at the Sunday morning, Youth-Center meeting. I sold them for 25 francs (10 cents) each, about half of the cost of having them printed. The BGMC of the A. G. paid for the entire cost of printing them, but we did not choose to give them away. I felt that anyone who received a copy of Mark in Wolof would value it more if he had paid something for it than if it had been given to him. What we received from sale of these Gospels helped with other literary needs of our mission in Senegal.

George Flattery, Sr. (right), presenting a copy of the Gospel of Mark in Wolof at Kaolack in May, 1963, to Simon Sarr, the informant who assisted him in translating it

Conclusion

On June 11, 1963, the Senegal Field Committee appointed David Wakefield to "make a monthly Wednesday night visit to Kaolack to hold a gospel service and take care of any matters pertaining to the work in Kaolack which need attention between the time the Flatterys leave and another missionary is stationed in Kaolack." The A. G. Foreign Missions Committee at Springfield chose the Homer Specter family from California to take our place at Kaolack. It was quite a while after we left Kaolack before Specters were able to get there. Nine months after we had gone, Margy Butler wrote from Kedougou to us in America on April 30, 1964: "Specters will go to Kaolack when they are through studying French in Dakar."

In their meeting of June 26, the Senegal Field Committee authorized the building of a wall across the interior of the warehouse on the Kaolack A. G. property to set off one third of it for a church auditorium. I built that wall and intended to have the first service in the newly prepared auditorium on July 21, the Sunday before leaving on furlough. But the church people were still meeting in our residence when we left, because the builders of our pews did not yet have them completed.

The final page of my diary of meetings (at our two Kaolack residences, the Kaolack Youth Center, and villages of the Kaolack district) indicates that I conducted (during the three-year term at Kaolack) a total of 647 gospel meetings (including Bible-study classes, but not including Bible-translation sessions). In addition, I conducted a few meetings which I did not record: for example, those in the home of Mossi preacher Etienne Miningou at the beginning of the term.

Having completed another fruitful term in Africa, I boarded planes (with Stella, Doris, and Sharon) on July 26, 1963 in Dakar at 3:30 a. m. for New York, and (later in the day) in New York for Dallas. That day, I was more grateful to God than I had ever known how to be, for His protection of Stella, Warren,

George, Doris, Sharon, and me, and for His deliverance of "us from the evil one" (Matthew 6:13, NIV), during all my time as a foreign missionary.

We'd gained a lot of time on the sun during our westward flights. What a joy it was to meet Jean, see little Mark for the first time, and be reunited with all the rest of our beloved family in Dallas about 10:30 a. m. on that memorable 26th day of July!

The next chapter describes the widest range of travel by George Flattery, Sr. He is ready in this 1973 picture, to board a plane at the Santo, New Hebrides, airport for Port Vila, New Hebrides.

PART THREE: *WORLDWIDE CHRISTIAN MINISTRY*

CHAPTER 9: EDUCATING AND EVANGELIZING

Must a Christian minister always evangelize people before educating them? The fact that a person must experience conversion to Christ before experiencing deeper things in Christ might seem to require an affirmative answer to this question. But we need to remember that no person is able to accept Christ as his Savior before he has been educated regarding who Christ is and what Christ can do for him. A person's knowing some things about Christ is necessary to his knowing how to accept Him and "know . . . the power of his resurrection" (Philippians 3:10).

Teaching at Evangel College

The year (more precisely, 13 and 1/2 months) between July 26, 1963 (the day we arrived in the United States from our 4th term in Africa) and the time I started teaching at Evangel College in Springfield, Missouri, was a period of transition between my 20 years as a foreign missionary and my 10 years as a teacher at Evangel.

My foreign missionary work during that period included: 1) The participation of Stella, Doris, Sharon, and me in the General Council of the Assemblies of God in Memphis, Tennessee, in August, 1963, 2) our participation in the

Memphis city-wide A. G. missionary convention at First Assembly in October, 1963, and 3) my holding of 44 individual missionary meetings (mostly in Kansas, but some in Oklahoma, Nebraska, Texas, and Florida) in the interest of Senegal. An important part of my transition from foreign missionary work to teaching at Evangel was my earning of a Master of Arts degree, with an English major, at the University of Oklahoma in Norman, between January and August, 1964.

Back in 1960 (right after I earned my Bachelor of Arts degree at Texas Wesleyan), a professor of English at Evangel invited me to join Evangel's teaching staff. But I could not do that then, because I was committed to a fourth term in Africa.

In 1964, I solicited a teaching position at Evangel, mainly because I felt (at age 50) that I could (in the future) do better work for God's kingdom through college teaching and holding Christian evangelistic meetings in French than by trying to return to French West Africa for more of the type of Pentecostal pioneering that I had been doing for 20 years. I was certain that I would not have (between 50 and 65 years of age) as much physical strength for that kind of Pentecostal pioneering as I had had between 30 and 50.

My French Sunday School Lessons were used in Senegal throughout 1961-1964, and in all of the four A. G. French-speaking mission fields in West Africa throughout 1962-1964. A further part of my missionary work in 1963 (after we returned to America from Africa) was to write those lessons for the last half of 1964. That was the end of my enjoyable four years of writing French Sunday School lessons for Africa. I wrote John Weidman on May 6, 1964, at the Ouagadougou press:

> *Evangel College has offered me a position as a teacher, beginning next September. I will not have time to do any more French Sunday School lessons for Africa. Please ask someone to do them, beginning with the first quarter, 1965.*

During the years that I taught at Evangel (and for several years after that), I occasionally translated French documents, and interpreted for French people, at the A. G. Division of Foreign Missions.

During my first year at Evangel, I taught Freshman English. During the next five years, I taught both Freshman English and French. Then during the last four years, I taught French only. At the end of my first year of teaching, Dr. Ward Williams, Evangel's Academic Dean, advised me to go to the University of Missouri at Columbia to begin work on a Master of Arts degree in French.

I completed that degree at Columbia in the summer of 1968, after four summers of study there—plus a few classes that I took at Southwest Missouri State University, during the academic school years of that period. During my last three summers at Columbia, I rented a room from Jim and Twila Edwards (my faculty colleagues at Evangel), and boarded with them. That was an excellent arrangement for me. I enjoyed it much more than living in the dormitory, and eating in the cafeteria, at Missouri University.

Evangel College Faculty and Staff retreat of August 30 to September 1, 1967; at Camp Aurora, on the Niangua River, at Windyville, Missouri (about 10 miles northeast of Buffalo, Missouri). President Ashcroft is at the center of the front row, and I am near the center of the third row.

After earning my M. A. in French, I taught all levels of undergraduate college French at Evangel. I enjoyed my teaching and my participation in recreational activities at Evangel College. The latter included my attendance at basketball and baseball games, and my participation at the excellent retreats planned by the capable college President, J. Robert Ashcroft, and his staff.

A student who completed a concentration in French under my teaching at Evangel, Lucinda (Saghin) Metzger (a worker in the A. G. Church of Painesville, Ohio), recently wrote me regarding her study of French in my classes: "I have fond memories of your singing 'Mervielleux' and bringing in movies of Upper Volta mission work . . . thank you for your godly example as my instructor." While I was teaching at Evangel, Stella and our daughter Doris were studying there. They earned Bachelor of Arts degrees together at Evangel in 1969.

Summer Evangelism in French

After having taught for two years at Evangel College, I began a program of worldwide Christian ministry which I titled "Summer Evangelism in French." In this program of Pentecostal pioneering, I went personally during 8 consecutive summers (while continuing to teach at Evangel) to 8 different French-speaking areas of the world to preach in French. In length, these French revival campaigns ranged from two weeks to two months. One summer, all of the mass meetings of the campaign were held at the same locality. During the remaining 7 summers, I went (not every day, but often) from one place to another nearby place to preach.

My 8 years of "Summer evangelism in French" were in: Quebec in 1966; Haiti in 1967; French Guiana in 1968; French-speaking Europe in 1969; Guadeloupe in 1970; Tahiti in 1971; Reunion and Mauritius in 1972; Tahiti again, New Caledonia, and New Hebrides in 1973. I was the first A. G. minister of the United States to hold protracted gospel meetings in French

Guiana, Guadeloupe, Reunion, and Mauritius. The positioning of the 8 dates (1966-1973) on the following map will help you to visualize the worldwide aspect of my summer evangelism in French.

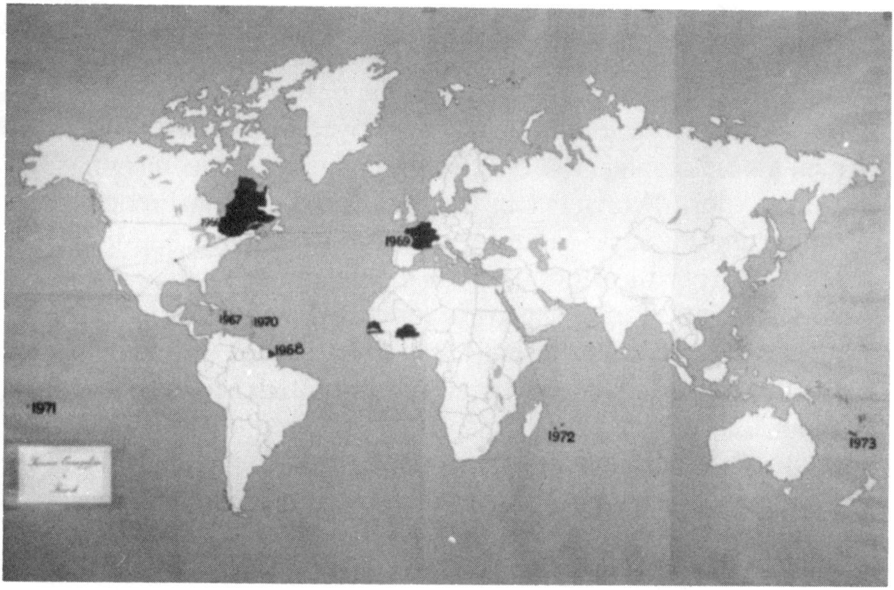

Map of dates and places of summer evangelism in French by George Flattery, Sr.

The two blackened areas in West Africa on the above map (Senegal, left, and Upper Volta) indicate where my wife, our children, and I were missionaries—before my engagement in these summer campaigns. Now, I will present, chronologically, a brief report of each year's activity in my summer evangelism in French.

Quebec, 1966

At the Des Moines General Council of the Assemblies of God in August, 1965, I saw Pastor E. L. Lassegues (whom I had not seen for 20 years) of the French-speaking Pentecostal church that we had attended in Montreal in 1945. After 20 years, he was still pastoring the same church, but in a fine new location. He arranged for me to evangelize at his church, at other churches near Montreal, and at Quebec City, in August, 1966.

Stella and I (accompanied by our daughter Sharon) went in our car from Springfield, Missouri, to Montreal, for our meetings in Quebec, from August 14 to 28. The congregations enjoyed my showing of films which I had made of our missionary work in Africa. They enjoyed also Stella's instrumental music and Sharon's singing during these meetings. During those two weeks in Quebec, I preached in French 14 times, and 8 people came forward for salvation. I had hoped that our freewill offerings from the people of Quebec would take care of all our expenses connected with holding those meetings. According to my letter to Lassegues of September 14, their offerings "paid for all of our cash expenditures with about $50 to spare!"

I was a Missionary Evangelist of the A. G. Division of Foreign Missions during all 8 summer campaigns. Quebec was the only place to which we drove our car to the locality of the summer campaign in French. Each of the following 7 summers required an overseas plane flight, which I made without my family. With the approval of the Division of Foreign Missions and Evangel College, I held promotional meetings in churches during each of the school years which preceded the remaining 7 summer campaigns. In these meetings, those churches gave enough money each year for my plane fare and other expenses connected with my French campaign abroad.

Haiti, 1967

Soon after my campaign in Quebec was completed, I began prayerful consideration of Haiti as the place for my 1967 summer evangelism in French. I wrote A. G. missionary Robert B. Turnbull of Port-au-Prince, Haiti, on September 24, 1966: "If you think my ministry in French could help your work in Haiti, I would be glad to come and preach there under your supervision between August 13 and 27, 1967." I wrote this to him after describing (in the same letter) God's blessing upon the campaign I had just concluded in Quebec.

In his letter to me of October 25, 1966, Turnbull replied: "In regard to your desire to come to Haiti to minister, we would be pleased to have you come. I am sure that you would be a blessing to our people." Then in seeking the approval of the A. G. Division of Foreign Missions on my project to evangelize in Haiti, I visited Melvin Hodges, A. G. Secretary for Latin America, and told him about the project. Hodges wrote me on December 14, 1966: "The Foreign Missions Committee has approved your visit to Haiti, as outlined in your conversation with me."

In the winter and spring of 1967, I visited 7 A. G. churches of Springfield, Missouri, and received help from them for expenses connected with my evangelism in Haiti. The Haitians responded enthusiastically to my ministry. They, too, enjoyed seeing my films of our terms in Africa. The churches were nearly always full, and sometimes people had to listen from outside the building because there was not enough space to accommodate them within the sanctuary.

About 15 people came forward for salvation, and many more raised their hands for prayer. I do not think I had ever heard more enthusiastic gospel singing than that of the Haitians. I spoke in 21 services between August 13 and 27. This included preaching in churches, lecturing in Bible classes, and witnessing at street meetings. Fourteen of the meetings were conducted in Port-au-Prince missions and the Petionville church. Seven meetings were in churches or on the streets of villages in northern Haiti. My messages in French needed no interpretation at Port-au-Prince and Petionville. But some of them had to be translated into Creole in the northern villages.

The spiritual and social fellowship which I enjoyed with the missionaries (Turnbulls and newly arrived Hittenbergers) helped me to minister successfully in Haiti.

George Flattery, Sr., teaching a Bible study class in the Petionville church, near Port-au-Prince, Haiti

French Guiana, 1968

Before I held the campaign in Haiti in August, 1967, I had felt that French Guiana might be a likely place for my 1968 summer evangelism in French. Right after that campaign, I felt more strongly that I should make plans to evangelize at Cayenne, French Guiana in August, 1968. I first told Melvin Hodges of my hope to go to French Guiana.

Hodges advised me to write the A. G. missionary in Surinam, John Verbarendse, about it. I then wrote Verbarendse on September 9, 1967 for his thoughts about my going to Cayenne to preach daily in French between August 11 and 25, 1968. In the same letter I solicited his help with preparations in Cayenne for such a campaign—if he thought I should go there at that time.

Then I talked to Verbarendse on October 17, by short wave radio from Evangel College. He had not yet had time to answer my letter, but invited me by radio to go to Cayenne to conduct a revival campaign in French at the time that I had mentioned in my letter. He assured me that day by radio (and two days later by letter) that he would do everything he could to prepare for my campaign in Cayenne. When I told Hodges of Verbarendse's response, he presented the matter of my going to French Guiana to the Foreign Missions Committee for their approval. The FMC responded as follows:

> *We think this is an excellent opportunity to reach this country with the gospel and warmly recommend your acceptance of the invitation. We also recommend that you present the need for fare and other expenses to any churches interested in backing you for this ministry.*

My first presentation of the need for funds to pay expenses connected with my going to French Guiana was on November 18, 1967, in the A. G missionary convention at my boyhood hometown: Wichita, Kansas. Then between February 11 and July 28, 1968, I presented this need in 14 Missouri churches.

(It was on July 7, 1968, that Talmadge and Margy Butler, and their son Stephen, 11, died at sea, between Florida and the Bahama Islands. We were deeply saddened by the death of these dear 1960-1963 coworkers in Senegal. I solemnly reflected on the time Talmadge and I escaped injury in our forced landing onto a rocky field at Toukouto, Mali, West Africa, on April 30, 1962.)

Between October, 1967, and August, 1968, Verbarendse did commendable work in preparation for the Cayenne crusade. Overcoming the handicap of 250 miles of rugged terrain and his inability to speak French, he made many trips to Cayenne from his home in Paramaribo, Surinam, to encourage people and distribute Light-for-the-Lost literature among them. Just before the crusade began, Verbarendse placed posters of it throughout Cayenne. William Charlet was the spiritual leader of the small group of believers in Cayenne. He helped Verbarendse with preparations for my meetings.

During the crusade, we continued to distribute Light-for-the-Lost materials, and distributed also some Scripture portions from the American Bible Society and the Scripture Gift Mission of London. Colportage was a more important part of this campaign than it had been during my two preceding summers.

In Cayenne, all of my mass meetings were held in an abandoned, centrally located pavilion that was large enough to hold several hundred people. The night crowds reached a peak of about 400, and the public-address system enabled many more hundreds to hear the services in nearby homes and adjoining streets. During the two-week campaign, I showed my 3 missionary films on Africa, and (for the first time) my new 8-minute missionary film on Haiti. I preached 15 times and conducted 5 afternoon Bible study classes. A total of 109 responded for salvation during this GOOD NEWS CRUSADE!

Harold Carpenter (an A. G. missionary in Bolivia) was interested in becoming a missionary to French Guiana. He went from Bolivia to Cayenne and helped in my crusade. While there, his desire increased to take his family to French Guiana for his next term of missionary service. With reference to my crusade in Cayenne, the *Pentecostal Evangel* of January 26, 1969, stated: "Results . . . were so encouraging that the Foreign Missions Board decided to enter . . . French Guiana, with a permanent witness. Present plans are that the resident missionaries will be the Harold Carpenters." Soon afterward, Carpenters went to Cayenne as missionaries and stayed about 3 years.

Three helpers in the Cayenne crusade (left to right): Robert B. Turnbull, William Charlet, and John Verbarendse

Robert B. Turnbull went from Haiti to Cayenne and gave valuable help to my crusade during the last four days of the two weeks I was there. Then he stayed on for a week after my departure to do needed follow-up work among the new converts, and to organize a local church.

French-speaking Europe, 1969

Before September, 1968, I had contacted the A. G. Field Secretary for Europe, Charles Greenaway, regarding the possibility of my engaging in summer evangelism in French-speaking Europe in 1969. In my thank-you letter of September 7, 1968, to Robert B. Turnbull for his follow-up work in Cayenne, I stated: "Brother Greenaway and Brother Kenneth Ware are already scheduling preaching . . . for me in France during next June and July." Before writing this to Turnbull, I knew that in their session of September 6, 1968, members of the A. G. Foreign Missions Committee had unanimously approved my proposal to minister in Europe during the summer of 1969.

I do not consider that my 8-summer program of evangelism in French attained true worldwide status until its final two summers with their meetings on islands of the Indian and South Pacific oceans. But the campaign in Europe would reach nearer to that status in 1969 than the three preceding campaigns (all in the Western Hemisphere) had reached. I knew in the fall of 1968 that expenses connected with my 1969 campaign would be more than they had been for any one of the three preceding campaigns.

Men's dormitory number 68 at Evangel College invited me to present (in their devotional service on October 24, 1968) the financial need of my 1969 summer campaign. At the close of my presentation, they gave me a small offering for that campaign, and promised to pray with me that I would receive all the financial help I would need for it. Then on November 3 and 15, 1968, I received more help toward this need through my presentation of it in three A. G. churches of central Kansas. Between November 17, 1968 and May 25, 1969, I presented this need in 24 Missouri churches.

I expressed gratitude to Kenneth Ware (Assemblies of God representative in France) for his arrangement of the itinerary for my preaching in French in Europe between June 5 and August 3, 1969. Before I went to Europe, I added the film of my French Guiana campaign to that of my Haiti campaign. Thus, I transformed the 8-minute Haiti film into a 15-minute film of the two countries. My European congregations thoroughly enjoyed seeing it, along with my three missionary films of our work in French West Africa that I had shown in Quebec, Haiti, and French Guiana.

Between June 5 and 8, I preached once in Compeigne and 4 times in Paris. Then on June 11-13, I attended the General Council of the Assemblies of God of France at Tours, where I was introduced as an American Missionary Evangelist who was currently working in French-speaking Europe. Most of the pastors who had me speak in their churches wanted me for only one service. But I spoke 7 times in 5 days (June 14-18) at Nantes in Brittany (the westernmost province of France) for Pastor Robert LeBel (now deceased). Twenty people were converted in his church. I was in and around Nantes long enough to understand why Pastor LeBel said to me: "Brittany is a section of France that remains a mission field for Pentecost."

After preaching twice at Angers, once at Blois, and twice at Tours between June 19 and 22, I had no meetings during the 12 days between June 23 and July 4. On Tuesday, June 24, I went by train from Tours, France, to Locarno, Switzerland, to attend a retreat for A. G. missionaries. Warren and Jean were among those missionaries and met my train in Locarno.

After the retreat ended, Warren, Jean, and I traveled together by train to the renowned city of Rome, stopping along the way to visit some other famous places. It was my first time in Italy, so I especially enjoyed seeing Rome, Florence, and other Italian sights. I was glad for my days of fellowship with Warren and Jean that followed the Locarno conference. Those days ended on July 5, when they went back to Jordan, and I went to Morges, Switzerland, to resume my evangelism in French.

Pastor Robert LeBel (Left) and George Flattery, Sr., in front of Pastor LeBel's church in Nantes

On Thursday, July 10, I preached in the A. G. church in Lausanne, Switzerland, where Andre Brisset (who had participated in the dedication of the Ouagadougou, Upper Volta, church, in 1957) was pastor. The next day I addressed the monthly ministers' conference in Brisset's church. Pastor Knops had me preach in both services at First Assembly in Brussels on Sunday, July 27. Three people were converted that day. I conducted the last five of my meetings in Europe during my 6 days (July 29 to August 3) at Agen (in the southern region of France, known as the Midi). Those meetings were in the A. G. church where Claude Tenneroni was pastor. Six people were converted in Tenneroni's church.

A main purpose of my summer program of preaching in French in various French-speaking areas of the world was to promote Pentecostal evangelism. But, inspired by Hebrews 5:12-14, I often preached beyond the ministry of the milk of God's Word to the unconverted, in an attempt to minister the meat of His Word to the converted—so that they could better understand and practice biblical "teaching about righteousness" (v. 13, NIV).

During the two months between June 5 and August 3, 1969, it was my privilege to preach in French 51 times in Europe (24 times in France, 18 in Belgium, and 9 in Switzerland). My congregations were larger in June than in July because many people had gone on vacations in July. But we had good meetings even when only a few people attended them. Thirty-nine came to the altars for salvation during the two months.

After two months of separation from Stella and our daughters, I arrived home on Monday night August 4, 1969. During our missionary furloughs from Africa, I had quite often been separated from my family for one month, but that European summer of evangelism in 1969 was the first project to separate me from them for two months. So, you can understand why I missed them more that time than ever before!

Guadeloupe, 1970

Abe Jacobson was a violinist with a burden for Pentecostal missionary evangelism in French. He had attended Evangel College and had been well received as a violinist by French Pentecostals in Quebec. I met him in the fall of 1968 when he attended the Homecoming activities of Evangel College. Jacobson wrote me on November 27, 1968: "Brother Flattery, let's keep the island need before God! There are over a half million souls in Guadeloupe and Martinique. There are no

Pentecostal missionaries there, as far as I know."

I had already thought of Guadeloupe as a possible place for one of my future summer campaigns. That contact with Jacobson helped to cause me to feel, by the time I arrived in Europe in the summer of 1969, that Guadeloupe should be the place for my evangelism in French in the summer of 1970. I went to the General Council of the French Assemblies of God at Tours, France, on June 11, 1969, with the hope of contacting someone who could help me to begin making preliminary arrangements for 1970 ministry in Guadeloupe.

At the French General Council, I was told that there were no Pentecostal missionaries already in Guadeloupe, but that the Jacques Giraud family (who were also attending the Council) hoped to go there soon to pioneer a Pentecostal work. At that time Giraud (whom I had not met before) and I made the preliminary arrangements for me to go to Guadeloupe in the summer of 1970 to minister under his supervision. My next step was to seek the approval of our A. G. Foreign Missions Department upon my proposed ministry in Guadeloupe. Foreign Missions Secretary, R. T. McGlasson, wrote me on January 8, 1970:

> *The Foreign Missions Department is deeply appreciative of your ministry in French-speaking areas of the West Indies and South America. The department is pleased to endorse your accepting invitations received from Guadeloupe to minister there in the summer of 1970. Any church in which you would be speaking and presenting your ministry, should be asked to indicate its interest with an offering towards your expenses for ministry.*

Between February 1 and May 31, 1970, I presented in 15 Missouri churches my need for plane fare and other items connected with my coming ministry in Guadeloupe. Most of these meetings had to be on Sundays to fit in with my teaching schedule at Evangel. My habit in these meetings was to show one brief missionary film (the one I had made most recently) then preach a short missionary message. In these meetings, I showed the film I had made in Europe during the summer of 1969.

Through its spiritual emphasis program called SCOPE, Evangel College sent Kenneth Lee (a student who was taking French from me) to Guadeloupe with me to lead singing, sing solos in French, and help with the distribution of gospel literature. We had little time for recreation in Guadeloupe. But Kenneth, some of the nationals, and I took time off one day and climbed the famous live volcano known as "La Soufriere." It has an altitude of 1467 meters. We had to keep proper distance from the flowing molten lava. What a sight that lava was from the close range from which we saw it!

Kenneth Lee in Guadeloupe with nationals of Guadeloupe

Our ministry in Guadeloupe began on Sunday, June 7, and ended on Sunday, July 5. It included a series of three campaigns: first, a 15-day meeting in Basse-Terre; second, a week in Capesterre; and last, a week in Sainte Anne. After the first campaign, we flew to nearby Martinique, and held a service in Fort-de-France. Then before the last campaign, we held a Sunday service in Pointe-a-Pitre, Guadeloupe's biggest city.

During the month we held 44 services, and 120 came

forward for salvation. Fifty-two of them came forward at Sainte Anne where no regular meetings had been held before our campaign. The meetings in Sainte Anne were held on the spacious veranda of a Christian's home, and those in Basse-Terre and Capesterre were held in rented halls. Crowds reached as high as 200. At the night meetings, people enjoyed seeing all of my missionary films of our family's early years in Africa, and my recent summers abroad. Each summer there was one more film to show!

The main purpose of my crusade in Guadeloupe was to proclaim the Pentecostal message in an almost entirely neglected place (until the arrival of Girauds less than a year before). Kenneth Lee and I joined hands with the French Assemblies of God mission in Guadeloupe in an effort to strengthen this new Pentecostal work.

Tahiti, 1971

While I was still campaigning in Guadeloupe in the summer of 1970, Jacques Giraud told me of his plans to go during the coming winter to Tahiti to evangelize. For several years, I had searched my map of the world for possible places in which to continue my program of summer evangelism in French. Tahiti was one of those places to which I had hoped (for some time) to go. Before I left Guadeloupe, I asked Giraud to try to make preliminary arrangements (through his forthcoming personal contact with the leader of the Pentecostal work in Tahiti) for me to evangelize there during the summer of 1971.

It was on August 24, 1970, that I made oral presentation to Wesley Hurst (A. G. Secretary for the Far East) of my tentative plans to evangelize in Tahiti during the summer of 1971. He assured me orally that if I could make arrangements with the Tahiti Pentecostal leader for such evangelization, it would have the approval of the Foreign Missions Committee. I outlined my plans to Hurst in writing, so he could present them to the committee. It was on September 17, that Hurst replied in writing (for the FMC) that my plans for Tahiti were "wholly acceptable."

Giraud held a 9-day Pentecostal crusade in Tahiti from December 2 to 11, 1970. Four days later he was in Springfield, Missouri, and told me that he had made arrangements with Pastor Ronald Ewart of the Chinese Pentecostal church in Papeete, Tahiti, to receive me for a Pentecostal crusade during the summer of 1971.

Something happened that made it easier for me to raise the money that I needed for expenses connected with my evangelism in the summer of 1971 than it had been to raise it for the summer campaigns of the preceding years: it was the institution by Evangel College in January, 1971 of their "Jan-Term." Since I had no teaching assignment in January, James C. Ellis (Superintendent of the Kentucky District of the A. G.) arranged a 3-week series (January 3-24) of daily missionary meetings for me. These meetings, 23 in all, supplied my entire financial need for my 1971 summer ministry. When I returned home, I wrote Superintendent Ellis that "I had a very fine series of meetings in Kentucky." He replied: "Please accept this invitation to come to Kentucky again."

Our missionary colleagues in Upper Volta, between 1948 and 1957, Howard and Charlotte Fox, were missionaries in New Caledonia when I was preparing to evangelize in Tahiti in 1971. Their prayers for my project helped it to succeed. Their mailings of gospel literature to me for distribution in Tahiti was another manner whereby I received help from them. I gave out more literature personally in Tahiti than in any of the previous 5 summer campaigns. This included distribution of the ICI course titled "Great Questions of Life."

Brother Fox had personal acquaintance with Pentecostal leaders and people in Tahiti which enabled him to help my work there in still other ways: 1) He wrote them a fine recommendation of me and my ministry, saying in his letter of March 10, to one of those leaders: "We collaborated with Pastor Flattery on a mission field in Africa for many years. We know him as a servant of God who is entirely devoted to the service of the Lord." 2) He shared information with me concerning needs and problems of the Pentecostal work in Tahiti which helped me to know how to pray more specifically for my approaching crusade.

Through SCOPE, Evangel college sent Sam Croutworst (one of my students of French) to Tahiti with me to help me with the crusade in the same ways that Kenneth Lee had helped me the preceding year in Guadeloupe. Sam and I flew from Springfield, Missouri, to Acapulco, Mexico, on Saturday, June 5, 1971. Right after we became airborne over Springfield, he brought Psalm 119:117 to my attention: "Hold thou me up and I shall be safe" (KJV).

A little after midnight on Sunday, June 6, as we started out from Acapulco on the almost 4000-mile nonstop flight over the Pacific Ocean to Tahiti, Sam was somewhat tense—it was his first long flight over water. (Although I had made many long flights over water, I gladly joined him in placing faith in Psalm 119:117!) We had an excellent westward flight and arrived in Tahiti a little before dawn. Ronald Ewart, pastor of Papeete's Chinese Pentecostal church, and Ernest Yune, its head deacon, met us at the airport and gave us a very warm welcome to Tahiti.

Between Sunday, June 6, and Sunday, July 4, I held a total of 30 gospel meetings in Tahiti, and had a total of 27 conversions. I spent the first two weeks in the Chinese Pentecostal church in Papeete (capital of Tahiti), where Sunday-morning attendance may have averaged 100 while I was there.

I especially remember the service at this church on Thursday night June 10, when, after my message on Pentecost, I called the people to the front of the church to seek the Holy Spirit. They prayed earnestly, some of them "in other tongues as the Spirit enabled them" (Acts 2:4, NIV). If none was baptized in the Spirit, certainly some must have been refilled with the Spirit!

"He's Everything to Me" was a popular gospel song with youth groups at that time. Sam and I translated it from English into French, then he sang it as a solo at the service for youth in the Chinese church on the final Saturday night that we ministered there. The young people thoroughly enjoyed his singing it.

During my third week in Tahiti, I preached to a group in a small Tahitian church in Papeete which had come out of the Reformed Church. I preached during the fourth week in another Tahitian church in the Papeari District, about 35 miles from Papeete, toward the peninsula. Neither of these two Tahitian churches had yet become Pentecostal, but I preached Pentecost to them, and they received my messages well. Since we began on Sunday and ended on Sunday, there were 5 Sundays during our month of meetings: Three in the Chinese church, none in the Tahitian church in Papeete, and 2 in the Papeari Tahitian church.

Only 2 people were converted during the first three weeks, then 25 were converted during the final week! At noon on our first Sunday in the Papeari Tahitian church, a picnic meal was served on the church grounds. While we were in church that morning, a large pig was being roasted for that picnic. It was roasted in a native-style, underground oven beside the church. All the people of the Chinese Pentecostal church at Papeete were invited to partake of that delicious picnic meal with the Tahitians of both churches. Many of the Chinese came and enjoyed precious spiritual and social fellowship with the Tahitians that day.

That meal on the church grounds probably helped to produce the immediate atmosphere of spiritual revival in the Papeari Tahitian church during the following week. And it undoubtedly helped to produce more friendly relationship in the future between Christians of the two races in Tahiti.

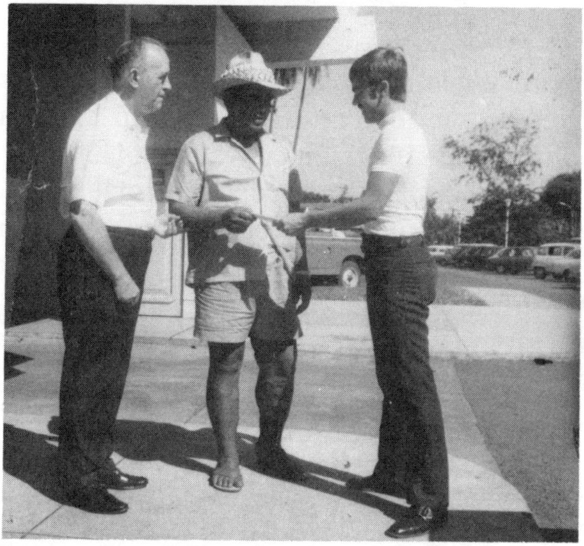

George Flattery, Sr., (left), with Sam Croutworst, (right), and a Tahitian, (center), to whom Sam is giving a gospel tract

The marriage of our daughter Doris Ann to Allen Frederick Repko of Rochester, New York, at the Central Assembly of God Church in Springfield, Missouri, on December 28, 1971, was an event of the same importance to Stella and me as had been (in earlier years) the marriages of our two sons. What a joy it was to me to attend their wedding, participate in it, and witness their marriage vows!

Allen completed a doctorate in history at the University of Missouri about 18 months after their marriage. Then both he and Doris taught at Oral Roberts University. Allen entered pastoral work at Virginia Beach, Virginia, in 1984. He and Doris spent several years there in successful pioneering of a new Assembly of God church. And now they are pioneering another new Assembly of God Church in the St. Louis, Missouri, area. They are carrying on the tradition of Pentecostal pioneering!

Reunion and Mauritius, 1972

Reunion and Mauritius are small (but main) islands of the Mascarene archipelago (to the east of Madagascar), in the

Indian ocean. When I visited these islands in 1972, Reunion was an overseas department of France, and Mauritius was a British colony where government was conducted in English, but the common people still spoke mostly French with the outside world. Mauritius had been a French colony until England wrested it from France about 1810.

I had learned about the beginnings of Pentecost in these islands from Jacques Giraud when I was with him in Guadeloupe in the summer of 1970. Aime Cizeron and his wife were the Pentecostal pioneers of both Reunion and Mauritius. They first went to Reunion as appointed missionaries of the Assemblies of God of France in June, 1966. Then they (accompanied by their son-in-law and daughter, Georges and Michelle Burki) took Pentecost to Mauritius near the end of 1967. Giraud had worked with Cizeron in Reunion as an evangelist, for about 4 months, in late 1966.

The A. G. Division of Foreign Missions in Springfield, Missouri, had approved my summer evangelism in French for 6 consecutive years. So, my procedure in making arrangements to go to the Mascarene islands was to first seek approval of my plans by the French A. G. missionaries working in those islands.

Before going to the Mascarenes, I had no personal acquaintance with any of the several French Pentecostal missionaries who were in Reunion and Mauritius. But in September, 1971, Giraud had written Cizeron a favorable report of my summer evangelism in French. His letter to Cizeron concerning my work helped me, through correspondence with the latter, to arrange to preach in Reunion from Sunday, July 30, through Tuesday, August 15; and in Mauritius from Thursday, August 17, through Sunday, August 27.

I wrote R. T. McGlasson, asking for endorsement by the FMC upon my 1972 summer ministry in the Mascarene Islands. And he answered: "The Foreign Missions Committee is pleased to advise you that this ministry trip is approved."

From Sunday, January 9, through Sunday, January 23, I held 16 missionary meetings in Kentucky. From those meetings I received a substantial part of the expense money I needed for my ministry in the Mascarenes. Then between March 5, and July 16, I held 13 more missionary meetings (all in Missouri), and received from them the balance of what I needed for it.

All of my 8 consecutive summer trips abroad to evangelize were memorable. But the stops during the 1972 flight to the Mascarenes made that trip even more memorable than the others. I left Springfield, Missouri, on Tuesday, July 25. There were routine stops at St. Louis and New York before the overnight flight to Paris, France. George, Esther, their sons, and Warren made the trip from Brussels to meet my plane in Paris. (Jean was not well enough to make that trip.) I had a fine 6-hour visit with my children and grandchildren in Paris, during which time we saw the famous painting "Mona Lisa" and other sights of Paris.

My plane left Paris at 3:00 p. m. on July 26, and arrived at Tel Aviv at 8:00 p. m. the same day. I took a taxi to the hotel room in nearby Jerusalem which Mrs. Kofsmann had reserved for me. I had only 30 hours in Jerusalem before my plane left to take me on towards the Mascarene Islands. During the morning of July 27, Mrs. Kofsmann took me to see Golgotha, the garden tomb of Jesus, the garden of Gethsemane, and the Mount of Olives. I filmed Jerusalem from the top of the Mount of Olives. Then while taking a guided tour of the Old City of Jerusalem in the afternoon, I walked along the route where Christ carried His cross, and went inside the "Dome of the Rock" or "Mosque of Omar." That has been my only visit to the Holy Land.

I stopped for two days in Somalia, at Djibouti, on the southern end of the Red Sea. There I distributed some gospel literature, including the ICI "Great Questions of Life." My plane arrived at St. Denis in Reunion at 12:30 p. m. on Sunday, July 30.

We began our Mascarenes outreach on Sunday, July 30, at 4:00 p. m., with a 17-day crusade in Reunion. Church buildings and rented halls were nearly always filled to capacity. The Reunion campaign culminated in an afternoon evangelistic rally held in the spacious city gymnasium of St. Denis on August 15. Attendance soared to 1200 that afternoon, and about 140 came forward for salvation. Two days later, we started Good News Crusades in Mauritius, and continued through Sunday August 27. The revival spirit prevailed there also. At the conclusion of the 45 services conducted in the Mascarenes, we had counted 969 (660 in Reunion and 309 in Mauritius) who came come forward for salvation.

George Flattery, Sr., praying for people who have come forward for salvation in the St. Denis rally. Only about half of the crowd shows in this picture.

From the very beginning of the meetings on the Mascarene Islands, there seemed to be a greater manifestation of the presence and power of the Holy Spirit than I had witnessed during the 6 preceding summers. On Monday, the second day of the meetings in St. Denis, the pastor was (according to my letter to Stella of August 1) "expecting a smaller crowd but it was even larger than on Sunday." On that Monday night, a young man testified in the meeting of having been healed of an abscess in his throat, when I prayed for him the night before. To God be the glory!

God said, "I will not give my glory to another" (Isaiah 42:8, NIV). But Paul assures us that God "will give to each person according to what he has done" (Romans 2:6, NIV). I feel that much credit for what was done in all those meetings, in which I preached the gospel in Reunion and Mauritius in 1972, belongs to the faithful French missionaries under whose supervision I worked.

I never met Aime Cizeron; he was on furlough while I was there. I worked under Georges Burki and Bernard Hascoet in Reunion, and under John Mattei and Vaughan Abeyssekera in Mauritius. Regarding me and my ministry in Reunion, Burki reported in a French Assemblies of God missionary publication: he was the first foreign missionary to visit the island of Reunion, and his coming "nous a fait du bien" (was helpful to us).

The French missionaries in Reunion had seen their Pentecostal work grow (between 1966 and 1972) to 15 churches attended by about 2000 adults and 600 children. The French missionaries in Mauritius had seen their Pentecostal work grow (between 1967 and 1972) to 9 churches with a total average attendance in the Sunday morning services of about 1300.

I showed all of my 16 mm. color films of Africa and summer French campaigns to the congregations in the Mascarene Islands. They enjoyed them all. At Reunion and Mauritius, I spent a considerable amount of time in making a film of the Mascarenes to add to my films for my summer evangelism of 1973.

Tahiti, New Caledonia, and New Hebrides, 1973

In my letter to Howard Fox of October 13, 1972, I mentioned my desire to go to New Caledonia to evangelize under his supervision in July, 1973. He replied on November 2, that Jacques Giraud had written of his desire to return to New Caledonia in 1973 (possibly in the spring), for another evangelistic crusade. In that letter Fox concluded that I should proceed, tentatively, with my plans to go to New Caledonia in July, while he waited to learn more precisely whether or not the time I wanted to be there would conflict with the time Giraud wanted to be there.

Then on November 20, Fox wrote me that it would not be possible for Giraud to come before the first part of 1974. On January 6, I answered Fox that I had reserved plane seats to arrive in New Caledonia on Saturday June, 30, and to leave New Caledonia for home on July 26. On behalf of the A. G. Foreign Missions Committee in Springfield, Missouri, R. T. McGlasson wrote me on January 8, 1973: "Your project for ministry in New Caledonia during July of 1973 has our fullest approval."

Between January 14 and June 13, I held 24 missionary meetings in Missouri, in which I raised the money that I would need for all expenses connected with my summer evangelism in 1973. I held the last one of these meetings in Central Assembly of Springfield, Missouri, my home church. Under the pastoral leadership of Thomas Zimmerman, Emil Balliet, David Hastie, James Van Meter, J. L. McQueen, E. E. Krogstad, and Philip Wannenmacher; Central Assembly had, in 1973, been my only home church for 29 years! And it has now been my only home church for another 19 years.

After carefully studying the situation in New Caledonia, Fox wrote me that he thought I should try to minister for a week in Tahiti again (while enroute to New Caledonia), then plan to divide my remaining 3 weeks between ministry in New Caledonia and the New Hebrides.

I answered Fox that I would follow his suggestion regarding times and places where I would minister during my month of summer evangelism in 1973. Christmas greeting cards to me in 1971 and 1972, from the Chinese Pentecostal church in Papeete, were indications of its appreciation for my 1971 ministry. This (together with my memory of the fine 1971, week-long revival at the Papeari Tahitian church) made me glad for the opportunity to visit Tahiti again.

Ernest Yune and Assam Lefait (Sunday School superintendent of the Chinese church) welcomed me back to Tahiti when I arrived at Papeete's airport, about 5:00 a. m. on June 29. A member of this Chinese church, Lai Tham Fo Lin, supplied me with a room (free of charge) in his new apartment house during the week I was there.

Between June 29 and July 5, I held 7 meetings in churches in Tahiti: three in the Papeari Tahitian church, where 25 had been saved during the final week of my month in Tahiti in 1971, and four in the Chinese church at Papeete. The deacons of the Chinese church treated me to a dinner on Tuesday night, July 3, at a restaurant in Papeete. My Scripture reading at that dinner was Psalm 100.

Both the Tahitians and the Chinese enjoyed seeing my 1971 film of Tahiti and my 1972 film of the Mascarenes. They were especially interested in seeing themselves in the Tahiti film. The Tahitians loudly applauded the scene where the husky Tahitian breaks coconuts open with an axe. These Tahitians and Chinese were the only people who had the privilege of *seeing themselves in my missionary movies* during one of my French campaigns, because Tahiti was the only place to which I returned after having made a film of it.

(Later on, the peoples of Guadaloupe, Reunion, and Mauritius, saw themselves in copies of these films that Jacque Giraud and Georges Burki acquired from me. My films helped Giraud and Burki with promotion in their homeland of their missionary work.)

My final meeting in Tahiti (before going on to New Caledonia) was a young people's rally in the Chinese church on Thursday night, July 5. At the end of that meeting, Assam Lefait gave the first lesson of the ICI course titled "Great Questions of Life" to every young person present. The Chinese Pentecostals had refused to use the ICI materials when I took them to distribute in Tahiti in 1971. They excused their refusal by saying that they preferred French gospel literature produced by French people. Their change of attitude toward ICI literature encouraged me!

My diary for June 30, indicates that I spent 2 hours that day listening to the reading in French of the "Great Questions of Life" by Jean Chahaut (Sam Croutworst's special friend in 1971). A few days later, I wrote Stella and Sharon that I spent 6 or 7 hours, altogether, in helping Jean to earn a certificate for answering all the exercises in all 6 lessons of the "Great Questions of Life." What I was able to accomplish for ICI during my week in Tahiti in 1973, helped to make that week very worthwhile.

Jean Chahaut in Tahiti with a lesson of the "Great Questions of Life"

My plane left Tahiti for New Caledonia on Saturday, July 7, at 7:15 a. m. I crossed over the International Date Line (for the first time) before arriving in Noumea, capital of New Caledonia. Flying west, I arrived in time to hold my first meeting in the Noumea French A. G. mission church during the evening of the same day that I left Tahiti. French A. G. missionary Ledru was in charge of that church and had been for 10 years. Howard and Charlotte Fox were in charge of the ICI work, and were very capably assisting Ledru with other missionary work in New Caledonia.

Between July 7 and 13, I held 8 meetings in the Noumea church. Twenty people were converted during those meetings. I showed the Noumea people all three of my films on Africa of 1950-1963, and 4 of the films of my French campaigns. The people thoroughly enjoyed seeing these films.

On Saturday July 14, I flew from Noumea to the town of Port Vila on a small island near the southern end of the New Hebrides chain. During the 3 days of July 14-16, I held 4 meetings in the A. G. mission church at Port Vila. As I was leaving for Santo (the chief town on the large island called "Espiritu Santo" at the northern end of the New Hebrides chain), Jim Williams (Fijian missionary to Port Vila) said to me: "I wish you could have stayed longer!"

God poured out His Spirit on all four services in Port Vila. In the 3 night services, 44 were saved or reclaimed. In the Sunday morning service, there were about 40 people at the altar. Some were speaking in other tongues. The church in Port Vila was a lively Pentecostal Assembly.

At Santo on July 17, I was warmly welcomed by A. G. missionaries Ronald and Joy Killingbeck, and their teen-aged daughter, Lori. The Killingbecks had spent a 4-year term in New Caledonia, but had just arrived in Santo for their new term when I got there. They were just camping in their house while they waited for the arrival of their furniture. They placed me in Santo's only hotel, and we ate together in a restaurant.

Killingbeck had tried unsuccessfully to locate a building where we could have a week of evangelistic meetings.

The management of the Burns Philip Department Store, on the central square of Santo, offered us use each night of the large paved parking area, in front of their store, for open-air evangelistic meetings. Killingbeck wrote in the August, 1973, issue of "Pacific Outreach," his missionary publication:

> *Eight nights of open-air services with Rev. George Flattery proved very effective with attendance of 150 to 350 every night. Many found Christ as their Savior and the town was stirred by the Spirit of God. Many of the converts are continuing to come to the Bible Studies and are showing growth in Christ.*

Paradoxically, God sometimes provides through refusal. At Santo, God's refusal of our quest for a building for our meetings was a necessary preparation for His granting of a better place for them in the open air. We could not have reached as many people for God in any building in Santo as we reached in the open-air. I used a 55-gallon steel drum as the stand for the projector which I used in showing all my missionary films to the people of Santo. The children all shouted "taxi" at each appearance of a horse-drawn taxi in my 1960-1963 film of Kaolack, Senegal.

George Flattery, Sr., showing film to a large crowd (mostly hidden from view) at Santo in July, 1973

On Wednesday, July 25, I flew back to Noumea from Santo. I preached that night in Ledru's church. The next night the Foxes had me preach in a new place in the industrial area to Hebredian Christians of Noumea. Many new people attended the service, and 17 of them came to the front for salvation. I held a street meeting in Noumea the night of July 27, and about 10 raised their hand for salvation. On July 28, as I flew homeward, I was rejoicing that I had been able to conduct (in my 1973 crusades) 32 meetings in which there were a total of 101 converts.

Conclusion

In the title to this chapter, the word "educating" refers more specifically to my teaching at Evangel College than it does to my summer evangelism in French. And the word "evangelizing" refers more specifically to my worldwide French crusades. But I did some evangelizing at Evangel, and also accomplished some educating in the crusades. I very carefully saw to it that neither my homeland itineration for crusade expenses nor my actual crusading in foreign lands hindered, in any way, my teaching at Evangel. And I will add that my teaching at Evangel did not hinder my foreign crusades in any way.

My two ministries (teaching and evangelizing) helped each other during my decade as a teacher at Evangel: just the fact that I held a teaching position there helped to produce openings for my evangelizing under the supervision of French pastors and missionaries around the world. And the documentary, silent, color films that I made in various places around the world helped me with my classroom teaching of French at Evangel.

Each film began with valuable travelogue-type information, and closed with local Pentecostal information which was, in some ways, even more valuable to Pentecostal students. I inserted frequent printed titles in English to groups of scenes in each film. I then gathered the printed titles from each film and stenciled them in outline form. I gave each of my students of French a copy of each film's outline.

After each student viewed each film in the classroom, he was assigned (as homework) the writing of a brief essay in French on the film. As a basis for his essay, each student had both the stenciled outline and any other notes he may have taken while viewing the film.

The administrators of Evangel College helped me to carry out my 8 consecutive summer evangelistic campaigns in French-speaking countries. For example: Evangel's Dean of Students, Don Argue, and its Campus Pastor, George Wood, were key persons in the decision to provide me with the excellent help (through Evangel's spiritual emphasis fund) of Kenneth Lee and Sam Croutworst in the 1970 and 1971 campaigns.

CHAPTER 10: EDUCATING BY CORRESPONDENCE

Editing, Revising, and Writing for ICI

My time as a teacher at Evangel College came to an end at the conclusion of the spring semester of 1974. As I contemplated, at 60, my future ministry; my desire was the same as it had been at 50, when I gave up my Pentecostal pioneering in French West Africa, and applied for a teaching position at Evangel: to accomplish all that I could in the future for the kingdom of God!

In 1974, I committed, anew, my "way unto the Lord" (Psalm 37:5, KJV), and my "works unto the Lord" (Proverbs 16:3, KJV). As I prayed about my future work, my desire to help God's kingdom was greater than my desire for personal advancement. One thing I knew at 60: the worldwide aspect of my Christian ministry became greater through my summer evangelism in French than it had ever been in the United States or French West Africa. Would God help me to continue to do something of a worldwide nature for His kingdom?

John F. Hall, my longtime friend and colleague in Africa, was teaching in Lome, Togo, at the West Africa School of Theology. He asked me to consider joining him as a teacher there. But Stella had already completed 6 of 11 years as a teacher at Fair Grove, Missouri. Neither of us thought that she should quit that excellent work. God in His foreknowledge had planned that I become an editor for the International Correspondence Institute of the Foreign Missions Department of the Assemblies of God of the United states.

The president of ICI (my son George) had invited me to edit for ICI in his letter from Brussels to me of November 28, 1972, saying:

We in the ICI central office would like to invite you to work with us . . . we are working hard to produce our Bible college level courses. All of these courses must be edited very carefully. Since you have done some of this kind of work for us before, you know basically what our requirements in this area are . . . we are very short of editorial help . . . your past experience in missions as well as your training in English and French would help us a great deal . . . our Bible college level courses are being well received by missionary educators overseas . . . please let me know whether or not you will be able to come.

I accepted this work with ICI and continued to do it for 18 years—until I laid it aside on April 1, 1992, to begin the writing of my autobiography. This work for ICI did not require that I move to Brussels (where the ICI International Office was located between 1972 and 1991), but during 16 years (1974-1989), I made 16 trips to Brussels in order to keep up with my job better than I could have done through nonpersonal communication (telephoning and letter-writing) alone. During those 16 years I spent (on the average) about a month out of each year in Brussels.

Those trips were not only times of fruitful work at ICI for me, they were also happy times of fellowship with my children (and their families) who worked there. I enjoyed even more family fellowship during the 6 of the 16 trips to Brussels that Stella made with me than during the 10 which I made alone. I enjoyed excellent fellowship with all the ICI personnel during each one of those 16 trips!

Left to right: Sharon Barefield, George Flattery III, George Flattery I, Mark Flattery, George Flattery II, Warren Flattery. Having family fun at ICI in Brussels in July, 1979

Once, while I was in Brussels, an ICI worker said, jokingly, to me: "Dad, you come over here each year just to check up on everyone!" Knowing that the ICI workers were doing a good job, I went to Brussels each year not to check up on them, but to check up on my own job in a way that would help me to continue to do it well.

During my time in Brussels during the summer of 1977, Mark Flattery wrote from Brussels to his Grandma Stella in Springfield, Missouri: "Everyone here at ICI really likes Grandpa. Everyone calls him 'Dad', which is pretty neat." It made me so happy when one of the ICI workers said to me: "Dad, everything seems just right when you are here."

When I began working full time for ICI in 1974, I was 60. For people who retire at 65, that would have meant only 5 more years of work. When the editor of my Kansas District's monthly paper *The Kansas Concept* noticed that I was 66 and hadn't retired, he inserted a brief article in the September, 1980 issue of the paper, titled: "Flattery Declines Retirement, Continues in Translation Work." That article states in part:

> *Reverend George Flattery, former Kansas missionary to West Africa, has returned to the United States after spending several weeks working with International Correspondence Institute in Brussels, Belgium. Brother Flattery has worked with ICI for the past seven years out of his home in Springfield, Missouri . . . as an editor for ICI. Reverend Flattery has the responsibility of making sure the ICI courses can be easily translated into another language.*

It is by counting my 1973 part-time work for ICI that this article has indicated seven years for me with ICI before September, 1980. Although I'm now 78, my retirement from ICI on April 1 of this year (to write my life's story) may not be permanent. If ICI needs my editorial assistance in the future, I will be glad to help—if my general health and eyesight remain equal to the task!

In the Summer 1992 issue of *ICI Datelines,* the Assistant General Superintendent of the Assemblies of God in the United States, Everett Stenhouse, says: "ICI is serving the Assemblies of God Fellowship, and, indeed, the larger church world in the significant responsibility of discipling the body of Christ. No other one entity in our lifetime, perhaps in the history of the church, has done more to fulfill Christ's command to "MAKE DISCIPLES OF ALL NATIONS."

David D. Duncan, Director of ICI college materials development, reported in his letter of April, 1992, that "the accumulated number of students in ICI's college program has passed 25,000. Current active enrollment is over 12,000. This is equivalent to a full-time student body of about 2,000." Through my work for ICI, I have attained worldwide Christian ministry to an even greater degree than I did through my summer crusades in French.

During my 18 years with ICI, I have spent 12 years (1974-1986) in major editing of 23 courses (21 college, and 2 Christian Service), almost 5 years (1986-1991) in major revision of 5 college courses, and a little over a year (1991-1992) in writing Instructor's Guides for 1 Christian Service course and 2 Christian Life courses. I used a typewriter during the first 13 years of this work and my computer during the last 5.

George Flattery, Sr., using a typewriter in editing at home in Springfield, Missouri, for ICI, in 1974

George Flattery, Sr., using a computer in editing at home in Springfield, Missouri, for ICI, in 1987

Here is a complete list of the major projects (in chronological order) that I accomplished in my 18 years (1974-1992) of work for ICI:

1. Editing of college *Gospel of John* by Peter Kuzmic
2. Editing of college *Old Testament Survey* by Fred J. Greve
3. Editing of college *Church History I* by George R. Stotts
4. Editing of college *Old Testament Historical Books* by Amos Millard
5. Editing of college *Old Testament Biblical Theology* by John Phillipps
6. Editing of college *World Religions* by John S. Thannnickal
7. Editing of college *Greek I* by Hobart E. Grazier
8. Editing of college *Greek II* by Hobart E. Grazier
9. Editing of college *Eschatology* by Andrew McDearmid
10. Editing of Christian Service *Christian Maturity* by Rick C. Howard
11. Editing of Christian Service *Understanding the Bible* by Dorothy L. Johns
12. Editing of college *Counseling* by Fred J. Greve
13. Editing of college *Bibliology-Ecclesiology* by Suwandoko Roslim
14. Editing of college *Theology Proper-Angelology* by Massyoshi Safu
15. Editing of college *Pentateuch* by George Assad
16. Editing of college *Journalism* by Rex Jackson
17. Editing of college *Speech* by Louise Kimberly Harrison
18. Editing of college *The Biblical Doctrines of Man and Sin* by Daniel B. Pecota
19. Editing of college *Principles of Preaching* by Jesse K. Moon
20. Editing of college *Introduction to Missions* by Hugh P. Jeter
21. Editing of college *Theology Proper-Angelology* by Paul Martin

22. Editing of college *Cross Cultural Communications* by Del Tarr
23. Editing of college *Daniel and Revelation* by George W. Westlake, Jr.
24. Revising of college *Apologetics* by William Menzies
25. Revising of college *Christology* by L. Thomas Holdcroft
26. Revising of college *Old Testament Survey* by Fred J. Greve
27. Revising of college *Pastoral Ministries* by Jack V. Rozell
28. Revising of college *Soteriology* by Daniel B. Pecota
29. Writing of *Instructor's Guide* for Christian Service *Prayer & Worship* by Morris Williams
30. Writing of *Instructor's Guide* for Christian Life *What Churches Do* by Robert and Evelyn Bolton
31. Writing of *Instructor's Guide* for Christian Life *We Believe* by Ralph M. Riggs

When I started my editing for ICI, I was glad for the help and advice of my colleague, ICI missionary Norman D. Anderson. He helped me to get started in the editing of the 2nd, 3rd, 4th, and 5th items of the above list.

On the 47th anniversary of my marriage to Stella, I was honored with a gift desk pen from ICI which reads:

Presented to
REV. GEORGE W. FLATTERY
In appreciation for his
labors of love in developing
the ICI ministry
"YOUR PEN IS BLESSED OF GOD"
May 8,1981

Mrs. Louise Walker was honored by ICI in the same manner and at the same time that I was. J. Philip Hogan, Executive Director of A. G. Foreign Missions, and my son, George M. Flattery, President of ICI, presented the gift pens to Mrs. Walker and me.

Left to right: George M. Flattery, George Flattery, Sr., Mrs. Louise Walker, and J. Philip Hogan. On the May 8, 1981, occasion of presenting gift pens to Walker and Flattery, Sr., by ICI

Other Ministry While Editing for ICI

During the last 18 years (1974-1992), my editing for ICI has required most of my time for spiritual ministry. During these years, I've had much less time to preach than I had during the 40 preceding years! But, I've continued to preach whenever I've had the opportunity. Between November 18, 1973, and March 21, 1976, I preached in 40 missionary meetings in Missouri and 20 in Kentucky, to raise my plane fares to and from Brussels in 1974, 1975, and 1976. Then ICI told me that they would pay my plane fare each year to Brussels, so that I could stop itinerating and make more rapid progress with my editing of their college courses.

It was my privilege to preach in French occasionally in Belgium, France, and Switzerland, during the annual times that I was working for ICI in Brussels. I preached for my grandson George, once in Switzerland and twice in Paris, while he and his wife Debbie were A. G. missionaries to France. Also, while working in Brussels, I preached frequently in English in the ICI chapel services, and a few times at the Christian Center church in Brussels.

The last time I preached in an ICI Chapel service was on

Wednesday, March 18, 1992, at Irving, Texas. In my message on "Life, Motion, and Balance," I used the words of Jude "God our Savior" (v. 25, NIV) "is able to keep you from falling" (v. 24) in emphasizing the fact that every Christian must have God's help in order to maintain his spiritual equilibrium.

I had the opportunity to address, briefly, the National Congress of the French Assemblies of God at Reims in May, 1986. Pastor Francois Forschle was pastor of the Reims church and one of the leaders of that Congress. When he spoke at Central Assembly in Springfield, Missouri, on Wednesday, April 19, 1978, I interpreted his message. He remembered me when he saw me in the congregation of the 1986 Congress, and called me to the platform to speak briefly. Pierre Dupret, with whom I had fellowship in Upper Volta between 1948 and 1957, was on the platform when I spoke.

At the 1986 Reims A. G. Congress, George Flattery, Sr. (left), and Pierre Dupret, standing in front of Dupret's booth for his Teen-Challenge type work

ICI's "World Alive" (television program for the American audience, video cassette number 5) features the work in Upper Volta of Stella and me, between 1945 and 1957. From April 3-20, 1987, Stella and I were in Upper Volta (now Burkina Faso) with George, Esther, John Merrell, and the ICI television crew, to make this television program. We visited Ouagadougou, Po, and Corabie.

It had been 40 years since we first lived at Corabie, 36 years since we first lived at Po, and 30 years since I built the downtown Ouagadougou church. It had been 30 years since Stella had been in Upper Volta, and 24 years since I had been there. When, in 1987, we stood side-by-side on the little knoll at Corabie (where rains had washed away the mud house we had built 40 years earlier); our reflection on what we had endured there, so long ago, almost caused us to swoon! We grabbed each other to keep from falling.

The missionaries and Mossi national church honored Stella and me during our visit to Burkina Faso in 1987. The Jim Bryants, Don Tuckers, and Randy Tarr sponsored a delicious dinner in our honor on Sunday, April 5, at Ouagadougou's finest hotel. On April 17, the national church leaders entertained us and the missionaries on the Ouagadougou mission compound with a lovely native-style *sagebo* meal. The nationals presented us with the gift of a beautiful, very thick, woolen rug which had been woven by Mossi girls at the Ouagadougou Catholic girls' school. And the missionaries gave us a beautifully carved ivory elephant.

I preached a few times while in Burkina Faso in 1987. At the downtown Ouagadougou church that I had built, my message to a capacity crowd of about 1000 people on Sunday morning, April 5, in French, was translated into More. After reviewing my materials in Kasem for about 2 months before going to Burkina Faso, I preached in Kasem (where our Corabie mission had been) on Saturday morning, April 11, to a crowd of about 250 people, from Mark Chapter 2, on the subject of the man healed of palsy. The Corabie church people served us a lovely native meal, and gave gifts to us, after the church service had ended.

On Sunday morning, April 12, I preached in More to a capacity crowd of 1200 people in the church on the Ouagadougou mission compound. Then on Sunday morning, April 19, I testified in the church at the French school which Pierre Dupret had founded at Ouagadougou. The crowd of about 1200 was very pleased when I told them about my cordial visit of the preceding year with Pierre Dupret at the French A. G. National Congress in Reims, France. While we were in Po, enroute to Corabie, Stella enjoyed a visit with Nongelem Esther (Belco's healthy 36-year-old daughter). Stella had performed the services of midwife at her birth.

Nongelem Esther (left), and Stella, the midwife who delivered her. Beside the A. G. Po mission house in April, 1987

When we were leaving Corabie, the day before we went back there for the church service and meal, we visited Nasia (our first Kasena convert in 1947) at his home. In 1987, he was probably about 85, but was alert! He still had the copy of the Gospel of Mark in Kasem that I had given him 40 years before. Stella feels that the greatest highlight of our 1987 trip to Burkina Faso was seeing Nasia, our first Kasena convert, still alive and serving the Lord. It was a great joy to see that several of our first group of Kasena converts were still preaching the Gospel of Christ. Outstanding among them was Alia, the presbyter of the Kasena Pentecostal Christians.

Stella in the center of the crowd to whom George, Sr., preached in Kasem at Corabie on April 11, 1987

Conclusion

I've ended many of the chapters in my autobiography with a subsection titled "Conclusion." In each case it has been a conclusion to only one part of the story of my life. I will not use the term "conclusion" in a way that would cause anyone to think that I am planning how and when to conclude my life. I've always had, and hope to always maintain, the healthy mental and spiritual attitudes of wanting to live on earth as long as God wants me to!

When Stella, Warren, and I, went to visit my dying brother Frank in March, 1991, he was 71, and I knew (as well as his dear family knew) that he could not live many weeks, unless God miraculously intervened for him. I was alone with dear Frank when I spoke these last words to him: "I am praying for you, just what I am praying for myself—that God will help both of us to succeed in remaining on earth as long as He wants us to."

Each of the first 9 chapters of my autobiography has dealt, in chronological order, with a different time of my life. But the same period of time will be dealt with in the next chapter (the final chapter) as has been dealt with in this chapter. The main emphasis of the subject matter will, of course, differ in the next chapter from that of this chapter. Both of these chapters deal with my "golden" time of life.

I am referring to that which is ripened to an advanced degree of maturity as "golden," and have chosen to consider from 60 years of age, upward, as my golden time of life. This calculation for a person who (like myself) is nearing 80 fits well with the Bible's statement in Psalm 90:10 about length of human life on earth: "The length of our days is seventy years—or eighty, if we have the strength" (NIV).

A picture of April, 1987, at Corabie. Alia Kasena, presbyter of the Kasena Christians of Burkina Faso (right), has presented those Christians' gift of a Kasena chief's robe to George Flattery, Sr., who is extremely well pleased with the nicely fitting garment.

CHAPTER 11: MY GOLDEN YEARS

Let's be careful lest we misinterpret "golden" as something that is all joy and no sorrow. "The blessing of the Lord" contains "no sorrow" (Proverbs 10:22, KJV), but because of man's fallen condition, sorrow is mingled with joy throughout his entire earthly lifetime. Revelation 21:1-4 indicates that "There shall be no more . . . sorrow" (v. 4, KJV) in the "new heaven and . . . new earth" (v. 1). As I have pressed forward from the time of my conversion toward my place in the new heaven and new earth, I have experienced decreasing sorrow and increasing joy throughout the successive stages of my life.

Golden Anniversaries

It may be too well known to even mention that, in our culture, the phrase "golden anniversary" refers to the 50th anniversary. But if we searched worldwide, we would probably find some cultures that attach a different numerical meaning to this phrase.

I experienced the golden anniversary of my natural birth when I reached 50. But it was on August 16, 1981, that I experienced, at 67, my first golden-years, golden anniversary celebration: the 50th anniversary celebration of my conversion to Christ in the Pentecostal Tabernacle at Lincoln and Main Streets in Wichita, Kansas.

I've indicated in the first chapter of this autobiography that it was in responding to Mrs. H. B. (Ruth E.) Garlock's sermon and altar call that I was converted. I telephoned her in Dallas, Texas, on August 16, 1981, from my home in Springfield, Missouri, to thank her for her part in my conversion. She is 95 and still lives in Dallas. About 4 months ago, Stella and I had a lovely visit with her.

Back: George Flattery, Sr., (left) and Stella Flattery. Front: Mrs. Ruth E. Garlock. At Dallas, Texas, in March, 1992

I had intended to talk only a few minutes on that 50th anniversary day, but Ruth Garlock was so delighted to receive my call that she kept me on the phone for perhaps 30 minutes! H. B. Garlock (now deceased) deeply appreciated my telephonic expression of thanks to his wife. He wrote his sister—Mrs. Wilson H. Frayer of New Castle, Pennsylvania—about it. Then about a year later (on August 8, 1982) Mrs. Frayer wrote me:

I am . . . H. B. Garlock's sister . . . some time ago

I received a letter from him telling about a telephone call Ruth had received from a George Flattery in Springfield, Missouri . . . you were expressing appreciation for her ministry in Wichita, Kansas, 50 years ago. It was under her ministry when you, a young man of high school age, gave your heart and life to Jesus. You went on to Bible School to prepare for the ministry, married, went to Africa as a missionary. The Lord blessed you with 4 children, one is George, Jr., who became head of ICI headquarters in Brussels.

On Sunday, November 22, 1981, Stella and I participated in the 50th anniversary celebration of the founding of the Wellington, Kansas, First Assembly of God Church. The February 1982 issue of *The Kansas Concept* stated that this church celebrated its fiftieth anniversary "recently with special services to which former pastors and members were invited. Four former pastors and their wives were present for this special occasion."

Back (left to right): Reverend and Mrs. Forrest Murray, and present pastor, Greg Mohr. Front (left to right): Reverend and Mrs. N. B. Rayburn, Reverend and Mrs. Wesley Goodwin, and Reverend and Mrs. George Flattery, Sr. In front of the Wellington church on November 22, 1981

Sunday School was eliminated for November 22, and each of the visiting four former pastors spoke briefly to the congregation (during the two-hour morning worship service which began at 9:45) of what had happened while he was pastor at Wellington First Assembly, and of what he was currently doing. Kansas District Superintendent, Reverend Derald Musgrove, ministered in the evening worship service.

On April 21, 1984, Stella and I celebrated our golden wedding anniversary with a reception at the Central Assembly of God Church Pioneer Center, at 1330 Boonville, in Springfield, Missouri. The day of our wedding was May 8, 1934, but we had to move our celebration up a few days, to a date when all four of our children and their companions could be present. About 200 people attended our reception.

George and Stella Flattery at the time of their 50th wedding anniversary celebration

Ralph and Evelyn Dunham singing at George and Stella Flattery's 50th wedding anniversary

On April 9, 1986, at the Kansas District Council of the Assemblies of God, in the Calvary Assembly of God Church at 2225 E. Central, Wichita, Kansas, I was presented with a certificate. It was a certificate of honor conferred upon me for my completion of 50 years as a minister with General Council of the Assemblies of God credentials.

Kansas District Superintendent, Derald Musgrove, presenting to George Flattery, Sr., in Wichita, Kansas, on April 9, 1986, a certificate of honor for having completed 50 years as a minister of the General Council of the Assemblies of God

I first met Pastor John L. Skinner at the 1986 Kansas District Council meeting. Pastor Skinner was and still is (in 1992) the pastor of the Leavenworth, Kansas, First Assembly of God Church, which Stella and I founded in 1939. In 1986, he was already planning a golden anniversary celebration for his church in Leavenworth in 1989, and invited Stella and me to participate in it. (I will tell, below, about our participation in the 1989 Leavenworth celebration.)

From November 5-7, 1987, I attended, with Stella, at Southwestern Assemblies of God College, in Waxahachie, Texas, the celebration of the golden anniversary of my graduating class of 1937. This celebration was described by Ann Ahlf (in her promotional circular) as a "GOLDEN - DIAMOND JUBILEE" because 1987 was the 60th anniversary of the beginning of Southwestern Assemblies of God College. Each of the 1937 graduates received from Southwestern the honorary Golden Anniversary Diploma. Mine reads:

Southwestern Assemblies of God College
has conferred on
GEORGE FLATTERY
Class of 1937
the Honorary
GOLDEN ANNIVERSARY DIPLOMA

After 55 years, I remember some of my 42 graduating classmates better than others. Two of them which I remember well are Lester McNabb (our class president), and Orville Mills (now deceased), who was a nearby neighbor to Stella and me in 1937 at Enid, Oklahoma. Both of them attended the 1987 golden anniversary celebration.

On May 26-28, 1989, Stella and I participated in the 3-day 50th anniversary celebration of our founding of the Leavenworth, Kansas, First Assembly of God church. Pastor John L. Skinner chose the Kansas District Superintendent (Reverend Derald

Musgrove) to preach at the opening service on Friday night, May 26; Reverend U. S. Grant to preach at the Saturday night service, May 27; Reverend Art Sorg (converted in this church after we left it in 1944 to go to Africa) to preach at the Sunday morning service, May 28; and me to preach at the celebration's closing rally on Sunday afternoon, May 28.

Orville Mills (left) and Lester McNabb. At Southwestern Assemblies of God College, Waxahachie, Texas, in November, 1987

God anointed Brother Skinner to lead the Leavenworth celebration, and blessed the messages of all 4 speakers. I spoke on "Togetherness," emphasizing that a church's proper attitude toward its past increases the brightness of its hope for the future. Our visit with Mrs. Faye Rutter was especially enjoyable. She has always been, and still is, one of the best supporters of the Leavenworth church.

My nephew, Larry Hammer, and his wife Gail kept Stella and me in their home in Leavenworth, during the 3-day celebration at the church. I was delighted to have them and their children as guests in my audience at the closing rally. The Leavenworth church made an audio-video recording of my message at the Sunday afternoon rally. I've had friends in our home view it and hear it on our VCR.

Faye Rutter (left) and Stella Flattery, in front of Faye's home (for over 55 years) in Leavenworth, Kansas, in May, 1989

Other Golden-Time Events

George and Esther's two sons, George and Mark, were born before Stella and I were 50. So, their births were not golden-time events to us. Considering that our golden-time of life began when we were 60, George and Mark were already 17 and 13 when it began. Not having been able to see either of them under 2 years of age, caused us to enjoy being with them even more, I think, than if we had been around them from the beginning. We might not have known how to enjoy newly born grandchildren as much during our forties and fifties as we have during our golden years!

The births of our remaining grandchildren were precious

golden-time events to us. I became 60 less than 2 months after the birth of Lisa Flattery to Warren and Jean on February 13, 1974; and was 3 months past 60 when Mark Repko was born to Allen and Doris on June 21, 1974. What a joy it was to be with them and rock them to sleep when they were tiny babies! And the same held true for tiny Ashli Repko who was born 3 years after her brother Mark.

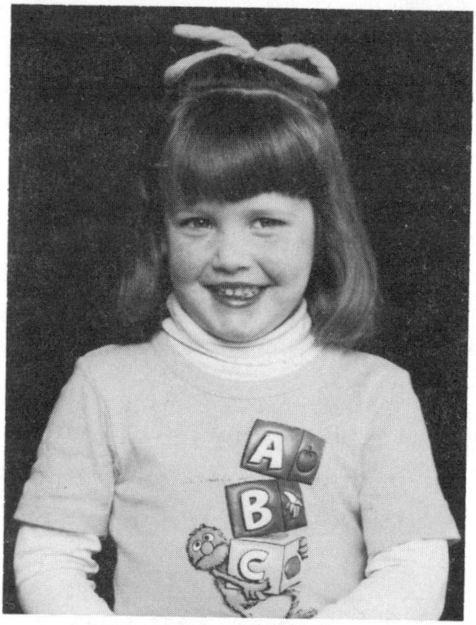

Lisa Flattery, about 4 years old

Mark Repko (left), about 3 and 1/2 years old; and Ashli Repko, about 6 months old

A memorable event, to Stella and me, at the beginning of our golden-time of life, was Warren's taking us on an 8-day automobile tour of a little of western Germany and Switzerland, and much of France. This tour began on Saturday, July 13, and ended on Saturday, July 20, 1974. We enjoyed seeing Mont Blanc, some of the great castles of France, and other great sights.

We reached Strasbourg (in northeastern France) at the end of our first day. The next morning we went to the small town of Mussig (a few miles west of Strasbourg), where many of the Engel side of Stella's family live, and have lived during past generations. Stella enjoyed walking through the Mussig cemetery, and reading inscriptions on tombstones of her Engel ancestors. She enjoyed, also, searching through registers at the Mussig town hall for names of her ancestors. She found many such names, including that of her grandfather George Engel who was born in 1837.

On the southern edge of our tour, we visited Jacques and Jacqueline Melon (with whom we had fellowship in Kaolack, Senegal, from 1960-1963) in their home at Bordeaux, France.

Front: The Mayor of Mussig, France (left), helping Stella to find names of her ancestors at the Town Hall in July, 1974

Our daughter Sharon Rose was married to Ronnie Gene Barefield in a beautiful ceremony at the Central Assembly of God church in Springfield, Missouri, on February 26, 1977. I enjoyed participation in that ceremony. In the early 1970's, Ron graduated from Southeastern College of the Assemblies of God in Lakeland, Florida; and Sharon graduated from Burge School of Nursing and Drury College in Springfield, Missouri. After graduation from Drury, Sharon became a registered nurse at Cox Medical Center North.

Ron and Sharon served as missionaries with ICI in Brussels for several years. Then, in 1989, Ron was appointed to the Foreign Missions Committee of the Assemblies of God of the United States. For the past 3 years, he has coordinated the production of an annual Missions Convention Theme Video. These 3 videos have greatly helped churches and missionaries to promote Foreign Missions. The births, to Ron and Sharon, of Kris on September 12, 1978; and Brooke on June 1, 1984, were precious golden-time events to Grandpa George, and Grandma Stella!

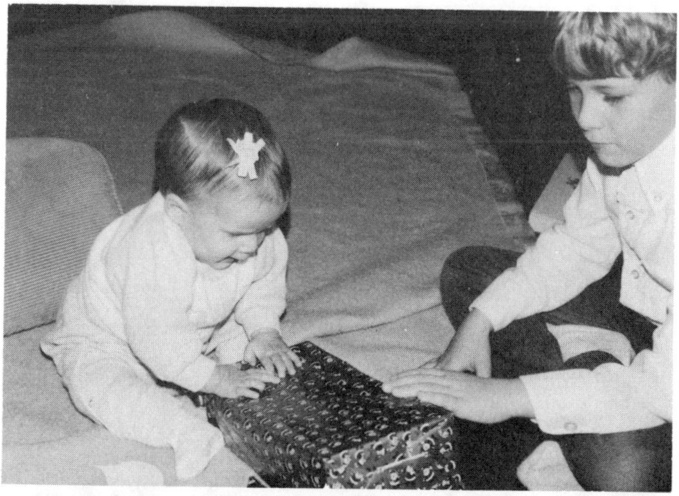

Brooke Barefield (left) and Kris Barefield. Christmastime, 1984, at the home of Grandpa and Grandma Barefield in Eufaula, Alabama. Kris was 6, Brooke was 7 months.

Stella began working on a Master in Education degree during the summer session of 1973 at Drury College in Springfield, Missouri. She kept on teaching third graders at Fair Grove during each year in which she worked on that degree. When I went on my annual summer work trip to ICI in Brussels on June 30, 1977, I knew that Stella was scheduled to receive her Master's degree during the commencement exercises at Drury on August 13. I wanted very much to be back in Springfield in time to watch her get that degree!

I did not anticipate any problem, because I had gone to Brussels expecting to return to Springfield at the end of July. But Hal Kohl (chairman of the ICI committee under which I was working) told me, near the end of July, that ICI greatly needed my help in Brussels for another month. I stayed on at ICI and did not get to attend Stella's graduation. This was the only time (other than the summer of 1969) that I was away from home for 2 consecutive months.

Stella Flattery, with the Master's degree she has just received, at Drury College on August 13, 1977

When Stella retired from teaching school at Fair Grove in May, 1979, the school paper reported: "Fair Grove is on the verge of losing one of its most valuable teachers—Mrs. Stella Flattery, one of the third grade teachers. Mrs. Flattery has been at Fair Grove for the past 11 years. Her retirement will be effective at the end of this school year . . . her hobbies are yard work, painting, entertaining her grandchildren, and traveling."

The writer of this school-paper article placed "painting" immediately after "yard work." Here, "painting" refers not to painting a house, but to painting pictures! Since her retirement, Stella has picked up in the painting of pictures where she left off as a teenaged girl and young lady. She has produced literally scores of beautiful oil paintings during the 13 years since she retired from Fair Grove school. At the end of the school-paper article, Stella stated to her Fair Grove associates: "I have . . . enjoyed the ride out here and back."

Stella Flattery, arriving home in May, 1979; after the last day of her 11 years of teaching school at Fair Grove, Missouri

The marriage of George Flattery III, grandson of Stella and me, to Debbie Sites was a precious golden-time event to us. Their wedding was at the Eastside Assembly of God Church in Tucson, Arizona, on January 2, 1981. (Debbie's father was pastor of that church, and has now been Arizona District Superintendent of the Assemblies of God for several years.) Officiating ministers were the fathers of the bride and the groom: Reverend Robert Sites, and Reverend George Flattery II. George, Esther, and their son Mark, accompanied Stella and me in our 1968 Chevrolet Impala on our enjoyable trip from Springfield, Missouri, to Tucson for this wedding. I was asked to pray at the wedding. This was my prayer:

Our heavenly Father, we thank you for creating man and woman for each other, and for placing godly love for each other in the hearts of George and Debbie. We thank you for the privilege of having enjoyed their fellowship in our own home at the beginning of their love for each other. Thank you Lord that the moment of their wedding has arrived. Help their love to stand firm against the trend in the modern world of unfaithfulness to wedding vows.

Cause their love not only to remain, but also to grow as long as both of them shall live. Bless them first of all in their life at home, and also in their work among other people for Thy kingdom. And may their faithful life together be a helpful example to other couples who live in the state of holy matrimony. If any wedded persons are here who are experiencing temptation to break their wedding vows, may their witnessing of this holy service encourage them to be faithful to those vows. We ask all this in Jesus' name. Amen.

As I write this autobiography, I am praying this same prayer for the wedding of Stella and myself, and for the weddings of all our descendants.

The births to George and Debbie of our first three great-grandchildren (Christie on October 22, 1982; Becky on

November 15, 1986; and George David on May 9, 1989) were precious golden-time events to Stella and me!

Christie Flattery, 4 years old holding Becky Flattery, 5 weeks old

Back: George Flattery III (left) and George Flattery I. Front: George Flattery II, holding George Flattery IV

I had neglected to get an annual physical checkup, for a few years, when I went to Dr. Andrew Evans for one in September, 1989. At that time, Dr. Evans noticed beginning symptoms of cancer in my prostate gland. He advised me to see a specialist about it, and arranged an appointment for me with Urologist Jeffrey R. Johnson. Dr. Johnson submitted me to ultra sound treatment which confirmed those symptoms of cancer, and recommended a series of 8 weeks of radiation treatments for me.

I received those treatments during October, November and December, 1989, at Cox Medical Center North, in Springfield, Missouri. My quarterly checkups by Dr. Johnson in 1990, and my semiannual checkups by him in 1991, showed at the beginning of 1992 that medical treatment, together with prayer unto God for my healing, had healed me of cancer! I am thankful that my cancer was discovered in its earliest stage.

James and Toby Gangwes were members of the First Assembly of God Church in Kansas City, Kansas; while I was pastor of the First Assembly of God Church in Leavenworth, Kansas. They attended the dedication of our church in Leavenworth in April, 1944. We renewed our acquaintance with James and Toby after they moved from California to Springfield, Missouri, in 1976. We have enjoyed precious spiritual and social fellowship with them as we visited in each other's homes since they moved here. During the last few years, we have especially enjoyed the Christmas parties in their home that they have given for us and other friends.

On Valentine's Day (February 14, 1992), Stella and I enjoyed a lovely dinner with a group of friends. We had worked with most of them (before World War II) in the ministry of the gospel of Christ in Kansas. The dinner was a gift from the Old Country Buffet of Springfield, Missouri, to couples who had been married for 50 years or more.

After the Central Assembly of God Church of Springfield, Missouri, moved into its new sanctuary on January 1, 1992,

Pastor Wannenmacher (and his staff) arranged periodical area prayer meetings at various homes of members of the church. These meetings have helped the church in general through the blessings they have imparted to people who have attended them. Stella and I have attended two of these meetings at the home of the Raymond Hudsons.

Left to right: George Flattery, Sr., Art Priest, Bill Wright, Melvin Hodges, Ralph Dunham, James Gangwes. December 18, 1987, at the Gangwes home in Springfield, Missouri

Left to right: Leona Liddle, Ann Ahlf, Stella Flattery, George Flattery, Sr., Charles Peak, Nell Peak, Lloyd Logan, Irene Logan, Ralph Dunham, Evelyn Dunham, Glen Ahlf, Cecil Liddle. February 14, 1992, at the Old Country Buffet in Springfield, Missouri

There was an appropriate, enjoyable, social time which followed the main spiritual emphasis at the Hudsons' prayer meetings. God has social blessings for His people as well as spiritual blessings for them—they need both! All people are social beings, and all of them who are "born of the Spirit" (John 3:6, KJV) are spiritual beings.

The marriage of Mark Flattery, grandson of Stella and me, to Angela Hunt was a precious golden-time event to us. Their wedding was at the Calvary Temple Assembly of God Church in Springfield, Missouri, on November 30, 1990. Officiating ministers were the fathers of the bride and groom: Reverend Eugene Hunt (A. G. missionary with his wife and family to Latin America for many years), and Reverend George Flattery II. I voiced the same burden of prayer at their wedding as I had voiced at the wedding of George and Debbie nearly 10 years before.

The wedding picture of Mark and Angela Flattery taken on November 30, 1990. Left to right: Kris Barefield, Sharon Barefield, Ashli Repko, Ron Barefield, Brooke Barefield, Doris Repko, Allen Repko, Mark Repko, Mark Flattery, Angela (Hunt) Flattery, Becky Flattery, Esther Flattery, Christie Flattery, George Flattery II, Stella Flattery, George Flattery I, George Flattery IV, George Flattery III, Debbie Flattery, Jean Flattery, Warren Flattery. Lisa Flattery, directly in front of George Flattery III

Up to this point, I've not placed the wedding picture of any couple in this book. I'm not showing partiality in placing the wedding picture of Mark and Angela in it. I've included this picture so that everyone of our descendants (except Ethan, of course) can be seen in one group.

The birth to Mark and Angela of our fourth great-grandchild, Ethan, on May 11, 1992, was another precious golden-time event to Stella and me. It is a remarkable coincidence that Ethan was born on the 114th anniversary of the birth of his great-great-grandfather (my father), James Perley Flattery, a thresher of wheat in Kansas when I was a little boy!

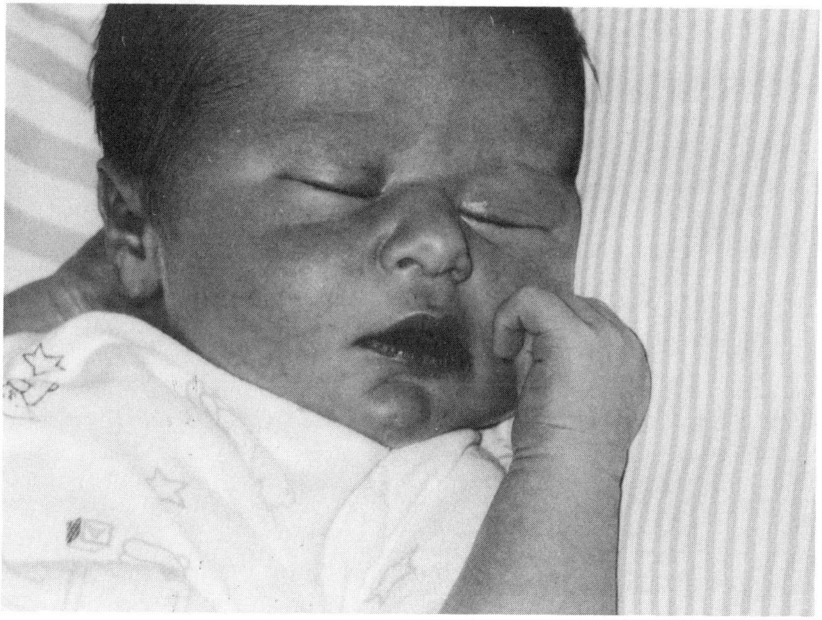

Ethan Flattery, soon after his birth

Now, I've come to the conclusion of this story of my life—but not to the conclusion of my lifetime. God alone knows just how and when my life on earth will end! My bright hope is to live on earth as long as God wants me to, then go to heaven and "be with the Lord forever" (1 Thessalonians 4:17, NIV). Mrs. Annie (Mother) Bamford, sponsor of my graduating class at Southwestern Bible School of Enid, Oklahoma, described what seemed to her to be my goal in life as: "To glorify God no lesser aim, my earthly life and power shall ever claim" (*The Southwesterner,* 1937, p. 35).

This inscription about me in *The Southwesterner* describes "the goal to . . . which God has called me heavenward in Christ Jesus" (Philippians 3:14, NIV), and has helped to keep this biblical goal before me—especially at times when I have failed to make as much progress toward this goal as I should have made. I sincerely desire that reading the story of my life will help many people to make good progress toward "the prize of the high calling of God in Christ Jesus" (Philippians 3:14, KJV)!

INDEXES

Index 1: to Bible Portions Quoted

Index 2: to Pictures